Chasing Zorba

A JOURNEY of SELF-DISCOVERY *in a* VW BUS

Jerry Steimel

Chasing Zorba

A Journey of Self-Discovery in a VW Bus

Jerry Steimel

Cover photo by Dianne Steimel

ISBN (Print Edition): 978-1-09833-462-8

ISBN (eBook Edition): 978-1-09833-463-5

For my wife, Dianne
Without your support, the journey was not possible.

For my daughters, Katie and Rebecca
My favorite road trips will always be the ones I took with you.

For my siblings Mary Lee, John, Jeanette and Sally
You have supported me, and put up with
me, longer than anyone else.

For my life-long friend Art
Your companionship has made me a better person

For the mechanics Damon, Dave, Jeff, Doug, Steve and Elliot
Your skills and generosity kept Zorba moving across the country.

For all the Zorbas I met along the way
You lifted my spirits, and your presence
gave the journey meaning.

CONTENTS

PROLOGUE

I paused and looked down the long row of corn ahead of me, the last row I needed to pick. It was late June and the Alabama sun had pushed the temperatures well into the 90s, showing no mercy on the pickers spread out in the field. Within ten minutes of stepping into the field that morning, my shirt was soaked and the red bandana tied around my neck offered little protection from the heat and humidity—or the constant itch the corn leaves created on my arms. Just one more row to go, I told myself.

I wiped the sweat from my forehead with the second bandana I carried in my pocket and allowed myself a brief reflection, wondering how I had arrived at this spot in my life. One month earlier, I had graduated from college with a degree in political science. While not an overly confident graduate, I had the youthful expectation that I would do something special with the life ahead of me. As I grasped my diploma, I was eager to begin. The possibilities were not endless—I was acutely aware of some of my limitations—but working with a crew of migrant farmworkers was not part of the vision. I laughed to myself. There was no need to wonder. I knew exactly how I had gotten to this hot and unforgiving field in Alabama.

I had put my college degree on the shelf and set off in a 1966 VW Beetle to see what was beyond the horizon. I wanted some distance from my roots and familiar surroundings. The road trip I embarked on was to take me across the United States to California. Along the way, I expected to learn much about myself and gain a deeper understanding of the country. In 1972, the nation was sharply and violently divided over the Vietnam War. I went searching for our common ground. Whether I would return to my hometown, Louisville, Kentucky, was an open question.

On the first day, my Beetle suffered total mechanical failure only 300 miles from home. I abandoned it in the small town of Warrior, Alabama, and made it down to Florida's panhandle. I had been trying to hang on, living in Pensacola, and doing whatever I could to make ends meet—like farm work. My childhood friend Art had accompanied me on the road trip, but he quickly concluded our prospects were bleak and had returned to Kentucky a month earlier. I was a little more stubborn about it.

On this day, as I stood in the cornfield, the rent was due on my apartment in Pensacola—and I didn't have it. The odd jobs I collected never amounted to enough to pay the bills. I had run out of options to keep the journey alive. Pick this last row of corn and then pack it in. My road trip had ended, and the attempt to break away and see distant horizons had failed. Return home where the journey had started, put the dream on the shelf, and remove the college degree. It was time to become an adult.

The above reflection occurred on a farm in South Alabama in the summer of 1972. I returned home, and with my degree, started a career in youth work. I believe I lived a life worth living. I married, raised two daughters, and had more than my fair share of enriching experiences. But the memory of the failed road trip in '72 always lingered in my mind and left me feeling I had some unfinished business. The bucket list I compiled as I neared retirement had only one item on it: drive an old air-cooled VW to California. I retired in 2016, showed my one-item bucket list to my wife, Dianne, and started looking for a VW bus that could get me to California.

My goals as I set out in 2017 were not much different from my goals in 1972. It was the first year of the Trump Presidency, and again the country was sharply divided. I wondered what I would see from the large bay window of a VW bus and whether I could find our common ground as I traveled the back roads of America. And again, I wanted to step out of my comfort zone and see what I could discover about myself. It was a dream deferred, but not forgotten.

I

*Once more there sounded within me the terrible warning
that there is only one life for all men, that there is no
other and that all that can be enjoyed must be enjoyed
here. In eternity no other chance will be given to us.*

—Nikos Kazantzakis, *Zorba the Greek*

THE BIG MUDDY

In 1969, the folk singer Pete Seeger wrote a song entitled "The Big Muddy." The song described an army platoon marching in a Louisiana swamp. First, they were knee-deep, then waist-deep, then neck-deep in the Big Muddy. It was an obvious metaphor for the Vietnam War and became more controversial and more popular after CBS banned it from being played on *The Smothers Brothers Comedy Hour*. Our country was neck-deep in the Big Muddy, and every young male had to decide whether they were going to wade in.

In 1970, I was entering my junior year of college and beginning to look ahead to graduation and the next chapter in my life. Some of my peers were preparing to launch their careers, had their first job secured, and were ready to begin the long march toward retirement. I saw that march as not much different from the march into the Big Muddy. Like others, after graduation, I wanted to take a detour before fully embracing the responsibilities of adulthood and launching a career. The options were varied, but there were some popular ones such as strapping on a backpack and hitchhiking around Europe or hiking the Appalachian Trail end to end. Others chose to join the Peace Corps or VISTA, providing service to others. Finally, there was the epic road trip, a detour from adult life that offered the possibility of never returning. It was an easy choice for me. I wanted to hit the road. But first I had to contend with the Big Muddy.

The country was torn apart by the war, and every draft-eligible young man weighed his options: voluntarily serve in the armed forces, flee to Canada, or claim status as a conscientious objector. Incarceration for failure to report for induction was another option. Or... you could do nothing and pray that your number wasn't called. The number I am referring to was the number you received in the draft lottery. In 1969, with the war becoming increasingly unpopular and the all-volunteer army becoming unfeasible, President Nixon directed the Selective Service Commission to develop a method for selecting inductees. The SSC decided to institute a lottery, a fair and random way of determining the order of induction. The system proved to be anything but fair and significantly less than random.

The drawing was held on December 1, 1969, for all males born during the years 1944–1950. The method selected was simple and could not have been more low-tech. All 366 calendar dates—February 29 included— were written on paper and inserted into capsules. Starting with January, each month was placed into a shoebox, mixed, and then dumped into a large glass jar. After all the months had been placed in the glass jar, the numbers were mixed again. The dates were drawn, one by one, with the first date drawn, September 14, assigned lottery number 1, the second drawn, February 10, assigned lottery number 2, and so on.

However, because the dates were placed into the glass jar by order of calendar month, it was later determined the mixing method was insufficient, and persons born in November and December—which were added last and were disproportionately near the top—had a much higher representation of low draft numbers. Only five birth dates in December escaped being called for induction, while the rules of probability would have predicted there would be three times that. But there was no "do over." My birthdate, August 7, was the 168th pulled from the jar. It seemed like a good number, and I certainly fared better than my brother John, one year older than me. His birthdate, February 19, put him 25th in line for the draft. Big brothers always have more responsibility.

Another ingredient in the draft that created inequity in the system was the deferment categories. These were many and varied and included involvement in agricultural work, persons studying for the ministry, and the most significant one of all, a college deferment. Any young man who could afford to attend college could defer his induction so long as he maintained passing grades in twelve credit hours each semester. As a result of this deferment, the poor and disenfranchised, many of whom could not afford to attend college, assumed an inordinate amount of responsibility for fighting the war in Vietnam. Poor people always have more responsibility.

When I initially registered for the draft at age eighteen, I received the deferment for persons pursuing religious studies. At the age of fourteen, I had decided to follow in my uncle's footsteps, a priest in Kansas, and entered the seminary. I enrolled at St. Thomas Seminary, a boarding school just outside of my hometown, Louisville, Kentucky. The year was 1964, and before the buildup in Vietnam, so the choice was genuine and not a calculated way to avoid the draft. At that age, I was sharing my parents' view of communism, and if asked—though no one did—I would have voiced support for the war effort in Vietnam. However, like many Americans, my view of the war evolved as the years passed, and the politics of the war became more apparent. My epiphany occurred when I read the ninety-six-page treatise on the history of US involvement in Vietnam written by famed pediatrician,

Dr. Benjamin Spock. *Dr. Spock on Vietnam* was published in 1968 and was such a compelling argument against our involvement in the war that the federal government indicted him on charges of conspiring to urge people to violate the draft laws. He was convicted and sentenced to two years in federal prison—the conviction later set aside on appeal.

In 1970, after six years of somewhat priestly studies (I worked more on my jump shot in the gym than anything else), I decided to leave the seminary. Despite the Second Vatican Council and the step toward enlightenment that the Catholic Church took in the early 1960s, I still had profound differences of opinion with church leadership—birth control and the ban on women priests among them. When I transferred from the seminary to the University of Louisville, the Selective Service Commission came knocking. Because my theology classes at the seminary would not transfer to a state university, I was behind in my credit hours and had lost my student deferment. Without a deferment, I was in the queue to be drafted, and suddenly, the number 168 became very important to me. My number was not low enough to be certain of induction, nor high enough to be certain of non-induction. Seeking advice, I went to the unadvertised office that existed on every college campus at the time, the one with the savvy long-haired people who knew the system and who could advise you on the "how-to" of avoiding the draft. They all looked like they owned VW buses.

When I entered their space, I saw it was adorned with anti-war slogans, black fists raised high, a wide variety of peace symbols, and sure enough, a portrait of a VW bus. They advised me that the government would not draft as high as number 168, and I was safe. "Relax and enjoy your college life" was the message I got. A month later, as I was relaxing, the letter arrived instructing me to report to the local selective service office for a physical. I returned to my VW bus friends, and they again told me to "chill brother" as the government was pulling people in with borderline numbers for physicals but assured me 168 was sufficiently high and I would not be inducted. I prepared myself for the probing the government wanted to do, but I can't say I was particularly "chill" about it.

SOCIALIST WORKERS PARTY

There were many strategies employed at this stage of the draft to derail one's induction. Convincing the army you were gay or showing up for your physical as a crossdresser were among those utilized. Many people stayed awake for days and took multiple drugs, hoping a sickly appearance and the various substances identified in their bloodstream would convince the army they were not fit to serve. And then there was noted rock musician Ted Nugent. Ted did not bathe for thirty days, took some crystal meth, shat in his pants before attending the physical, and successfully secured a 4-F draft rating, which grouped him in with mass murderers and unfit to serve. Ted would go on in life questioning everyone else's patriotism, most notably Hillary Clinton's during her run for the Presidency in 2016.

But I didn't need any of that. I was told to relax, chill. I reported at the appointed time and place, and the probing commenced. My biggest hope lay in the fact that I was severely nearsighted and had been wearing eyeglasses since second grade. God help my platoon if my glasses broke in combat and I continued firing my M16. But when they tested my vision, they seemed only concerned about my sight with glasses, not without. After several hours of standing around in my boxers with my fellow inductees and visiting several stations crewed by probers in white coats, everyone was told to get dressed and take a seat in a small classroom.

The final step in the process, before they released the group of potential inductees, was some non-physical probing. A young Army Lieutenant was handing out a list of all the known radical elements in

American society at the time. Being a member of Ted Nugent's band was not one of them, but it was still a very extensive list. He told us to check off any groups we had ever been in contact with. I scanned the list, and there it was—"Socialist Workers Party." The memory brought a smile to my face, but I also became less relaxed.

The previous summer, I had been working as a bottle inspector on the production line at the RC Cola plant in Louisville. My responsibility was to sit and watch empty bottles race by on the assembly line, yanking off the line any that had not been properly cleaned. Dead mice and toothbrushes—I can't explain the toothbrush phenomenon— seemed to be the most frequent violators of the RC Cola code of cleanliness. After thirty minutes of empty bottles, you switched to watching filled bottles go by, illuminated by a backlight so you could see any dead mice or toothbrushes that the guy up the line had missed. After an eight-hour day of this—empty bottles–full bottles–empty bottles–full bottles—you went home with a headache, blurred vision, and a commitment never to drink RC Cola.

I had been at the bottling plant for a week when my brother John informed me he was going to Chicago to live with his girlfriend for the summer and asked if I wanted to come along. His girlfriend's dad had some connections and could get us jobs at a local factory. Summer in Chicago versus protecting the public from contaminated soda pop? I broke the news to my boss at RC Cola, who muttered something disparaging about college kids, and I headed north to Chicago.

In Chicago, I found factory work that paid more than inspecting bottles. More importantly, my migraines went away, and my vision was ensured for later use in life. I also met Judy Campbell. Judy was a college student at Northern Illinois University. She was both attractive and connected to the radical lifestyle in Chicago—which for me heightened her allure. My summer in Chicago was only two years after the police riot at the Democratic National Convention, and an air of tension and upheaval was still present.

The previous summer, the Weathermen Underground conducted their first public demonstration, a riot in Chicago timed to coincide with the trial of the Chicago Seven. Also, the previous year the Students for a Democratic Society had held their annual convention in Chicago. I felt I was breaking out of the bubble I had spent my life in—family, seminary, and the conservative, don't-challenge-authority environment of Kentucky. Having watched it all from a distance, I had a sense of excitement as I put myself closer to the unrest growing in the country.

One day, Judy suggested I attend a meeting of the Socialist Workers Party cell she belonged to, and I eagerly accepted the invite. We took the bus—good socialists always take public transportation—and arrived after dark at a house in a working-class neighborhood north of downtown Chicago. There was no porch light illuminating the entrance, and few lights were on in the house. We wandered through several rooms where various conversations were taking place, all dimly lit. Judy found some fellow socialists she knew, and we settled onto the floor and joined in. The mood was tense, and the exchanges were edgy. The joint being passed around did nothing to lighten the mood. Challenging authority and creating upheaval in the system was serious business.

Passed along with the joint was a flyer with the letters KKK in boldface type. I assumed the Socialist Workers Party was taking a stand against racism, and I was ready to jump in, but then realized the letters referred to something else—"Kopechne Killer Kennedy." It was one year after the tragic accident on Chappaquiddick Island in Massachusetts, which killed Mary Jo Kopechne, her body found underwater in a car driven by Senator Ted Kennedy. The connection between this accident and the agenda of the Socialist Workers Party wasn't clear to me, but my attraction for Judy was only strengthened by the dark intensity in the room so I let it slide. I don't recall saying much at the meeting, which would be typical of me. When in new environments, I become more an observer and, from a safe distance, carefully weigh my options. Judy's intensity grew with the others, and I could feel the temperature rising in the room. I'm not sure that a plan of action was ever agreed upon, and Judy and I departed the meeting with only one of us fully committed to the agenda of the Socialist Workers Party. But I was fully committed to Judy.

My job at the factory paid well and while I earned my money, my last day on the job may have negated most of the contribution I made to industrial America. With only one hour to go in my workday, my floor boss finally uttered the words I had been wanting to hear all summer: "Hey college boy… would you like to drive the forklift?"

Having never driven a forklift, I jumped at the opportunity. He directed me to deliver a load of rebar to the next warehouse over. The rebar was already loaded onto the forklift. My job was a simple one, just drive to the open bay in the neighboring warehouse and deposit the load. A glorious end to my summer employment.

I hopped onto the forklift, fired it up, and began my journey. As I neared the bay door where I was to make my delivery, I realized the load was wide and would be a tight fit entering the warehouse opening. I slowly eased up to the opening with my head on a swivel, ensuring the rebar would have sufficient clearance on both sides. I had inches to spare, but due to my now proficient forklift skills I was going to make it. However, I was so focused on the width of the load and the narrow bay opening, I failed to notice that the lift cylinders were extended up and at a height that would not clear the bay door hanging above the opening. This became apparent to me when the door came crashing down on top of the forklift.

After I extracted myself from the wreckage, the floor boss was standing by the forklift shaking his head. He had only one thing to say: "Do me a favor, okay? Go back to college." I assured him I would and promptly punched out, my last day at the factory. I'm sure if he had talked to my RC Cola manager back in Louisville, they would have had similar thoughts about the efficacy of hiring "college boys" in the summer.

Now a year later and back in Louisville, sitting in the cramped classroom during my army physical, I dutifully made a checkmark next to the Socialist Workers Party. I did this not in hopes it would discourage the army from drafting me, but rather, at that point in my life I felt lying to the government was probably unwise. I also wondered what information they already had on me. I don't remember signing anything when I joined Judy in her Socialist Workers Party cell, but I did take a hit or two off the joint, so who knows?

The young Army Lieutenant collected the forms and after a brief review he dismissed everyone but me. The Lieutenant wished to have some private time with me, and he wanted to hear a little more about my ties with the Socialist Workers Party. I don't remember the exact conversation we had, but I'd like to think it went something like this:

"Thank you, Mr. Steimel, for staying to talk to me."

"I didn't think I had a choice."

"Well, the US Army just has a few questions for you."

"Ask away."

"Are you a commie?"

"Nope."

"Well, what's your association with the Socialist Workers Party?"

"Well, there was this girl. Very attractive."

"I understand. You may go now and please have a nice day. We will be in touch."

Okay, it probably didn't go like that, but the good Lieutenant did release me, and sure enough, they were in touch. After my physical, I returned to enjoying campus life confident that my "draft advisors" were accurate in their predictions regarding the Selective Service and number 168. However, only four weeks passed before I received my next letter from the United States Government. Induction letters were infamous for both being directly from the President of the United States and their opening line: "Greetings… You are hereby ordered for induction into the Armed Forces of the United States." "*Greetings*," it's a nice touch. The letter ordered me to report in two weeks for induction into the US Army. They do not give you much time to get your affairs in order—or consider other options.

At this point in my life, I was morally opposed to the war and I felt my best option was to inform my parents they could visit me whenever they wanted over the border in Canada. Before heading north, and I'm not sure why given their track record so far, I took the letter to my now not-so-savvy but still long-haired draft advisors on campus. I assume I did this only to see the embarrassed look on their faces and who knows, maybe they knew the best places to cross the border. Instead, they showed me another path, one that did not lead north. I learned I could request a delay in my induction for six months, and if at that time, I had caught up on my college credits, I could regain college deferment status. I made my calculations and determined that enrolling in seven college classes during the next semester would put me back on track. Seven courses in one semester was a bit overwhelming but better than getting shot at in Vietnam. And I did not have to defecate in my pants as Ted Nugent did.

I successfully navigated my way through a challenging semester, passed my seven courses, and reclaimed my student deferment status.

I completed my studies in 1972, and by then, my friends in their VW buses were finally correct. Number 168 was beyond the reach of the government. With the Big Muddy not in my future, I could begin planning my detour from a responsible adult life—an epic road trip.

I share all of this not out of a sense of pride that I managed to avoid the draft. I did nothing deserving of admiration. That should be saved for the people who answered their country's call and served, and for the people who saw the injustice of the war and actively opposed it. While I participated in one anti-war march in the Kentucky state capital of Frankfort, I can't say that I ever resisted in any way that put me in jeopardy. My brother John served, as did my cousin Gregg. John returned safely, but Gregg did not. My admiration is reserved for them and the others who, no matter what kind of marching they did, paid a price for their convictions.

On a final note, and in an odd twist of fate, Judy graduated from Northern Illinois University with her degree in art history and, unable to find a job, enlisted in the US Army. She had a twenty-five-year career, was honorably discharged with her full pension, and last I heard, was living with her husband and kids in the south of France. Well played, Judy.

WHEELS

I can recall only two occasions in my life when I heard my father use a curse word. Once was when I was very young, and I put too much bathwater in the tub. Coming into the bathroom, he quickly reached for the faucet, and while shutting it off, the words "Why is there so much damn water in the tub?!" flowed from his mouth. To this day, I think of that every time I fill the tub, and even my showers are astonishingly brief so as not to use up a lot of "damn water." The second time was my senior year of college, and it was in reference to my very first car, a 1947 Willys Jeep. I have always been attracted to the unusual in my vehicles, and when I saw the old Willys for sale, resting in someone's yard, I pulled together the $300 I needed to make the purchase.

The Willys–Overland Company had beat out the Ford Motor Company in its bid to produce a lightweight four-wheel-drive vehicle for the US Army in 1940. After winning the bid, Willys shared the design with Ford, and together they manufactured over 700,000 Jeeps for the Army during World War II. After the war, Willys marketed a civilian version until 1953, creating the "Jeep" brand in 1950. The brand has changed hands several times since then, but like the Volkswagen Beetle, the look has remained relatively unchanged.

My Willys was a mobile class in automotive repair—because everything on it at one time or another broke down. My personal nemesis was the starter. It had the annoying habit of engaging and then freezing in place without turning the engine over. Its favorite time of doing it was first thing in the morning as I was rushing out the door to class at the University of Louisville. Holding the starter in place were two bolts, and I became very adept at removing the bolts, resetting the starter's drive gear, and then reinstalling it. I became so adept at it that the problem at most created a three-minute delay at the start of my day.

But that was just one of many problems associated with the Willys, and it was not unusual for me to be stranded somewhere and, needing a ride, call my dad. I think there is a counter in every dad's head that keeps track of all this, and at some point, you exceed the limit. It had the same effect as putting too much water in the tub. He finally exclaimed one day, "When are you going to get rid of that damn car?!" When you hear a word only twice in your life from your dad, it has an exaggerated effect. It took me less than a week to find a buyer.

Even without my dad's "encouragement," the clock had been ticking on the Willys. I had made up my mind to take an extended road trip after college, and a vehicle that had a maximum range of one hundred miles before breaking down would not get me very far from my parents' driveway. As I studied my options, my mind kept returning to the VW Beetle. It got great gas mileage, was fun to drive, had a counterculture feel to it, and was affordable. My search took me to a local used-car lot, and a Beetle sitting next to a '65 Ford Mustang caught my eye. The Beetle had a shiny black finish that made it look a little badass—as much as a Beetle could—and bright chrome bumpers front and back. The dealer seemed a little surprised by my choice of the Beetle over the Mustang but was happy to take my money. When I returned home I discovered my dad wasn't much of a VW fan—"No Fords available?"—but I'm sure he felt it was an improvement over the Willys, since the Beetle got me through the final weeks of college without any rescue calls to him.

Every road trip vehicle needs a name since it will be your companion on the journey, and I christened my Beetle with the name of Zorba. I don't recall how I was first introduced to the writer Nikos Kazantzakis, but I began reading his novels during my college years. The spirit of Zorba—*Zorba the Greek*— particularly captured my imagination. The novel relates the tale of a young Greek intellectual who seeks to escape his books and experience life directly. After his encounter with the boisterous Alexis Zorba in a cafe, he hires Zorba to assist him in an ill-fated endeavor to revive a coal mine in Crete. Zorba is spontaneous and fearless in his approach to life.

Zorba's guiding philosophy was to be totally absorbed in whatever you are doing and whomever you are with. You only have the present within your grasp—embrace it! To this end, Zorba celebrated the experience of failure as much as success. No matter the result— have a shot of ouzo, spread out your arms, and dance. I knew I was no Zorba—more like the bookish narrator of the story—but I strived to acquire his outlook on life and felt that naming my vehicle after him would keep him present on my journey.

I also knew I needed more than imaginary companionship given the challenges I expected along the way, so I turned to the person who knew me best, a lifelong friend. Art and I first met when we were two years old and our families moved to the same street. Art lived three doors down on Eagle Pass, and we became inseparable. We attended eight years of elementary school together at St. Stephen Martyr, often walking the half-mile to and from school together. Sometimes we even ran home together for lunch. Yes, there was a time when you could leave school if you lived nearby and go home to have lunch with your mom. I believe it's called the 1950s.

After finishing eighth grade at St. Stephen Martyr, Art and I both decided to attend St. Thomas, the local Catholic seminary just outside of Louisville. It was a boarding school, and when it came time to say goodbye to my family at age fourteen, having Art there made all the difference. We shared six years together, studying for the priesthood and then chose different paths. Art continued in the seminary in Baltimore, Maryland, while I ended my priestly studies and attended the University of Louisville.

Two years later, 1972, having graduated from college, I needed someone foolish enough, or perhaps loyal enough, to join me on this journey west to California in a very small VW Beetle. Art was still in the seminary, struggling with the decision to return or not, and felt he could use some time outside of his bubble as well. He was up for a road trip. We planned to head west until we got to California, and beyond that, there wasn't much of a plan. Neither of us needed to march into the Big Muddy, and we found the call of the open road irresistible—and requiring a lot less effort than hiking the Appalachian Trail.

WARRIOR, ALABAMA

Following in the footsteps of other travelers, Art and I chose to keep a journal of our trip just as the legendary Marco Polo did in the thirteenth century. The journal notes that we departed Louisville on Friday, May 26, at precisely 6:47 am with the sun rising on the horizon. (While our trip planning may have lacked some attention to detail, the journal we kept did not.) We had placed one bag of clothing each in the small trunk under the front hood of Zorba, and in the back seat, we loaded our tent, camp stove, and a bag of assorted gear. Art was at the wheel as we headed south on I-65, out of Louisville. Our objective that first day was to arrive in Pensacola, Florida, 615 miles away, where my brother John was in the US Navy's Aviation Officer Training Program. He was to become an officer and a gentleman, courtesy of the US Navy. Pensacola was an ambitious target for the first day, but we had gotten an early start, and we were confident in ourselves and Zorba.

The journal mentions only one delay to our departure that morning: a quick repair of the racing grip I had put on Zorba's steering wheel—yes, a racing grip on a '66 Beetle. As I said, we were confident. The next detail noted in the journal were the numerous fireworks stores we passed when crossing the state line into Tennessee. Because fireworks are illegal in Kentucky, there is a parade of stores just over the state line, and they all seemed to imply that anyone who plays with fireworks is not playing with a full deck. Loco Joe's, Crazy Ed's, Looney Luke's, Crazy Cecil's, and finally Crazy Jerry's flew past Zorba as we "raced" south on I-65.

A photo in the journal, from a stop for gas, shows me sitting on a swing set—not a care in the world. The photo also captures the price of gas—37.9 cents a gallon. There is a passing reference to the starter not turning over and the need to push-start Zorba. One would think the need to push-start your car a hundred miles into a road trip would raise some concerns, but none noted, just a mention that we may need to purchase a new solenoid. After the stop for gas, the journal notes passing a billboard of a smiling George Wallace welcoming us to the great state of Alabama and telling us to "Take a Fun Break!" We gave George the one-finger salute and headed into the Deep South with our shaggy hair.

The next entry in the journal simply states: "*The 'planned' trip is over.*" I cannot recall whether the quotation marks around "*planned*" were meant to mock ourselves over the lack of planning—or we were just indicating that although the trip was continuing, it was not in the way we planned. Either way, the news was not good. Thirty miles north of Birmingham, the green light on Zorba's dash lit up. It's important to know that the 1966 Volkswagen has an uncomplicated dash and the only warning indicator that lives on it is the green light. We weren't sure what it meant, but we noticed the car seemed to be losing some of its power, which in an old Beetle is limited to begin with.

As we continued down I-65, we next heard a ticking sound coming from the engine. We tried to ignore it along with the green light, but it insisted otherwise. It was time for an intervention. Pulling off the interstate, we parked on an overpass while pulling out the manual I had purchased after I had acquired Zorba—*How to Keep Your Volkswagen Alive—A Manual of Step by Step Procedures for the Compleat Idiot* by John Muir. John Muir was a structural engineer who worked for NASA before dropping out, '60s style, to become a writer and a long-haired car mechanic with a garage in Taos, New Mexico. First published in 1969, it opens with the quote, "Come to kindly terms with your Ass for it bears you." Its philosophy was born out of the counterculture of the '60s, and it was as much a guide to finding Zen with your car as it was a repair manual. I know of no other auto repair manual that uses words like "feel," "love," and "karma."

Before delving into the workings of an air-cooled VW, John Muir lifts up the hood on the driver's inner workings and attempts a little adjustment:

While the levels of logic of the human entity are many and varied, your car operates on one simple level and it's up to you to understand its trip. Talk to the car, then shut up and listen. Feel with your car; use all of your receptive senses and when you find out what it needs, seek the operation out and perform it with love. The type of life your car contains differs from yours by time scale, logic level and conceptual anomalies but is "Life" nonetheless. Its Karma depends on your desire to make and keep it—ALIVE!

I share this not to diminish in any way its scope and range as a repair manual. Nearly 500 pages of detailed instructions and illustrations address any possible maintenance or repair issue a Volkswagen owner may encounter. It just asks that whatever you do to your car, you do with love. And that's a beautiful thing.

It probably would have been a good idea to have read John Muir's book in its entirety before beginning our odyssey, which in fact, he tells you to do, but we didn't have time for that. Besides, we were "Compleat Idiots." We would learn as we went. Art and I searched out the section that explained the green light and found forceful directions, highlighted in all CAPS, for when the light comes on: "STOP THE CAR—RIGHT NOW!" Too late for that. Muir then instructs you to go to the back of the car, open the engine compartment, and attempt to touch the dipstick. *"Too hot to touch?"* Art confirmed that it was.

Here Muir's instructions get very specific:

Do nothing until the engine cools! Read, enjoy the scenery, take a walk. If you have a bus, and a friend, it might be a good time to go in the back and ball. Eat your lunch. Give

*the engine at least a half-hour or more to cool before you
take any further action. Ya hear?*

Luckily, Art and I did not have a bus because, at that point, we
were trying to do everything John Muir told us to do. We enjoyed the
scenery instead. Our journal includes a picture of Art striking a pose
on the overpass, with no obvious concern reflected in his face. There
should have been. After we let the engine cool for the length of time
Muir requested, we restarted Zorba, the green light returned, and the
engine continued to make a ticking sound.

We turned to the section in the *Compleat Idiot Manual,* where
Muir describes engine noises. On page 87, under the heading *"Listen
for Expensive Noises,"* he states the following:

> *A connecting rod about to burn out its bearing will make a
> tick-tick-tickety-tick sound changing to a tock-tock-tockety-
> tock sound, usually associated with a loss of the oil pressure
> causing the green light to come on, but not until the rod is
> really gone.*

We leaned in, tilting our heads toward the engine, and jointly
concluded we had a tickety sound, not a tockety sound. Muir is adamant that you do not drive the vehicle when making a ticking sound
because you don't want it to evolve into a tocking sound. It's the difference between a minor overhaul to replace the rod bearing and a major
overhaul calling for a new crankshaft. He instructs you to take what is
important to you out of the car and seek help.

This created a problem. Art and I were on an overpass in the
middle of Alabama, having recently given the Governor a rude gesture,
and according to our map, there was no place within walking distance
where we could seek help. Having no other option, we decided that
perhaps John Muir was an alarmist. We restarted Zorba and limped

onto I-65 south, heading for the closest town, Warrior, Alabama, fifteen miles away.

After ten minutes on I-65, we reached the Warrior exit, and by then, even two *Compleat Idiots* could tell the engine's ticking sound had transformed into a tocking sound, which to us felt more like a mocking sound. It turns out John Muir was not an alarmist. We sputtered and jerked our way into Warrior, Alabama, drawing looks from the locals as Zorba noisily made his way down Main Street, tocking and mocking away.

At the time, Volkswagens were still considered an oddity, and Muir advises you not to let a mechanic learn on your car. He implores you to seek out someone who has some experience with air-cooled vehicles or be prepared to spend twice what you should pay. We rolled, barely, into the first gas station we encountered and inquired if they worked on VWs.

"Nope. You need to go see Slick. He works on them things."

We got some directions and luckily it was just down the street. Actually, in Warrior, everything is "just down the street," and we pulled into Slick's Automotive Shop on the corner of Fifth and Main right behind the OK Garage. Slick heard us coming, stopped what he was doing, and wiping his hands on a rag, walked out to Zorba. After confirming he worked on "them things," he lifted up the engine cover and told me to start it up. He pulled the throttle cable a few times revving the engine, and put his ear up close to the tocking sound.

"You done blow'd it up" was his diagnosis.

I'm sure John Muir was shaking his head somewhere, saying, "Told 'em not to drive it." Slick said he could fix it, but it would cost us $400. Between Art and me, that was pretty much all the money we had brought on the trip. Having paid a total of $600 for Zorba a few months earlier, I wasn't ready to make a deeper investment.

Seeing my hesitation, Slick added that if I didn't want to repair it, my best option was to rent a car and "Drag its ass back to Louisville." That meant ending our trip and reversing our direction, and I wasn't ready to do that. I figured if Art and I could get to Pensacola, then we could find jobs and plan a way forward. I could not let go of the dream of living on the open road, even if I didn't have a functioning car. Dreams die hard.

"Hey, I know you in a tight spot. How 'bouts I buy the car from you?" Slick offered. "I'll give you $175, and you leave it here. I'll give you thirty days to figure out what you want to do with it. I won't touch it for thirty days. If you want to come back and reclaim it, you can do that and give me my money back." Slick added that this would give us some time to figure out the "situation you in."

Art and I looked at each other, shared a nod, and after I talked Slick up to $200, we shook on it. Slick pulled an 8×11 mimeographed "Bill of Sale" from his desk and called his brother Billy asking him to drive to the shop with $200. I made a plea for the new tachometer I had installed in Zorba just before Art and I left Louisville, and Slick graciously let me remove it from the steering column. Billy pulled up in his pickup truck, and Zorba changed hands.

After Art and I removed our gear from Zorba and changed clothes in Slick's garage, we headed over to the phone booth outside the OK Garage. We needed a way out of Dodge. It was a roll of the dice, but I called the only number I had for my brother John at the Pensacola Naval Air Station. The number was for the watch station on the base, and it was the Friday before Memorial Day weekend. We did not know if John would be able take a call, let alone get off the base and come pluck us out of Warrior. But our options were even more limited than when we were standing back on the overpass. I dialed the number, and the voice on the other end shouted back at me, "Naval Aviation

Officer Candidate John C. Steimel, sir!" My brother happened to be on watch duty.

John was enrolled in the same naval training program on which the movie *An Officer and a Gentleman* was based. In the movie, Mayo (Richard Gere) meets Paula (Debra Winger) at the Regimental Ball on the base. Ultimately, after multiple tests of his character, and a direct blow to his balls, Mayo has an epiphany. He becomes an officer and a gentleman and, for the big climax, goes to Paula's place of work and sweeps her off her feet—all very romantic. For my brother, it was the night before the Regimental Ball—his chance to meet his Debra Winger.

I explained that Art and I were stranded in Warrior, Alabama, and requested him to pick us up if he wasn't too busy. My brother had other plans. The Navy employed a woman, let's call her a "Social Director," whose primary task was to ensure that all the Naval Officer Candidates had a date for the Regimental Ball. She had on her desk— and Mitt Romney stole this idea forty years later when he ran for President—a binder full of women. The ladies in the binder were all local single women within a designated age range who had volunteered to be dates for Officer Candidates at the Regimental Ball. The previous day John had met with the Social Director and selected a young woman from the binder.

The Ball was held on a Saturday night. On Friday night, the night we called, the Candidates were allowed to leave the base and have a meet and greet with their dates so they would know a little bit about each other before the Ball. My brother had a decision to make. Get off the base for the first time in his training program and meet an attractive young woman or rent a car and drive up to Warrior, Alabama, and drag his brother's ass down to Pensacola.

Anyone who has ever met my brother knows what he did. He gave his regrets to the attractive young woman and headed north on

I-65 in a rental car to get his little brother out of another jam. I say "another" because that was not the first time nor the last time that he has had to do this. As I mentioned before, big brothers always have more responsibility. Whether they choose to accept it or not is another question. I was fortunate to have a big brother who always did.

Since John was several hours away, Art and I wandered around Warrior and found ourselves at the 5th Annual Warrior Horse Show on the football field of Warrior High School. We grabbed a couple of hot dogs from the food stand and climbed up into the bleachers. The public address announcer was a well-known radio DJ from Boaz, Alabama, fifty-two miles away, and while we concluded he knew very little about horses, he was entertaining.

"What did the horse say when it fell? I've fallen, and I can't giddyup."

"What do you call an Amish guy with his hand in a horse's mouth? A mechanic."

The mechanic joke hit a little close to home, but we laughed anyway. We ate our dogs and got a few looks from the locals who probably thought we needed a visit to the Warrior barbershop.

After the horse show, we headed back to Slick's where we settled in on the sidewalk waiting for my brother to arrive. Around 11 pm, the local police came by.

"Why you layn' on my sidewalk, boy?" Officer Obie inquired.

Leaning out of Officer Obie's squad car window was a double-barreled shotgun. Feeling like we were in a scene from *In the Heat of the Night*, we gave him straight answers and several times mentioned that we knew Slick. That seemed to satisfy him, and he gave us permission to remain on his sidewalk. We respectfully thanked him. A shotgun demands courtesy. Shortly before midnight, one of the locals wandered by, or rather staggered by, and relieved himself in the middle of the intersection. Officer Obie did not question him. He did have a nice haircut.

My brother pulled up a little after midnight. We loaded the gear into the car, put Warrior in the rearview mirror, and, given the lateness of the hour, headed to a Ramada Inn just outside Birmingham to spend the night. The entry in our road trip journal simply states:

Funny, life never quite turns out the way you plan it—I guess that's why it's so darn interesting.

Deep.

SQUIRREL CITY

The next day we continued down I-65 to Pensacola, Florida, and made our first stop an auto parts store. John owned a turquoise 1965 Mustang convertible. It was not the one I saw in the used-car lot next to Zorba a few months back, but it did make me reflect on my choice that day. Since John did not need his car while stationed on the base, he loaned it to Art and me for use while we were in Pensacola. But first, it needed a new alternator and regulator. John had the Regimental Ball to attend that night, so having picked up the parts we needed, Art and I made the repairs in the parking lot at the Navy base.

From there we drove to The Townhouse Motel at the intersection of US 90 and 98 and got a room for the night. ABC was broadcasting the Indy 500 that day, but the picture on the television was fuzzy with the sound cutting in and out. We did hear Jim Nabors sing *Back Home in Indiana* for the first time at the Indy 500, which he continued to do for thirty-six consecutive years. While Art played with the rabbit ears antenna, I grabbed a local newspaper and began looking for a job—although the photo in the journal shows me reading the comics. I guess I did that too.

The next day we called the campground at Fort Pickens State Park, which sits on the Gulf of Mexico, and discovered that all the campsites were occupied; it was a busy Memorial Day weekend. Art recalled passing an establishment called Squirrel's Tent City on the way into Pensacola, so we headed back in that direction. The first thing we encountered upon entering Squirrel's store was a mynah bird. Whenever a young woman passed by, the mynah would let out a wolf whistle. We laughed at that, but later, when we went to the back of the store to grab some batteries, the mynah did the same for us. Maybe we did need a haircut.

Squirrel's given name is Frontis William Sherrill Jr., and he welcomed us to Tent City, where we had our pick of campsites. Squirrel was a local entrepreneur, and in addition to operating an RV park and campground, he had established a zoo on the site. Based on the conditions we witnessed, we concluded that regulations for caging animals were pretty loose in a state where alligators freely roam the street. Squirrel's other operations included Sea Shell City, Souvenir City, and the Shark Museum in Navarre, Florida. Not satisfied with providing tacky souvenirs just to Florida's visitors, he later opened souvenir shops in Costa Rica and Liberia. Squirrel obviously planned to dominate the world's souvenir market.

We spent only one night at Squirrel's Tent City. A picture in the journal shows me hunched over the camp stove, preparing a meal of franks and beans, and Art enjoying some Southern Comfort by the tent. Because Tent City was not on the Gulf of Mexico, and because we wanted to wake up to an ocean breeze, we moved on the next day. It was now Monday, Memorial Day, and we drove out to Fort Pickens State Park, where we figured the campsites would be opening up as the weekenders departed. We were correct and found a spot on the beach with a view of the deep blue Gulf waters. Wanting to be as close to the ocean as possible, we set up our tent on the sandy beach where we could hear the waves gently lapping at the shore and crawled into our sleeping bags for the night. This was when the boys from Kentucky learned a valuable lesson about tides. Those waves that lulled us to sleep entered our tent shortly after 1 am. We retreated back into the palm trees with our wet sleeping bags.

The next day—and I blame the damn tides— Art decided to return to Louisville. His last journal entry states his belief that back in Louisville, "things are a bit better off for me." He hopped on a Greyhound bus heading north. I wrote the final entry in our trip journal the night he left. Prepare yourself for some melancholy.

Wednesday Nite, May 31st

Well it is the end of May and the end of Art and I's trip together and I guess this will be the end of the log. Art took the 1:15 pm bus back to Louisville today, and with him went one of my silly childhood dreams. I'd always dreamed of Art and I taking a long trip and getting away from it all together. My dream never ended so abruptly, however. I'm signed up for 5 more nites at Fort Pickens. It seems so dead now that Art has left. It's been a long time since I can remember being really alone. I have a feeling I'd better get used to it. Sometimes I really feel doomed to be a lonely person. Well, my spirits are falling with the sun. They'll rise with the sun in the morning. Good bye Art. Good bye dreams.

I tried to warn you—pretty dramatic stuff. (Note to self: don't write journal entries at night during your darkest moments. And if you do, don't keep the journal for forty-five years.)

My spirits did rise in the morning, and I got to work trying to find a job and a place to live. I had my brother's Mustang convertible, and with the top down, I set out to find my future. My first stop was the State of Florida's Office of Employment Assistance. After waiting for my turn, I sat down with one of the employment counselors. She was middle-aged, friendly, and seemed sympathetic to my plight. I don't recall her name, but she had red hair and reminded me of my mother. I felt I was in good hands. I mentioned I had seen in the newspaper they were hiring on the shrimp boats, and the pay was three times what I had ever made on a summer job in Kentucky. Employment Mom shot that down right away.

"Hun, you have a college degree. I'm going to find you something where you can use that education of yours."

Sounded like something my mother would say. I let go of the notion of working the nets on a shrimp boat, and she told me to come back the following Monday, and she would see what she could find for me and my college degree.

Trusting she would make me her number one priority, I began searching for a place to live. I had some quick success and used most of my money to secure a third-floor efficiency apartment on East Cervantes Street. There was a view of a park across the street, but most critically, it had an air conditioner. Having grown up in Kentucky, I thought I knew what summer heat and humidity were, but Pensacola was beyond anything I had ever experienced. A few hours in the sun sucked the life out of you, and it was easy to lose five pounds every day from sheer perspiration. I found myself looking forward to that cushy air-conditioned office job my Employment Mom was going to find for me.

I returned to her office at the appointed time on Monday but found I needed to remind her who I was. She seemed to recall after a couple of hints and informed me no, she hadn't found anything for me yet. I brought up the shrimp boats again, but she put her foot down.

"No, no. That is not pleasant work. You have a college degree. Give me another week to find you something, hun."

The "hun" was reassuring, but then that term is employed rather generously in the South. I should have been suspicious, but as one can see from my last journal entry, I was feeling a little vulnerable.

I continued to trust Employment Mom but started working on a backup plan. I returned to the ads in the newspaper and found two part-time jobs I could do while I waited to use my BS in Political Science. It was a Presidential election year, and the McGovern campaign needed people to do door-to-door canvassing for them. I combined that with a job delivering discount coupons books that people had purchased through the newspaper. Doing both, I earned just enough to pay for the gas I used driving around town. Things were slipping away from me.

My growing sense of desperation may have been the thing that led me to an experience both odd and awkward. Heading home one evening after a day of doors slammed in my face when residents of the Florida Panhandle realized I worked for McGovern and not the true American patriot Nixon, I stopped to pick up a hitchhiker alongside the road. As we rode, he told me about the commune he lived in and asked if I was interested in joining them for dinner. It must have been the combination of desiring some companionship and the idea of a free meal that drew me in. I accepted the offer, and we headed for the commune.

It was located in a rather ordinary-looking house with no outward sign that anything deviant was occurring inside. Once in the door, I realized that the commune was organized around some rather rigid religious beliefs, although I never could figure out its particular variety. When the topic of books came up, I mentioned some of my favorite authors, and they countered with the Bible. It was the only book they were allowed to read. Okay. My favorite authors could not compete with God, so we moved on to another subject. The food was vegetarian, and the conversation centered around life at the commune and the joy it brought them.

After dinner was when things got a little weird. We gathered in a circle holding hands, and after they welcomed me into the group, and after a few shared thoughts on peace and love, the speaking-in-tongues commenced. That was the first and only time I had experienced the phenomenon. Various people were moved to shout out words and phrases that had no meaning whatsoever—at least to me, and I suspect everyone there. I was terrified it would become my turn and did everything I could to make myself invisible. When the inspired gibberish ended, I quickly thanked them for their generosity and slipped away. Back at my apartment on East Cervantes Street, I made myself a hot dog. For perhaps the only time in my life, it had a cleansing effect.

The next day I returned for the final time to see Employment Mom in the state office building. She remembered me this time but had not found anything that fit my particular skill set. My "skill set," a college degree, seemed to be holding me back, and I again inquired about the shrimp boats.

"You know, I really wouldn't mind working the nets on a shrimp boat. The pay is good, and the ocean breeze might be kind of nice this time of year. I'll hold onto that college degree of mine and use it another time." I gave her my most charming smile.

"Well, they're no longer hiring, hun."

Thanks, Mom. As I headed for the door, she asked me to return in a week, but I left knowing I wouldn't. I was on my own when it came to finding a job, and I concluded the State of Florida only had jobs for their own. I'm sure all of "Mom's" relatives were making good money on a shrimp boat, even the ones with college degrees.

I remembered seeing on one of my drives outside Pensacola, a sign in a field that said: "Hiring Pickers." Desperate, I returned to the spot, which was just over the state line in South Alabama. I knocked on the front door of the farmhouse and inquired if they were still hiring, or like the shrimp boats, had the golden opportunity slipped away? I was in luck, and my career as a migrant farmworker began. On the farm, they raised corn and cucumber. The pay was 50 cents for every bushel of corn picked and $1 for every bushel of cucumber picked. They handed me a bushel, and I headed out to the field.

For the next four weeks, I returned to the farm every day except Sunday and picked both corn and the big-money crop, cucumbers. The family was kind, and recognizing I was not their typical picker—"that boy has a college degree"—they began inviting me into their home where I had lunch with them each day. The heat in the fields was the worst I can remember in my life, and I'm confident it will never be matched. It seduced you to take off your shirt, but the rows of corn would create small scratches on your exposed skin, and the itch would become unbearable. I learned that migrant farmworkers preferred loose-fitting long-sleeve shirts in the cornfields, but I hadn't packed any. Somehow, I had not anticipated this situation.

I spent my nights cooling off in my East Cervantes apartment with an occasional trip to the Flora-Bama, a dive bar straddling the Florida–Alabama border. The beer was cold, there was live music, and there was all the shrimp you could eat. The shrimp sometimes left a bitter taste in my mouth as I thought about the cool breeze blowing over the deckhands as they hauled in their catch and cashed their large paychecks at the end of the week. I had one shot at working for Bubba Shrimp, and I missed it. To this day, I still think of my missed opportunity whenever I eat shrimp.

After four weeks of picking corn and cucumbers, delivering coupon books, and having doors slammed in my face on behalf of McGovern, I had run out of money. Rent was due on the East Cervantes apartment, and I did not have it. The irony of living on a street named after someone who wrote *Don Quixote* and of the folly of tilting at windmills was not lost on me. My personal windmill was getting the best of me, and after I had delayed it for as long as I could, I reached the same conclusion that Art had reached: things would be better for me back in Louisville.

I called my brother, and again he made time to get his brother out of a bad situation. In his '65 Mustang, we drove the final leg of my epic road together, up I-65 past Warrior, past the George Wallace sign, past Loco Louie's and Crazy Jerry's and back to my parents' driveway where the trip had begun. The attempt to break loose from my bonds with Kentucky had ended, and the plug was pulled on the idea of traveling west to a new life in California.

Jerry cooking franks & beans at Squirrel City

Art seeking Southern Comfort at campsite

II

Man is able, and has the duty, to reach the furthest
point on the road he has chosen. Only by means
of hope can we attain what is beyond hope.

—Nikos Kazantzakis, *Report to Greco*

MENTORS & THE ROAD TAKEN

The first mentors I had in life were my father and my older brother. They instructed me in the building blocks of character: finish what you start; if it's worth doing, then do it well; and your word is your most valuable commodity. Using few words, they taught me well through their example. My subsequent mentors I discovered in literature I read as a young man. The words I found on those pages had a powerful impact on me.

J. D. Salinger through Holden Caulfield in *The Catcher in the Rye* was the first to attain mentor status for me. Holden taught me that questioning authority isn't just hip, it is the only way to find your true path in life. If you never bump up against the edges of the envelope, then you are forever defined by someone else. And the angst Holden feels so profoundly, the teenage angst most of us try to shed for the rest of our lives, well, it's okay to carry a little of that around. It makes us a little more genuine. And more than anything, Holden implores us to be authentic.

> *I was surrounded by phonies....They were coming in the goddam window.*

> J. D. Salinger, *The Catcher in the Rye*

In many ways, Holden also pointed me down a career path. Near the end of the book, he is having one of his revealing conversations with his sister Phoebe, and he shares the thing he most wants to do in life.

> *You know what I'd like to be? I mean if I had my goddam choice? [...] I keep picturing all these little kids playin some game in this big field of rye and all. Thousands of little kids, and nobody's around—nobody big, I mean—except me. And I'm standing on the edge of some crazy cliff—I mean if they're running and they don't look where they're going I have to come out from somewhere and catch them. That's all I'd do all day. I'd just be the catcher in the rye and all. I know it's crazy, but that's the only thing I'd really like to be.*

> J. D. Salinger, *The Catcher in the Rye*

I loved the image, and since I had a choice of what I could be, I became a catcher in the rye of sorts. In 1976, I traveled back to Chicago, where I still had fond memories of summer nights with Judy, to work on a Master's in Social Work at the University of Chicago. For forty-five years until my retirement in 2016, I chased Holden's image and did youth work. The rye fields varied—the Chicago court system, a residential care facility in Maine, an outdoor program for abused and neglected youth, a shelter for teenage runaways, and Boys & Girls Clubs of Boston. I did my best to protect the children running in the field of rye from the cliff they could not see.

Siddhartha by Hermann Hesse gave me another mentor. Through Siddhartha's search for meaning, I learned that life is a journey and that I needed to stay alert to events I encountered along the way. If I focused my vision only on a particular goal or the destination of my journey, then life would pass me by unseen and unexperienced.

What could I say to you that would be of value, except that perhaps you seek too much, that as a result of your seeking you cannot find.

Hermann Hesse, *Siddhartha*

Live in the moment and stay alert to what is happening around you. Embrace it, whether good or bad, and your journey will have meaning.

I have always believed, and I still believe, that whatever good or bad fortune may come our way we can always give it meaning and transform it into something of value.

Hermann Hesse, *Siddhartha*

I was fortunate that the road I took brought me more good fortune than bad. The greatest fortune I experienced was my two daughters and the love they have given me. Children expand our capacity for feeling in every direction. I felt love and connection more profoundly than I ever thought possible, and I became vulnerable in a way I had never experienced. My greatest misfortune was that their mother and I could not successfully navigate the road we had started down together. Through that failure, I became responsible for causing my daughters great pain. Hurting the ones you love creates a lasting sorrow. It lives inside me to this day. And the love my daughters continue to give me heals me a little more each day.

Joseph Heller's fiction *Catch-22* introduced me to John Yossarian, a bombardier serving in WWII. If Yossarian had been a flower child of the '60s, I believe he would have embraced a common sentiment of young people at that time. That sentiment was expressed in a simple saying which he would have embroidered on his jean jacket, bumper-stickered on his VW bus, and shouted at demonstrations: "Question Authority." The authority in Yossarian's world told him to go to war, and the only thing that would exempt him was insanity. Ah, but there was a catch...

> *Orr was crazy and could be grounded. All he had to do was ask: and as soon as he did, he would no longer be crazy and would have to fly more missions. Orr would be crazy to fly more missions and sane if he didn't, but if he was sane he had to fly them. If he flew them he was crazy and didn't have to; but if he didn't want to he was sane and had to. Yossarian was moved very deeply by the absolute simplicity of Catch-22 and let out a respectful whistle.*

> Joseph Heller, *Catch-22*

Sometimes the rules we encounter in life are an obstacle to discovering ourselves. They reflect someone else's value system and someone else's moral compass. I grew up embracing rules as one would a life preserver. They made me feel safe from the uncertainty of living in a dynamic world, providing a false sense of predictability. Only gradually, and after much urging from Siddhartha, Yossarian and Zorba, did I learn to paint outside the lines.

One of authority's greatest allies is inertia. Inertia—the law which states that things in motion tend to stay in motion, and things at rest tend to remain at rest—may be the most significant influencer in our lives. We start in a particular direction, and the effort required to change course prevents us from redirecting—no matter what the signs tell us along the way. Or we become stuck in an environment—career, relationship, hometown—and cannot move from it. Rules reinforce inertia, and change becomes more difficult.

"How do you feel, Yossarian?"

"Fine. No I'm very frightened."

"That's good," said Major Danby. "It proves you're still alive. It won't be fun."

Yossarian started out. "Yes it will."

"I mean it Yossarian. You'll have to keep on your toes every minute of the day. They'll bend heaven and earth to catch you."

"I'll keep on my toes every minute""

"You'll have to jump."

"I'll jump."

"Jump!" Major Danby cried.

Yossarian jumped. Nately's whore was hiding just outside the door. The knife came down, missing him by inches, and he took off.

Joseph Heller, *Catch-22*

Yossarian learned to jump just in time. He now knew that any-one trying to move oneself to a better place, one more faithful to their vision of themselves, needs to be ready to "Jump!"

Be nimble in life. Adapt as the world changes around you. Question the rules and authority you encounter along the way. Most importantly, know your own rules. If your path conflicts with the rules of the world, remain true to your own compass. And always... be ready to "Jump!"

I learned much in Chicago, described by Carl Sandburg in the poem "Chicago" as "stormy, husky and brawling"...the "City of Big Shoulders." The diversity, the rush of humanity, the edginess of the big city honed my senses and raised my awareness. And when it was time to jump, I jumped. I left the city behind me, packing everything I owned into a small red Datsun pickup truck moving east. On the East Coast, first in Maine, then in the Boston area, I stood in the rye fields and I raised my two daughters. When my marriage ended I pulled back within myself and lost some of my daring. But my mentors stayed with me and reminded me of what was essential to living. As I healed, and as I regained my footing, life told me it was time to jump again. John Burroughs, the American Naturalist, said: "Leap and the net will appear." I leaped—Dianne appeared—and I was again married.

I discovered my most influential literary mentor, Nikos Kazantzakis, during my senior year of college. I found in his books— *Zorba the Greek*, *The Last Temptation of Christ*, and *Report to Greco*— guideposts and lanterns that provided direction for my life's passage. Zorba came first—this loud and combustible man who always embraced the now, and seemingly lived only for that one moment. The contrast with my self-image and those I had modeled myself after, my father and older brother, could not have been more stark. Spontaneous and impulsive versus reasoned and methodical. Valuing both, I struggled continuously to find the balance.

> *When everything goes wrong, what a joy to test your soul*
> *and see if it has endurance and courage! An invisible and*
> *all powerful enemy—some call him God, others the Devil,*
> *seem to rush upon us to destroy us; but we are not destroyed.*
>
> Nikos Kazantzakis, *Zorba the Greek*

I could not resist the gravitational pull of Zorba. I pursued his likeness throughout my life. While this chase never brought me close enough to be burned by his fire, I learned to be more present in the moment and perhaps, at times, a little impractical. Not irresponsible, just impractical. So impractical that forty-five years later I would make a second attempt at driving an old air-cooled VW across the country—hoping to catch up to Zorba the Greek along the way.

The Last Temptation of Christ took the moral compass I received through my religious training and turned it upside down. In Kazantzakis's book, the *Last Temptation* is the temptation that came to Christ as he neared death on the cross. He had the power to come down off the cross and live out his life with his love, the prostitute Mary Magdalene. Scandalous. The Church threatened to excommunicate Kazantzakis when it was published and there were worldwide protests when the movie version was released in 1988.

In the book, Kazantzakis reveals the life that Christ would have lived as a human, loving Mary Magdalene and raising children together. In the final chapter, the reader is brought back to Calvary, where Christ rejects the temptation and dies for our sins. The very human image of Christ created by the narrative stayed with me. The Bible also teaches us that Christ was both human and god, and yet we insist on thinking of him only as a god. Kazantzakis allowed me to see the human Christ as my guide and encouraged me to find him in every person I encountered.

> *There in the desert, there's hunger, thirst, prostrations—and God. Here there's food, wine, women—and God. Everywhere God. So, why go look for him in the desert?*
>
> Nikos Kazantzakis, *The Last Temptation of Christ*

Did not Christ say, "Truly I tell you, whatever you did not do for one of the least of these, you did not do for me" (Matthew 25:45). I embraced a literal view of that—every person we encounter is god. Kazantzakis returns to this message in *Report to Greco*.

The truth is that we are all one, that all of us together create
god, that god is not man's ancestor, but his descendent.

Nikos Kazantzakis, *Report to Greco*

Report to Greco, Kazantzakis's final book, is a partly fictionalized autobiography published in 1961, four years after his death. It tells of his personal journey to find meaning in his life. As Kazantzakis searches, he experiences life and culture in many countries and environments. He is married and unmarried. He follows Marx. He rejects Marx. He tries on various religious beliefs and dons many philosophies along with their instructions on living. More than anything, he struggles with the questions that are central to all of us. Why do we exist? What gives our lives meaning?

What one takes from *Report to Greco* is personal for every reader. The message I received from Kazantzakis, verily a command, was to embrace the struggle. To live is to struggle. Only by embracing it will each person find meaning in their life. The experiences which hold the most profound value for us in life, the things we treasure most, we gain through doing the difficult things that create struggle both external and internal. As Zorba says, "… what a joy to test your soul…."

In *Report to Greco*, Kazantzakis instructs us to "Reach what you cannot." And in the reaching, amid your struggle, embrace your fellow travelers along the way:

The sole way to save oneself is to save others. Or to struggle
to save others—even that is sufficient.

These were the lessons my mentors taught me. They've accompanied me throughout my life. But there was something else that also accompanied me—a lingering feeling that I had some unfinished business. I had begun a road trip in 1972 which had ended far short of its goal. I sometimes wondered how different my life would have been if I had gotten to California. I knew that question could never be answered, and loving the life I have lived, I feel fortunate that the attempt was a failure. But still, the dream remained. Perhaps it was because of the early lesson—"Finish what you start"— taught by my first mentor, my father, that I felt compelled to try again. Other mentors, Jack Kerouac (*On the Road*) and John Steinbeck (*Travels with Charley*) reinforced my dream along the way.

Whatever the reason for this folly, as my retirement date neared, I told my wife, Dianne, what I needed to do—drive an old air-cooled VW to California. She was surprised at first—I had held this dream close and not shared it with anyone for a long time. But she accepted it and promised to support it in whatever way she could—as long as she didn't have to experience it with me. She vowed to meet me in California, where she knew a nice hotel and spa would be waiting for her. Smart woman.

lll

*Every man has his folly, but the greatest
folly of all... is not to have one.*

—Nikos Kazantzakis, *Zorba the Greek*

THE PEOPLE'S CAR

In 1908, Henry Ford introduced the world to the Model T and a revolution in transportation began. For the first time, a car became affordable to the vast majority of Americans and it was a runaway success. It was reliable, easy to maintain, and because it could be mass-produced, the price was low enough for the growing middle class in America to own one. Henry Ford told his management team, "Any customer can have a car painted any color—as long as it is black." The base price was $825 in 1909, but by 1925, thanks to greater efficiency in production, the price had dropped to $260. On May 26, 1927, the fifteen millionth Model T was driven off the line by Henry's son Edsel, and its production ended that day. More Model Ts were manufactured than any other car in history— until 1972, when an odd-looking car from Germany surpassed it.

In the 1930s, the transportation revolution embodied in the Model T had not arrived in Germany, and only one out of fifty German families could afford to buy a car. Adolf Hitler informed the German Government he wanted to produce a vehicle for the masses, and in 1937 a state-owned automobile company was formed named Volkswagen, which translates to Folks' Wagon, or, more commonly, The People's Car. The criteria set forth by the Fuhrer were that it be air-cooled, seat two adults and three children, be able to reach a speed of 100km/h (62 mph), and be sold for under 990 Reichsmark ($396 in 1930 US dollars). Finally, and surprisingly, given its Nazi origins, the car was required to have the additional effect of giving its owner "joy."

On May 26, 1938, Hitler laid the cornerstone for the Volkswagen factory in Wolfsburg and in his speech, referred to the vehicle as the "Kraft-Durch-Freude Wagen" or "Strength through Joy Car." Ferdinand Porsche designed the unique bug-like shape, and it was one of the first cars designed using a wind tunnel. The German people called it the "Kafer," or "Beetle," although its official name given to it by the engineers who created it was the less joyful "Type 1." Only a few cars rolled off the line before the invasion of Poland in 1939. Production at the plant shifted to support the war effort producing the Type 82 Kubelwagen, the Wehrmacht's version of the American Jeep. Eighty percent of the workforce at Wolfsburg was slave labor brought in from the concentration camps. There was no joy at Wolfsburg.

In April 1945, American forces captured the heavily bombed factory, and production ended. Most of the Allies felt the factory could best be used for military vehicle maintenance, and if not that, wholly dismantled. The factory was offered to the Ford Motor Company at no cost, but they declined after Edsel Ford visited the plant and determined it was not worth investing one dime of American money. In the end, the Allies decided to make Volkswagen the centerpiece of their effort to resuscitate the German auto industry. The "Strength through Joy Car" was reincarnated and began rolling off the line.

Volkswagen introduced The Beetle in the United States in 1949 and sold only two cars that year. Americans viewed it as a relic of Nazi Germany and were in no mood to be seen driving their family around in "The People's Car." Sales were tepid throughout the 1950s when

Americans were in love with large, stylish cars with prominent fins, hood ornaments, and excessive horsepower, and hooked on the idea that car models should change in design every calendar year, which the Beetle never did. Adding to the mix, Americans were suspicious of foreign cars, and the Beetle was foreign in every sense of the word. How do you market a small, round, underpowered vehicle named after a bug in that environment?

In 1959, Volkswagen sent a man named Carl Hahn to America to meet with various ad agencies and find one that could convince Americans to buy a Beetle. After visiting several ad agencies on Madison Avenue, he found the Mad Man he needed in Bill Bernbach at Doyle Dane Bernbach. The resulting "Think Small" ad is considered by many to be the greatest ad campaign of all time and changed many of the practices on Madison Avenue.

The ad had a small image of a Beetle on the top left corner on a large blank field of ad space and below it, the phrase "Think Small." Even the ad print at the bottom was unusually small, encouraging the consumer to think small as in "parking space," "insurance bill," and "repair bill." Everything about the ad was honest, straightforward, and in black and white. For an audience that thought bigger was always better and drawn to flashy images, somehow it worked. And it didn't just sell Volkswagens. It launched a surge in demand for Detroit to produce smaller, more efficient automobiles. By 1972, the fifteen millionth Type 1 rolled off the assembly line, and the Model T became the second most produced vehicle in automotive history.

While the Beetle certainly belongs in any automotive hall of fame, the VW bus may be the most iconic vehicle of all time. Its origins can be traced to a Dutch businessman named Ben Pon, who, while visiting the Volkswagen plant in Wolfsburg, noticed a small utility truck workers used to move parts about the plant. He was inspired to sketch out the design of a vehicle that could transport people. The drawing appeared to be a loaf of bread on four wheels. The people at Volkswagen liked the idea, and using the Beetle's chassis as its foundation and keeping the engine located in the rear, the first loaf of bread on wheels rolled off the line in 1950. Pon's drawing now hangs in the Rijksmuseum Museum of Art in Amsterdam.

I do not know how many German engineers were involved in the naming of the vehicle, but there had to be more than a few as they joylessly decided to call it "Type 2". Its fans, however, found many names for it. It was called a "microbus," "Kombi" (for combined-use vehicle), "Splittie" (for models with a split windshield), "Samba" (for models equipped with a cloth skylight), and after being adopted by the counterculture in the United States, the "Hippie Van." Hippies loved it because it flew in the face of the muscle cars and large, luxurious sedans most popular during that era. It was anti-style and anti-success and easy to maintain and work on.

It also attracted many surfers who could fit their boards inside, and with rubber mats instead of carpets, saltwater dripping off the boards was not a concern. And one more thing—you could live in it. Hippies embraced that feature as they traveled to concerts and protests and adorned their buses with a multitude of psychedelic colors and images. While the engineers may not have shown much creativity in the naming of the vehicle, they had exceeded all expectations in the amount of joy they designed into it. No vehicle makes people smile quicker than a VW bus.

WRONG TURN

Since I failed to reach California on my first attempt in a Type 1, I chose a Type 2 for my second. And while I didn't own a surfboard, the idea of living in my vehicle appealed to me. This feature gave me an increased sense of security as I assumed history would repeat itself, and when my vehicle broke down, I would have lodging readily available. So after my retirement in 2016, I set off in pursuit of a VW bus, a camper that was sturdy enough to get me to California.

My initial search led me to a company in the panhandle of Florida, which restored old VW buses. This company was a small operation and turned out only two restored vehicles each month. Their business model required the buyer to make a $10,000 down payment, which would lock them into a completion date twelve months in the future. The restoration company would search for the model you desired, and once found, purchase it with your down payment, then transport it to their shop. Based on your specifications, they would restore the bus as you made monthly payments of $5,000 until it was complete. A husband and wife team, Annie and Bill, operated the company, and I had several conversations with Annie by phone. I liked what I was hearing, the photos on the website were phenomenal, so Dianne and I booked a flight to Florida to check out the operation firsthand.

When we arrived, Annie greeted us warmly and, along with one of her employees, showed us around. The employee was a young Army vet who told us he was so committed to what Annie and Bill were doing that he hitchhiked across the country from Oregon to work with them. We saw two buses undergoing restoration with one very near completion. The craftsmanship appeared to be outstanding. Everything looked so new on the nearly completed bus, you would have sworn it had just rolled off the line in Wolfsburg. It was painted cherry red, the chrome finishes reflected in the Florida sun, and everything about it made my heart beat faster.

As my excitement grew, we sat down with Annie to discuss the model year I preferred—the early '70s—and the various features I wanted in the vehicle that would be my home for however long it took me to get to California. The more we talked, the higher the price went, but this was my lifelong dream. Can you ever put a price on that? Apparently, you can, and the price came to nearly $45,000. Dianne, to her credit, never gave me her "Are you out of your mind?" look.

Annie informed me that the next available slot for delivering a finished vehicle was ten months away and that I could lock myself in with a check for $10,000. I caught my reflection in a chrome bumper leaning against the wall, and my face had the look I had expected to get from Dianne. I needed some time to reflect on this decision, and frankly, a check written in that amount from me would have the same properties as a psychedelic bouncy ball. Annie must have seen the look on my face as well, and she offered to hold my spot for the reduced amount of $1,000, but I needed to ante up the remaining $9,000 by the end of the month—three weeks away. I wrote the check for $1,000, then signed a contract she pulled out of her desk drawer that looked eerily familiar to me. It reminded me of the one Slick had produced in his garage in Warrior, Alabama, only this time I was the one handing over the money—and not yet getting a car in return.

Dianne and I flew back to Boston, and I had three weeks to figure out how important it was to fulfill this deferred dream of mine. I was almost hoping Dianne would tell me I was nuts, but she didn't. Instead, she supported my dream, and told me whatever I decided, she was all in. In other words, she did not give me an easy out. I wrestled with it for three days, crunching the numbers and working on a business plan for making this happen. I had retired with a pension and would be receiving social security, but our nest egg was relatively small. The $45K for the bus would have to come from earnings I made with a part-time retirement gig, and I was exploring my options when the email arrived.

Jerry and Dianne......Before you make a decision regarding your purchase from the company you visited in

Florida, Google the owners' names. In particular look for information on a similar company they ran in New Mexico.

End of email. No name or identifying information of any kind. I began Googling. I discovered that Annie and Bill had operated a similar business not just in New Mexico, but in Colorado and North Carolina as well. They had left a mix of customers in their wake—some happy—some not so happy—some furious. I wrote back to my anonymous tipster.

Thank you for your email, and I have learned quite a bit from my online search. I would really like to talk to you and wonder if you could call me so I can learn more before deciding whether to move forward with this company.

I included my phone number. The following day my cell phone rang, and I recognized the Florida area code. It was the young Army vet who had hitchhiked from Oregon to Florida to be a part of restoring old VW buses and fulfilling the dreams of people like me.

"Thanks for reaching out to me," I told him.

"First, you should know I no longer work there. I quit the day after your visit. You and your wife seemed like good people, and I just wanted you to know who you were dealing with."

"I appreciate that. I did some research as you suggested, and it sounds like Annie and Bill have bounced around a bit."

"Yeah. I think they mean well, but always end up getting in over their heads. Every month they are running out of money and then rely on new customers to cover the costs of keeping their doors open. The vehicles always cost more than what they estimate, and customers keep writing checks because they are $30,000–$40,000 in, and it's the only way to get their vehicle finished. After all that, a lot of the vehicles come back due to mechanical problems."

"Annie seems genuine."

"Yeah, but did you notice her husband never came over and talked to you? There's a reason for that, but I don't want to get into it. Let's just say he is fighting his own demons. But that is why a lot of the buses come back with mechanical problems."

He added that he was about to head back to Oregon and glad to be out of there. I wished him well and thanked him again for contacting me.

"You didn't have to do that."

"Heck, I hope you get your bus one day. You've waited a long time. And dreams are important."

By the end of our conversation, my mind was made up. I knew I was getting only one shot at this dream of mine, and I could not risk it on a shaky business model. I called Annie and told her my decision. She suspected I had talked to the man from Oregon, and she refuted some of his information but did not give me much of an argument. She promised to return my money, but it would have to wait until the end of the month. I wasn't holding my breath on that. I could live with a $1,000 mistake, just not a $45,000 mistake.

To Annie's credit, however, the check appeared as promised, and I can't say I know for sure what the real story is about the operation in Florida. In the end, it was probably too high a price for getting to California, and the vision of the cherry-red bus with the shiny chrome faded from my mind. I let it go and renewed my search for an early '70s bus that would meet my needs and leave me with enough money to repair it along the way. And I would be flexible regarding the color.

ZORBA REBORN

I found Mike and his VW bus on the Samba website. Samba is an online site for people who appreciate old VWs, whether it's a Microbus, Beetle, Karmann Ghia, or even the godawful Thing—available in the

United States for only two years in the early '70s. (The Thing was an ugly boxy vehicle—the German version of the American jeep—and I'm sure it contributed to the German war machine's failure.) I wasn't certain of much, but I knew a Thing could not get me to California, and like Americans in the 1950s, I would not want to be seen in it.

My experience in Florida had left me with a healthy dose of skepticism, and I peppered Mike with questions before again hopping on a plane to check out a VW bus. I flew into Charlotte, North Carolina, and found my way to Mike's house on backroads outside of Danville, Virginia. The bus was sitting in his driveway. After exchanging a few pleasantries, he handed me the keys, and I climbed into the driver's seat of a VW bus for the first time in my life. With Mike as my copilot, I backed out of his driveway and proceeded to have more fun driving a vehicle than at any other time in my life. We explored the winding roads near his house, and as I shifted the gears and swung around the bends in the road, I could feel the joy engineered into the bus. The joy increased each time a passing motorist flashed us the peace sign, and Mike said I would need to get used to that. I felt confident I could.

By the time we returned to his house, he had answered every question I had, except one. The bus was not cherry red and not any traditional VW bus color. Mike, as part of his restoration work, had painted it blue and silver.

"Why blue and silver, Mike? Not your classic VW bus colors."

"Yeah, my daughter is a Dallas Cowboy fan. She had some influence on me there," he said with a smile.

Having two daughters of my own, I recognized the smile. In some small way, it convinced me that this was the vehicle I wanted. If Mike had transferred just a little of that love for his daughter into the bus, I figured it stood a good chance of getting me to California. We executed the sale, and before I left, Mike told me about two resources I would want to keep close at hand. Number one was the Samba website, which listed by state all mechanics proficient in air-cooled repair. I wondered if Slick in Warrior, Alabama, was there. The second was an organization called Air-Cooled Rescue Squad. This group of air-cooled enthusiasts was available to assist any traveler who happened to break down on the road. I left Danville in my blue and silver hippie van to begin the 600-mile drive back to Massachusetts, curious to see if I would need either of these resources before I got home.

The thing I remember most about the drive home from Virginia was the heat. It was mid-September and unseasonably warm with temperatures in the 90s. Mike had shown me how to operate the "A/C" on the bus before I left. It consisted of opening the small vented window on the driver's side and letting the warm outside air blow onto you. The faster you drove, the more air you got. It was old-school but better than nothing. The other notable part of the trip was the brakes. Mike told me they would feel different from the power brakes I was used to, but I found I was nearly standing up out of my seat from the pressure I needed to apply to slow the bus down. I always allowed sufficient space between the bus and the cars in front of me in the event of a sudden stop, but that was just an invitation for other vehicles to cut me off. Which they did. Repeatedly.

Halfway home, I stopped at a roadside motel in Maryland, not mentally prepared nor equipped to sleep in the bus yet. The trip was giving me some time to get to know the Type 2, and that night I spent as much time in the parking lot hanging out in the bus and exploring its contents as I did in the motel room. Mike was a MacGyver type, and his ingenuity ran throughout the bus. He had created a bench seat that folded down into what looked to be a very comfortable bed. The sink had a water source, seven-gallon capacity, and a receptacle that collected the water that drained from the sink. The faucet had a hand pump that Mike had replaced with an electric pump, activated by pressing your knee against the counter door beneath the sink. There was a cooler hidden in the compartment next to the sink, and he had even installed a microwave in the bus. Attached to the back of the bus was a DIY bike rack Mike had created which hung off the roof rack. This was particularly beneficial as I planned to take my bike on my journey.

Mike had designed a white-gas stove specifically for the bus. After he demonstrated the stove to me in his driveway, I was convinced that I was likely to set the whole bus on fire if I ever tried to use it. As Mike proudly demonstrated it, I made a mental note to bring along my propane camp stove. Hidden away under the reverse facing seat was perhaps Mike's proudest creation—a sawdust toilet created out of a five-gallon utility bucket. If you have trouble imagining what that looks like, just think human litter box. He was quite adamant that it was utterly odorless, but I made a second mental note—purchase a marine toilet. That night I used the bathroom in the motel room.

The bus had an auxiliary battery and electrical outlets that operated off a power converter neatly tucked away next to the spare tire. The engine compartment contained an electrical cord that could connect to a power source at a campsite. The radio with CD player was erratic, but the speaker system was outstanding. Mike's wife had made curtains that provided privacy in the living compartment and which matched the gray upholstery throughout the interior. Finally, there was a countertop that converted into a table for fine dining.

But of all the characteristics of the bus, perhaps the features I loved most were the steering wheel and the big bay window. The steering wheel on a microbus is large, sits low, and tilts away from the driver, similar to one on a public transit bus. I loved the feel of it, and sitting directly over the front wheels, the turning action was different from any vehicle I'd ever driven. The wide sweeping turns, as I wrestled—no power assist—with the oversized steering wheel gave me the feeling of handling a big rig, although the overall length of the bus is only a few inches longer than the Beetle.

I also found that during long stretches on the road, I could lean forward, resting my forearms on the wheel, giving me a comfortable position of repose similar to leaning into your favorite bar. Don't look for that driving position in any instruction manual, but it felt good and also got me closer to the wind rushing in the side window vent as I drove. I anticipated this posture being invaluable when I found myself crossing the hot, dry western deserts. Finally, there is no better view of the world than the one through the big bay window of a VW bus. The road and everything ahead seem magnified. With your elevated sightlines, no roadside attraction slips by unnoticed, and every vista has a wide frame. You are forever in Montana, Big Sky Country.

For two days, the engine kept running, the brakes were sufficient to avoid collisions, and I covered 600 miles finding myself back home in Massachusetts. Along the way, I was greeted with peace signs, multiple thumbs-up gestures, and countless friendly waves. Bikers, in particular, especially those on Harleys, seemed to most appreciate the sight of an old VW bus. By the time I got home, I had my lists of what I loved, what I didn't love but could live with, and what I needed to change.

The trip also gave me two days to think about what name to give the bus. Knowing the adventure and challenges ahead, I wanted a name that captured the spirit of the trip and did not fear failure. I also wanted a name that felt familiar to me, like an old companion. Showing the same imagination the German engineers had when they designated it the Type 2, I decided to christen the bus Zorba 2. I was confident—somewhat—that together we could exorcise our shared demons and find our way across the country to California.

As I prepared for my trip, I thought of my mentors who had accompanied me through life and who would be with me on my journey west. Would I be faithful to them as I renewed my quest? Would I embrace the journey as Siddhartha taught me, or be only focused on my objective, California? Would I be spontaneous and able to "Jump!" as Yossarian did—changing my course when a new opportunity presented itself, or when one of "least of these" put out their hand? And would I be Zorba, seeking the uncomfortable, opening my arms to everyone, and always willing to dance?

Or... would the case be, as Zorba once said, "*You can knock on a deaf man's door forever,*" ... and I had learned very little from my mentors?

I packed all these questions into an old VW bus. It was time to finish what I had started—forty-five years ago. My journey with Zorba would reveal who I had become.

IV

You have everything but one thing: madness.
A man needs a little madness or else he
never dares cut the rope and be free.

—Nikos Kazantzakis, *Zorba the Greek*

"LIGHT THIS CANDLE"

At 5:15 am on May 5, 1961, Alan Shepard entered his Freedom 7 Mercury space capsule atop a Redstone rocket and prepared to become the first American launched into space. After the launch of Sputnik, and followed by cosmonaut Yuri Gagarin becoming the first human in space, America was falling behind the Soviet Union in the Space Race and was desperate for a positive step forward. Alan Shepard was ready to take that step. The launch was scheduled for 7 am.

Then the delays began. Clouds closed in prompting a pause in the countdown. As the weather cleared, other problems continued to pile up. A power converter failed and needed to be replaced. A computer error at NASA's Goddard Space Flight Center created another delay. By the time NASA overcame these obstacles, Shepard had been sitting in the cramped Mercury capsule for more than three hours. Then a more personal problem arose as Shepard needed to relieve himself. (He later blamed it on too much coffee during his pre-launch meal.) He requested to exit the capsule and take care of business, but

Wernher Von Braun, head of NASA's space flight program, denied his request.

Shepard then requested to urinate in his spacesuit. The engineers had never anticipated this circumstance, particularly when planning for a scheduled fifteen-minute flight. After some prodding from his fellow Mercury astronauts, the engineers decided to turn off the electrical current to the suit, and permission was granted—although Shepard made it clear he wasn't giving them much choice. A drawn-out "Ahhhhh" emerged from the capsule, and there were a few chuckles among the team monitoring the launch in the control room.

With two minutes remaining in the countdown, there was another delay when pressures inside the Redstone's liquid oxygen tank climbed unacceptably high. The safest option was to reset the pressure valves, which would necessitate the scrubbing of the mission—or they could bleed off some of the pressure by remote control. At this point, Shepard had been secured in the Mercury capsule for four hours. Given the rather dramatic failure of many previous unmanned launches, one could understand the flight engineers' reluctance to take any chances. Shepard put the issue to bed with his now-famous quote, "Why don't you fix your little problem and light this candle?" The other astronauts in the control room echoed Shepard's feelings and convinced the flight controllers that it was indeed time to "light this candle." Shortly after 9:30 am, Shepard became the first American in space, and the country's space program took an important step toward catching the Soviets and putting a man on the moon.

Now, after all the prep and all the endless talk of taking this road trip, and after a wait of forty-five years, I was finally ready to set out on my journey. A local mechanic, Damon, who specialized in old VWs, had been working on Zorba. When I said I was ready to go, Damon said he wished he had gotten to some "other things," ...but time was up. As I have learned about a VW bus, there are always "other things."

I was no Alan Shepard, and Zorba no rocket, but it was time to light the candle—time to launch what I was calling my Peace Out Road Trip.

On a bright and sunny Sunday morning in August 2017, I fired up Zorba, waved goodbye to Dianne, and uttered something hopeful like "See you in California." On the way out of town, I stopped by to see my newly minted three-month-old, and very first grandchild, Gretyl. In the event that I never made it back, I whispered into her ear:

"Don't ever buy an old air-cooled VW."

Soon I was westbound on the Mass Pike feeling like Matt Damon in the final scene of *Good Will Hunting,* driving to California "to see about a girl." Except "the girl" was behind me, and Will Hunting was "wicked smaht" and probably knew how to fix his car if something went wrong. But I liked the feeling, so I held onto it.

It didn't take long for traffic to back up and for the mid-August heat to build up inside the bus. As I slumped over the wheel, wondering why Matt Damon didn't hit traffic on the Mass Pike, I heard a high-pitched whining sound coming from somewhere in the bus. I cocked my head in every direction but could not determine where it was coming from. I pulled into the next rest stop along with many desperate others traveling the Mass Pike that weekend. By the time I parked, the whining sound had disappeared. Feeling I needed to do something, I did the only thing I really knew how to do—check the oil.

After only an hour on the road, the oil level was already low, so I stood in a long line of miserable travelers to purchase a quart. I suspected that none of them were starting a lifelong travel dream that day, but my attitude at the time was not much different from theirs. When I returned outside and opened the cover to the engine, I looked around at the crowded parking lot and had a brief moment of panic. I felt the crush of too many people, the heat, and I saw the lines of traffic waiting for me back on the Mass Pike. Suddenly Zorba looked like a too small space to be living in, and California was a long way off. To abort the trip was out of the question, but I was already slipping into survival mode after only an hour on the road. Just get through the day. After all, the rest of America can't be as insane as the Mass Pike in August. At least that's what I told myself.

WOODSTOCK

I rolled into Bethel, New York, the evening of the first day, 290 miles from home. The distance I covered on Day 1 would exceed all the other days on the trip. Like a satellite being launched into orbit, I wanted to thrust myself down the road and break away from the gravitational pull of home. Also, the idea of spending my first night on the road in Bethel, site of the historic Woodstock Music Festival, had a certain appeal.

I was eighteen when nearly 500,000 people gathered at Woodstock in July 1969. I was spending my summer driving an ice-cream truck through the neighborhoods of my hometown, Louisville, Kentucky. My soundtrack during those summer months was not Hendrix or Joe Cocker or Creedence Clearwater Revival. Instead, I heard the ditty "Bicycle Built for Two" emanating from the speakers on my ice-cream truck—over and over and over again. It became a slow form of torture.

I never considered driving to upstate New York to experience Woodstock, and not having a car may have influenced my thinking. But for my generation, Woodstock was a pivotal event whether you attended the concert or not. I identify myself as a member of the Woodstock Generation, which has either positive or negative connotations for people. For some, it represents peace, social equality, and unselfishness, while for others, it connotes drugs, youthful hedonism, and social irresponsibility. I drive an old VW bus, so my view is on the more positive side, not that I didn't indulge in a little youthful hedonism now and then. In any case, I was forty-eight years too late but still wanted to stand where Jimi Hendrix stood, and it seemed like a symbolic place to begin the Peace Out Road Trip.

As I approached Bethel on Route 17B, I saw the sign welcoming me to the "Home of the 1969 Woodstock Festival." The music festival was originally planned for Wallkill, New York, but the town fathers found a way to block it. Other locations were considered, and when time was running out, and with the festival in jeopardy, Max Yasgur stepped up and offered the organizers his 600-acre dairy farm in Bethel, NY. The reason the festival is known as Woodstock—Woodstock, New York, is fifty-five miles away—is that Bob Dylan was living in Woodstock, and the organizers believed if they put the Woodstock name on it, he would be tempted to attend. Bob had other plans and became irritated by the hippies who kept showing up at his house. He took off for England.

Thinking the welcome sign would be an excellent backdrop for my first "on the road" photo of Zorba, I pulled over to take the shot. The sun was setting, and as I contemplated returning in the morning when the light would be better, I noticed a young woman running up the road toward me. She didn't appear to be out for an evening jog and had a panic about her that made me take notice. As she approached, I could see that she was in distress with a red mark on her neck and a torn blouse.

The young woman had a small frame and wispy blonde hair, but a look on her face that told me she was nobody's pushover. Between quick breaths, and as she repeatedly looked back over her shoulder, she asked if I could give her a ride home. I had committed, when I began the trip, that I would pick up hitchhikers, a way of paying forward all the help that others had given me to make this journey possible. But I had not envisioned this scenario.

I said, "Hop in," and Naomi, as she had introduced herself, began to give directions to her house. I tried to lessen the anxiety that hung in the air by commenting, "I don't know what or who you are fleeing, but I just want to point out that you picked the slowest possible vehicle to flee in."

I thought there was some humor in that, but I can't speak for Naomi. As I drove, the retired social worker inside me took over, and I wondered if I should be doing more than just driving her home. "You know, I'm happy to take you home. But I can also drive you to the hospital. Or the police station?"

"No, I just had an argument with a guy, and I wanna go home. But thanks." After a pause, she added, "People suck!" And after another pause, "But not you."

"You grow up here in Bethel?" I asked, moving the conversation in another direction.

"Yeah, but I can't wait to get the hell out. This place sucks."

Along the way, I discovered that a lot of things in Naomi's life "sucked." She reminded me of many of the teenage runaways I had worked with, needing to escape something but no place to run to.

We passed a roadside bar, and she gave it a good long stare. As she continued to glance over her shoulder, I did the same, cursing the small amount of horsepower in a 1700cc VW air-cooled engine. Her directions took us up into the hills surrounding Bethel until we turned onto an unpaved dead-end road where the trees closed in, and little sunlight got through. I kept one eye on the road, one eye on my rearview mirror, and one eye on her, looking for a sign that I was being played. My eyes were moving a lot. This was the only time on the trip when I gave Zorba better odds of surviving than me. A fresh paint job, a forged title, new plates, and one of us would live on.

At the end of the road sat a house not dissimilar from many homes I had visited while working for an anti-poverty program in Kentucky. The house had a look of despair, and it also had the requisite car on blocks and abandoned appliances that often accompany houses on the back roads of Kentucky. Zorba and I ignored the multiple signs, some unwritten, telling people to keep their distance, and we pulled into the driveway. Slouching on a stuffed chair on the front porch was a rather sullen-looking young man. I looked at him in the same way Naomi had looked at the roadside bar and asked if she was sure she was okay. She picked up on the vibe and responded, "It's okay. It's my brother." She added, "I really appreciate this. Let me run into the house and get you some money for the gas."

I declined, wanting nothing to delay my exit from the driveway. Putting Zorba into reverse and grinding the gears a bit, I backed away. The old bus seemed to have a little more zip as we headed back into Bethel. It was too early in the trip for Zorba and me to start having conversations—these became much more frequent the farther we headed west—but I could have sworn I heard him say, "Let's not do that again."

I nodded in agreement. We found our way back into Bethel where the sun had set, and the opportunity for the iconic photo of Zorba the VW bus and the Woodstock sign had passed.

HECTOR'S INN

My first night on the road was the only one for which I had made plans. Knowing it would be a long day of driving, I intended to reward myself with a nice meal at the Dancing Cat Saloon in Bethel on 17B, which cuts through the center of town. I had even taken the step of perusing the menu in advance and was looking forward to their specialty—roasted rabbit. Part two of the plan, after complimenting the manager on my outstanding meal, was to ask if he objected to my spending the night in his parking lot.

When I arrived at the Dancing Cat, I found only a scattering of cars in the gravel parking lot. I attributed this to it being Sunday night and probably not a big drinking night in Bethel. Entering the front door, I found all the tables empty with the staff huddled together, having a meeting. A young man in his late twenties stepped out of the group and informed me they were closed. This fact torpedoed my plan immediately, and without the ability to compliment him on anything other than his expansive parking lot, I was at a distinct disadvantage. But I plowed ahead.

"Sorry you're not open. I hear the food is really good here."

"Come back tomorrow. You won't be disappointed."

"Fact is, I'm just passing through. I'm driving an old VW bus and trying to get to California. Any chance I could park in your lot and spend the night?"

"Sorry, man. Can't let you do that. But you should check out Hector's Inn. It's just down the road. I think that's the place you're lookin' for. At least your VW bus will be welcome."

He added, "It's not really an inn. It's just a bar with a field, and they let travelers spend the night."

"Thanks. Sounds perfect."

Back on the road, I found the sign on Route 17B directing me to turn right for Hector's. I didn't feel the time warp as I drove through it, but I knew it was there. On the other side, down an unpaved road, there was a variety of old vehicles and what appeared to be many authentic replicas of people who attended the concert in 1969. They were more antiqued than their vehicles. I pulled into a spot, and the first words spoken to me when I stepped out were, "Nice bus, my man. Do you have jumper cables?"

I did and handed them to Ricky the Red, who had long red hair held together with a red bandana. He was standing next to his red pickup truck. Ricky had his thing and was working it. He told me he had come to Bethel in 1969 and had never left. I had already suspected that.

As I walked around the field, I met many others who had come and never left. Their hair, clothing, and language were frozen in time, and, despite my now regrettable pre-trip haircut, they made me feel welcome. "It's all cool, man."

I learned that Hector's was a gathering spot for people attending Woodstock in '69 and continues to be a way station for travelers on the road. It had a bar with limited food options, an open area where people could gather around a bonfire, and many symbols of an era long gone. Jerry Hector passed away in 2012, but the hippie culture is still celebrated at Hector's, and all are welcome. I could tell Zorba felt at home.

I asked one of the hippies whom I should talk to about spending the night, and he directed me to Dee, who was apparently responsible for keeping things somewhat organized in the field. Herding hippies—not an easy task. I headed over to Dee, who had the look and demeanor more of a trucker than a hippie, and she looked suspiciously at my neatly trimmed hair. Her mood brightened when I pointed to my old VW bus, and she directed me to a grove of trees bordering the field—the first, but not the last time, Zorba opened a door for me. Dee and some friends were manning a grill, and I was able to secure a nondescript hamburger and a beer. Not the roasted rabbit I had planned on, but the beer was cold, and I had a place for the night.

I drove Zorba back among the trees avoiding several large mud pits along the way—apparently a constant at Woodstock—and found a spot next to a 1972 Ford Econoline. I heard the owner before I saw him.

"Welcome to Hector's Inn! Looks like we both drive classics." He pointed to his green Scooby-Doo van, as I climbed out of Zorba. "I'm Curtis."

I introduced myself and asked Curtis how long he had been at Hector's.

"Two weeks now. No plans for leaving any time soon." No check-out time at Hector's.

"You traveling on your own?" I asked.

"I'm not sure at this point. I met a lovely lady on the Internet and convinced her to come join me. At least that's what I thought. I bought her an airline ticket, and she flew up from Florida three days ago. She spent one night with me in the van then said she needed to visit a sister who lived nearby. She hitched a ride with one of the hippies, and I haven't heard from her since."

I sneaked a glance over at Curtis's van, and I had my doubts as to his lady returning. I remembered what Dianne told me when she realized I was serious about crossing the country in an old VW bus: "You go live in your old bus. I will meet you wherever there's a nice hotel and a spa." Dianne is a smart woman, and maybe Curtis had found one too. He might want to check out the local spa, and hopefully, he will recognize his woman under a mud mask.

I spent my night among the trees at Hector's Inn, listening to the periodic beating of drums and feeling very far from home indeed. I could see neon lights flickering among the trees and heard the occasional strum of a guitar. I don't know what I expected to find when I got to Woodstock, but I was a bit unsettled by the number of people I met who seemed stuck in time. They were friendly and welcoming, but I felt out of place and had no sense of belonging there.

I have two friends who attended the music festival in 1969. Both took the message of those three days back to their communities and lived it fully. Peace and love can change the world, but one has to engage the world for that to happen. It appears the gravitational pull of the moment and place was too strong for some, and they were never able to break away and return home. But..."It's all cool, man."

Before leaving Bethel, I stopped at the museum that commemorates the three days of traffic jams, rain, mud, and medical emergencies—there were two deaths and two births—but also the music, love, and sharing that took place. The museum also told the lesser known story of Woodstock—the story of the residents of Bethel, and how they responded to the event.

Bethel is a sleepy little town a hundred miles north of New York City and had a population of only 2,750 at the time of the festival. Its only distinguishing feature was the many youth sleepaway camps on Silver Lake, part of the "Jewish Alps" in the Catskills, providing summer escapes for many of the Jewish families of New York. David Berkowitz, later known as "Son of Sam," had spent a summer in Bethel in 1961 but was sent home when his cabin mysteriously caught fire— an omen of what lay ahead for Berkowitz when, fifteen years later, he terrorized New York in eight separate shootings.

The people of Bethel were, of course, unhappy about the masses descending on their community, and their fears were heightened further when the estimated number of attendees grew from 50,000 to 500,000. While most cursed the dairy farmer Max Yasgur—a popular sign read: "Buy no milk. Stop Max's hippy music festival"— there were many others, seeing the potential for disaster, who opened their homes and their hearts to the young people cascading into their little town. They shared their food and offered help in ways that kept people safe. The American tradition of assisting travelers and refugees who show up on our doorsteps was alive and well in Bethel in 1969. That spirit of Woodstock—that we all share this communal earth equally—was sparked as much by the residents of Bethel as it was by the festival attendees.

Max Yasgur summed it up when he took the microphone on the third day and shared his thoughts with the thousands gathered on his land:

"The important thing that you've proven to the world is that half a million kids, and I call you kids because I have children older than you are, half a million young people can get together and have three days of fun and music and have nothing but fun and music, and God bless you for it."

In fact, for three days, 500,000 people gathered, weathering terrible conditions, and there were no reported incidents of violence. The only recorded conflict occurred when Abbie Hoffman rushed the stage during a break in the music. He grabbed the mic and began a semi-coherent rant about freeing John Sinclair—a poet arrested for possession of marijuana in 1969 and sentenced to ten years in prison. The Who was waiting to perform, and getting impatient, Pete Townsend yelled at Hoffman to "get off my stage," then hit him in the head with the neck of his guitar. Hoffman got the message and departed from the stage.

Guest at Hector's Inn   Curtis's Scooby Doo van

SPEED BUMP

Leaving Woodstock and Hector's Inn behind me, I headed south on Highway 55, crossing the Delaware River into Pennsylvania over a bridge designed by John A. Roebling, famed builder of the Brooklyn Bridge. Located in Lackawaxen, Pennsylvania, the bridge is simply called the "Roebling Bridge." The wooden structure is the oldest existing wire suspension bridge in the United States and was originally built as an aqueduct connecting two parts of the Delaware & Hudson Canal. It is now open to automobile traffic but has only one lane and requires courtesy. Drivers are to refrain from entering the bridge unless it is clear. "Oh, the humanity!" if this bridge ever existed in Boston.

After crossing into Pennsylvania, what had been only an annoyance earlier in the trip worsened. Engaging first and second gear went from difficult to impossible. Unable to use either, I had to get Zorba moving from a stop in third gear, lugging the engine terribly, one of the worst things you can do to an air-cooled engine. It was time for an intervention. I was not ready to hit the panic button and call the Air-Cooled Rescue Squad but turned instead to the list of mechanics who specialized in air-cooled vehicles on the Samba website.

The first call resulted in a "number no longer exists" recording. Billy answered the second call, but he said he only did it as a sideline and only on weekends—it was Monday, and the weekend could not have been further away. Billy did say he knew a guy in Bethlehem who had a VW repair shop, and he was the guy I needed to see. I called Dave Sterner at Kresge Foreign Cars, and he confirmed that he was indeed the guy I needed to see. Zorba and I headed for Bethlehem, eighty-five miles away, avoiding as many lights and stop signs as we could along the way, using only third and fourth gear.

I was encouraged when I pulled into Dave's shop and I saw several old air-cooled VWs in various states of repair. He even had an old Austrian army vehicle that was air-cooled, but he wasn't quite sure what to do with it or why he kept it in the shop. I briefly considered a trade, but immediately felt guilty about it. Zorba and I would get through this together.

Dave was quick to diagnose the problem as a bent shift coupler, and he happened to have a used one on hand that he could install. But—and this would be a frequent occurrence on my trip—he found another problem, a brake line that had a bubble about to burst. He did not have the part to repair it but felt he could get his hands on one the following day. Dave changed out the shift coupler, and I had Zorba back for the night with an appointment to return to the shop in the morning.

Having already compared myself to Alan Shepard, I won't compare myself to Mary and Joseph, but I was in Bethlehem and needed a place to park the bus for the night. My first choice was by the abandoned steel mill that I had passed on the way into town, but there were too many signs discouraging overnight parking. Being a Marriott Gold Member, and membership having its privileges, I decided to use the parking lot of the local Marriott. Most hotels don't keep track of the cars in their parking lots, and given my frequent stays at Marriott hotels over the years, I felt I had earned the privilege of free parking. I put Zorba in a spot away from the front entrance and settled in for the night without turning on the interior lights of the bus. I was being discreet—not always easy to do in a vehicle that attracts as much attention as an old VW bus.

The next morning I casually walked in the front door, got the friendly greeting the Marriott staff always provides, and took a left into the breakfast area. I got my cup of House Blend and helped myself to a little sugar. The breakfast buffet was inviting, but there were limits to how much I wanted to push my luck. I wished the staff a good day as I headed back out to Zorba. After departing my Marriott "accommodations," I returned Zorba to Dave's shop, took my bike off the rack hanging on the rear end of Zorba, and decided to make the most of my day in Bethlehem.

BETHLEHEM STEEL

Just as Woodstock was an iconic location for my generation, the now silent Bethlehem Steel Plant was, in many ways, an iconic location for my father's generation. This was the generation that came of age during the Depression, fought World War II, and built many of the most recognizable structures we see across our country today. Bethlehem Steel was used in the construction of the Golden Gate Bridge, the Hoover Dam, the George Washington Bridge, the Empire State Building, Madison Square Garden, the Verrazano Bridge, and even Alcatraz. Every tunnel bringing traffic and trains into Manhattan from New Jersey was built with Bethlehem Steel. At one time, 85 percent of the New York skyline had Bethlehem Steel in it. It was also the number one contractor with the US Government during World War II, building the ships, guns, and ammunition that helped the country win the war. My father's generation did not have time for music festivals on dairy farms in upstate New York.

But some had to pay a horrific price for that steel. Immigrant workers, primarily from Europe, Puerto Rico, and Mexico, were the lifeblood of the plant and died in large numbers making steel. From 1905 until 1941, more than 500 workers died in the plant—one worker's body per month carried out of the plant over a thirty-six-year period. The dangerous conditions compelled the steelworkers to organize in 1910, but efforts to form a union were blocked by company management.

Subsequent attempts also failed until the workers went out on strike in 1941. The strike was marked by police teargassing and striker vandalism but ended in 1942 with the Steelworkers Organizing Committee being recognized by the company as a legitimate bargaining unit for the workers. Substantial improvement in workers conditions followed, and from 1942 until 1995, when the last blast furnace was turned off in Bethlehem, "only" 100 workers died in the plant. Still tragic, but progress had been made in worker protection.

There are many reasons behind Bethlehem Steel's failure, and the museum at the site fairly spreads the blame. Poor management decisions, a failure to adapt to new practices in the industry, an aging workforce with rapidly increasing pension liabilities, and finally increased competition with foreign steel all led to the shutdown of the mill. But as I cycled through town and spoke to the people I encountered, their reason for the failure was singular: "foreign steel." Sometimes it is easier and simpler to blame "the other."

The plant stands intact today, an apocalyptic structure of rusting steel that rises up to the sky. The City of Bethlehem has rebranded the mill as Steel Stacks where a catwalk leads visitors up and along the maze of pipes, cranes, and stacks from the blast furnaces. One can imagine the cacophony of sounds that would emanate from the site when it was fully functioning, but the people of Bethlehem knew the most frightening sound would be the silence heard on the day they extinguished the furnaces. Even without the roar of the blast furnaces, it is both awe-inspiring and terrifying to gaze upon. It stands as a testament to the workers who died there.

The downtown streets of Bethlehem were a surprise. They do not resemble what you see in many of the old mill towns in New England, towns built around a single enterprise that failed and could not regain their vibrancy. Downtown Bethlehem is a collection of shops, outdoor cafes, and restaurants reflecting a diverse and thriving community. I could conclude only that the descendants of steelworkers are a resilient lot.

I cycled back to Dave's shop, and he told me Zorba was ready to roll. This early delay in my journey had shaken my confidence, so looking for a boost, I posed the question to him:

"So, Dave, do you think I will get to California?"

"I think so. That's a pretty solid bus."

"But will it get me back to Massachusetts?"

He paused, then said with a laugh, "You might want to sell it when you get to California."

I laughed too—but not as hard as Dave.

Bethlehem Steel Stacks

Dave at Kresge's Foreign Cars

THE LINCOLN HIGHWAY

I am not sure why I selected mid-August as the time to begin my journey west, but clearly I intended to share the road with as many people as possible. Also, I must have wanted it to be as hot as possible in my air-cooled bus with no A/C. I was successful. Winding my way west on Highway 23, the traffic and the heat impaired my march toward Gettysburg.

During Civil War times, soldiers on the march would often shed blankets and other gear as the heat and weight became too much to bear. I briefly looked around Zorba to see if shedding anything would improve my situation but then remembered that the soldiers often regretted ditching their blankets when the cold nights came upon them. They resorted to spooning to stay warm, and I had no one to spoon with. I also considered taking my shirt off so the hot air coming in my side vent would have a more significant cooling effect, but the sight of a shirtless old hippie in a VW bus, although one with short hair, might be enough to cause an accident. I kept my shirt on.

Highway 23 took me to Lancaster, Pennsylvania, where I hopped onto Route 30 heading west, a four-lane highway. Here I could speed up a bit and magnify the breeze entering the bus. Route 30 traces the route of the legendary Lincoln Highway, the first transcontinental highway in the United States. Conceived in 1912, it stretched from Times Square to Lincoln Park in San Francisco. Formally dedicated on Halloween 1913, that date seemed to foretell the horror of highway traffic that lay in our future.

The surface was crushed stone, and the first name considered for the roadway was the Coast-to-Coast Rock Highway, which portended a rough ride. I suspect the engineers on the project, not hired for their marketing skills, came up with that name. Instead, they wisely decided to name the highway after the country's 16th President, the first such memorial to Lincoln in the country, predating the Lincoln Memorial in Washington, D.C. by ten years. The road was also affectionately known as "Main Street Across America" and brought prosperity to the towns fortunate enough to be included on the route. What many people today might find peculiar about the Lincoln Highway is that its construction was initially privately funded.

It was the brainchild of an Indiana entrepreneur, Carl Graham Fisher, owner of the Indianapolis Speedway. Fisher had made his money producing headlights, and his product was used on nearly every model of car at that time. Promoting automotive travel was good for business: more roads, more automobiles, more headlights needed. The estimated cost of the road was $10 million, and Fisher began collecting donations from his wealthy friends.

Frank Seiberling, president of Goodyear, and Henry Joy, president of the Packard Motor Car Company, reached deep into their pockets. But when Fisher approached Henry Ford with his hand out, Ford refused to contribute because he believed it was the government's responsibility to build roads. Why pay for something out of your own pocket when you can get the drivers to pay for it through such inventive things as gasoline taxes. Thanks, Henry.

I stopped to fill up Zorba at a gas station along the Lincoln Highway and experienced something that would become a rather frequent occurrence on the trip. It seems that having an old VW bus is the mechanical equivalent of having a puppy. People want to talk to you and see the bus up close. It generally starts with "Love the bus!" but on this occasion, it took an odd turn.

Maggie saw me at the gas station across the street from her house and made the effort to cross over to talk to me. I noticed that she didn't take a particularly straight line coming toward me, and when she spoke, it was confirmed that she had started her sippin' early that day. The conversation started with Maggie revealing her love for the bus and asking me where I was going.

"California or bust!" I replied enthusiastically.

She just as enthusiastically responded, "You're crazy if you think this thing will get you to California."

I shrugged and said I was going to try. After a few more non-flattering comments, and giving the bus a once-over, Maggie's attitude did an abrupt U-turn, minus a signal.

"Take me and my dog with you."

I explained that I would not be doing her a favor by bringing her along and asked her to take another look inside the bus—not much space. As she did that, I added: "Some people think I'm crazy for even trying." I smiled at her and getting the point, she smiled back.

In the time it took me to fill Zorba's tank, Maggie managed to share most of her life's story. She had hit on some hard times and probably could have benefited from a change of scenery, and while California was her first choice, I suspected that any place far from where she stood now would do. Her husband had left her, taking their car with him and leaving her only bills. She was facing an uphill battle, but I could tell she had a good heart as she offered me her driveway to park in if I needed a place for the night. I thanked her, told her I needed to get to Gettysburg, and wished her the best.

I often thought about Maggie and her dog as I traveled west. As wealthy as this country is, there are too many people living in the shadows, on the fringes where they can't be seen, just getting by in life. Good fortune has overlooked them, often through no fault of their own, and, like Maggie, they deserve passage to a better place. I'm sorry I couldn't give her that.

HALLOWED GROUND

Returning to the Lincoln Highway, I made good time and rolled into Gettysburg around noon. It was close to 90 degrees outside, and the temperature inside the bus seemed even higher. As I drove, I repeatedly wiped away the sweat that was dripping onto my glasses, trying not to swerve into oncoming traffic in the process. Annually over a million people visit Gettysburg, and the day I chose to visit was getting more than its fair share. The parking spot I found required a forced march to the visitor's center. I blunted my self-pity by reminding myself of the conditions the soldiers faced in 1863, marching hundreds of miles to arrive at this historic crossroads, many of whom would never get home again.

Exiting Zorba, I grabbed a hat for protection from the sun and headed for the Visitor's Center to get oriented. The park ranger who greeted me immediately made me aware of the mistake I had made.

"Patriots fan, I see," he said with a smirk.

I had grabbed my cap with the New England Patriots emblem, the old Pat Patriot, not the Flying Elvis replica, but that didn't seem to make a difference to the ranger. One would think that at a place where thousands of patriots died preserving the Union, Pat Patriot would be welcome. Not the case, and his friendly ribbing taught me a valuable lesson. As divided as this country appears to be at times, there is one thing that binds everyone outside of New England together—they all hate the New England Patriots. To his credit, he still performed his duty as a ranger and gave me a map of the battlefield.

I headed back to the car, and despite the heat, decided to cycle the ten-mile battlefield loop. My first visit to Gettysburg was many years earlier and was prompted by the historical novel *The Killer Angels*, written by Michael Shaara. I have returned several times after that first visit and always found it to be inspiring with each visit broadening my perspective on the battle. This visit occurred shortly after protests over the planned removal of the Robert E. Lee statue in Charlottesville, Virginia. The protests resulted in the death of one young, peaceful participant, Heather Heyer, killed by a white supremacist, and with President Trump declaring there were "very fine people on both sides."

The struggle over how to remember the Civil War continues 150 years after it ended, and the challenge of what to do with Civil War statues and monuments is driving much of the debate. There is certainly no shortage of statues and memorials at Gettysburg, and they represent both sides. However, the Union memorials dominate the field just as the Army of the Potomac did during those three days of battle in July 1863. As I cycled the circular route, which begins on the Southern side of the line, I halted at the statues and considered my position on all this. Growing up in Kentucky, a border state, I always felt I could see and understand both sides as they wrote their separate histories of the war. I know now that much of the Southern account, the Lost Cause narrative, is false and a distortion of history.

The ideology of the Lost Cause holds the Confederate cause to be heroic and endorses the supposed virtues of the antebellum South. It celebrates that the Southern soldier was chivalrous, fighting against long odds, and losing only because of the greater number of troops and the industrial might on the Northern side. But the central falsehood of the Lost Cause narrative is the myth that the war was about States' Rights and not about slavery. The reality, the factual history, is that the war was about preserving slavery, and if you have any doubt, read the articles of secession written by the states.

Mississippi Declaration of Secession:

Our position is thoroughly identified with the institution of slavery - the greatest material interest of the world [...] a blow at slavery is a blow at commerce and civilization.

South Carolina Declaration of Secession:

*they {the federal government} have denounced as sinful
the institution of slavery; they have permitted open
establishment among them of societies, whose avowed
object is to disturb the peace and to eloign the property
of the citizens of other States. They have encouraged and
assisted thousands of our slaves to leave their homes; and
those who remain, have been incited by emissaries, books
and pictures to servile insurrection.*

But as we know, nobody does it bigger than Texas. Slavery is
mentioned no less than twenty-one times in their articles of secession, and there is nothing ambiguous about their position regarding
African Americans:

*We hold as undeniable truths that the governments of
the various States, and of the confederacy itself, were
established exclusively by the white race, for themselves
and their posterity; that the African race had no agency
in their establishment; that they were rightfully held and
regarded as an inferior and dependent race, and in that
condition only could their existence in this country be
rendered beneficial or tolerable.*

The Lost Cause narrative found its way into our textbooks and
by 1940 dominated the classrooms in this country. It wasn't until the
1970s that the textbook industry made significant changes, and the
teaching in our classrooms began to reflect the actual history. Sadly,
the Lost Cause narrative so effectively promoted during the post–Civil
War period by the South is held not only by a fringe group in America.
The Pew Research Center in 2011 found that 48 percent of Americans
believed that we fought the Civil War over States' Rights, and only 38
percent thought it was fought over slavery.

Most of the Confederate statues we argue over today were not erected at the end of the Civil War, but at a time when African Americans were starting to assert themselves following World War I. Black soldiers, such as the historic Harlem Hellfighters, were returning home, and having fought to "make the world safe for democracy," they were looking for some democracy for themselves. Their demand for their rights was met with violence, lynching, and the proliferation of statues honoring Southern Civil War generals. The Confederate battle flag was revived in the 1950s and 1960s as a response to the Civil Rights Movement, and seven Southern states still retain symbolism of the Confederacy in their state flags.

So I pondered the statues that stand in town squares throughout the South. Symbols of proud southern heritage or symbols of white supremacy? To me, there is no difference between the two. The states' declarations of secession are unequivocal; the southern heritage that the Confederate States were fighting to preserve was the institution of slavery. (I would also like to add that this sacred "heritage" some southerners refer to, the Confederacy, lasted a scant four years. The Hula-Hoop craze of my youth lasted longer than that.)

When we decide to place someone in our town square, we are obliged to select someone whom all of us can celebrate and admire— someone whose values are inclusive, not exclusive. They should be persons who represent our "better angels" as Lincoln referenced in his first inaugural address. I see no honor, only shame, in keeping these statues and monuments, and as long as they stand, they exclude many among us from our common spaces.

The first road trip book I ever read was John Steinbeck's classic *Travels with Charley*. On that trip, Steinbeck made New Orleans the last stop on his circular journey around the United States. It was 1960, five years after the Supreme Court decision in *Brown* vs. *Board of Education*, and New Orleans was finally taking steps to desegregate their schools. One solitary black girl, Ruby Bridges, age six, was attending the previously all-white William Frantz Elementary School. When she enrolled as the sole black student, every other student in the school withdrew. Little Ruby was the single student walking in the doors of the school each morning, and she did so alongside Federal Marshals, who walked with her to protect her from the angry crowd outside. Norman Rockwell painted an iconic image of the scene.

Steinbeck went there to observe a group called the "Cheerleaders," a group of protesters who got more than their fair share of national attention. They frequently appeared on the evening television news and in most media accounts of the happenings in New Orleans. These strident white women were not there to cheer on Ruby for her bravery but rather to shout taunts and threats at a six-year-old child. Ruby never wavered and completed her school year at Frantz Elementary. Sixty years later, Heather Heyer was killed in Charlottesville because she was willing to confront the modern-day cheerleaders for hatred and white supremacy.

My final stop at the National Park was the site of Lincoln's Gettysburg Address—that immortal speech dedicating a national cemetery at the battlefield. I read the text, which still resonates powerfully today.

...It is rather for us to be dedicated to the great task remaining before us - that from these honored dead we take increased devotion to that cause for which they gave the last full measure of devotion....

Our country could benefit from another Lincoln. The great task he spoke of still remains before us. But with increased devotion, we will carry on—for Heather.

COWEN'S GAP

Icontinued west on the Lincoln Highway out of Gettysburg and allowed myself one last reflection on the statue debate. Perhaps we are a little too quick to turn to our military figures when honoring the best among us. Many deserve it, but thinking back to Bethlehem Steel and the hundreds who died there, also in service to the country and in sacrifice for their families, I wondered if more statues to them shouldn't stand in town squares.

Stopping for provisions in a shopping mall outside Chambersburg, west of Gettysburg, I had the pleasure of meeting Roni and her daughter Maddie, still in her preteen years. Roni told me she loved the bus, but Maddie went a step further.

"I'm going to own that bus one day."

She seemed pretty sure, so I didn't argue with her. In fact, I told her I would probably be selling it in a few years and asked how much longer until she got her driver's license.

"Five years," Maddie responded.

I gave Roni and Maddie the web address of my travel blog and invited them to follow along on the trip. I doubted there was anything that would happen that could dissuade Maddie from her belief she would own my bus one day, but I wanted her to be fully informed regarding what she was signing up for.

As a parting gift, Roni told me about the delicious peaches grown in the area and directed me to a farm stand nearby where I could purchase some. I wondered if some of the members of Lee's army, particularly the ones from Georgia, had the opportunity to experience them as they marched through in 1863. I fear the debate over who grows the best peaches could start a whole 'nother war, but I will say that Roni was right about the local crop—delicious.

I spent the night at Cowen's Gap State Park in central Pennsylvania, and there I made a rather startling, and briefly painful, discovery. I had been a little careless that morning when setting out and had failed to adequately secure the propane tank, which fueled my camp stove. The tank had found its way to the heating vents on the floor of the bus and nestled up against them. One would not think that a problem, since who would drive with open heating vents when the outside temperature was nearly 90 degrees?

Apparently, I would. When I reached to pick up the tank, it was red hot, and I dropped it like a hot potato, albeit a hot potato that had the potential to explode. It took me a minute to figure out what had happened, and I wondered how close the propane tank had come to overheating and engulfing Zorba and me in a ball of flames. I ran some cold water over my hand and made a mental note to get more organized.

A closer examination revealed that the floor heating vents were stuck open, and I could not close them using the limited, and apparently faulty, controls on the dash of the bus. I now understood why the temperature in the bus was always hotter than outside. After the delay in Bethlehem, I decided to live with the condition until I got to Louisville and my planned layover there. I did, however, use a different propane tank for grilling my steak tips that night. Brilliant.

Jim, the ranger at Cowen's Gap, stopped by to see me at my site that evening, and I did not bring up the fact that I had almost blown up his park. I asked Jim who "Cowen" was and how he got a gap named after him.

"He was from your neck of the woods. A Boston guy. Came here after the Revolutionary War. He fought for the British, actually, but his wife Mary was from a Patriot family."

"That must have created some tension," I opined.

"Apparently, Mary forgave him for his Loyalist ways but her family not so much. John and Mary eloped and began looking for a less hostile environment."

"Sounds like a good idea. Nobody likes angry in-laws."

"They were on their way to Kentucky, and their wagon broke an axle coming through the gap in the mountains here."

After my delay in Bethlehem, I identified with John and Mary. Pennsylvania is a tough state to cross.

"The Tuscarora tribe considered this to be their land, but the chief took a liking to John and gave him 'tomahawk rights,' which allowed him to mark a large chestnut tree on his property with three slashes, a sign of peace with the Tuscarora. They never got to Kentucky."

I thanked Jim for the history lesson and shared how I was also on my way to Kentucky, and I feared he might have jinxed me.

Jim laughed and added, "Well, maybe you'll get a gap named after you," and then continued with his rounds.

"LET'S ROLL"

Heading west on Route 30 and continuing on the Lincoln Highway, I passed through rolling farmland and encountered my first hard rainstorm. It didn't help much with the temperature, and the open heating vent continued to guide all that air from my "air-cooled" engine directly into the bus. Generally, old VWs are considered to have very inefficient heating systems, but I can assure you they are very efficient in August when the outside temperature is in the 80s. It was sapping the energy out of me.

I was heading toward the Flight 93 Memorial in Shanksville, Pennsylvania, which is only a few miles off the Lincoln Highway. On the morning of September 11, 2001, I had just arrived to work at the central office of Boys & Girls Clubs of Boston located in the Financial District in the heart of downtown Boston when news of the unfolding events spread through the office. Given the uncertainty of what might happen next, buildings in the Financial District were being evacuated, and by 10 am, I was on my way home. Like many Americans, I watched the horror unfold on television and gave my kids a longer hug than usual when they got home from school that day.

There were a lot of heroes that day, people who put themselves in harm's way to try and assist others. Everyone on Flight 93 met that criteria. Todd Beamer, who worked for Oracle Corporation and was flying to California for business, was among them. He had passed on an opportunity to take an earlier flight, delaying his departure so he could spend more time with his family. Flight 93 was relatively uncrowded with only thirty-seven passengers, and after the hijacking took place, the terrorists isolated all the passengers in the back of the plane. The passengers became aware that three planes had already crashed into the World Trade Center and the Pentagon, and their fate became increasingly clear.

Most tried to reach their loved ones through their cell phones or the phones provided on the backs of the seats on the plane. Todd was able to contact a telephone operator, and with the FBI listening in, told them of the situation on Flight 93. Anticipating the intentions of the hijackers, he informed those listening on the other end that the passengers had decided a group of them would storm the cockpit and attempt to take control of the plane. His voice conveyed the futility of the situation, since both pilots had been killed, but the passengers knew if they did nothing, others on the ground would die. He concluded with, "If I don't make it, please call my family and tell them I love them." That was followed by the final words heard from him: "Let's roll."

That phrase was the signal to storm the cockpit and retake the plane. Based on what we know from the cockpit recorders, they successfully breached the cockpit. When that happened, the hijackers put the aircraft into a dive, and everyone on Flight 93 met their end in a farmer's field outside Shanksville. It is still uncertain whether the hijackers' target on Flight 93 was the White House or the US Capitol building. We can thank the passengers on that flight for the uncertainty.

I did not know how visiting the Flight 93 Memorial would affect me. It was history I had lived through, and while I remembered my feelings of loss and anger on that day, it was beginning to fade on me. Sixteen years had passed, and while I wanted to honor the passengers of Flight 93, I was feeling a little disconnected from the event as I drove into the parking lot of the Memorial.

The Memorial is composed of a Wall of Names and a museum which overlooks the location in the field where the plane crashed. Walking through the front doors, I saw the obligatory gift shop one sees near the entrance of every museum and felt a little disappointed that this would not be the exception. I bypassed the gift shop and moved into the museum display area where the story of September 11 is recounted. The timeline of events that day is laid out in various displays, and I walked through trying to remember where I was at each moment that day and what I was feeling at the time.

I was successful at keeping my emotional distance until I got to the wall of photos. Represented on the wall was every passenger and crew member on Flight 93, and each photo captured them at what appeared to be a happy time in their life. I realized that each person's family had selected the photo that would go on the wall and that this was how they wanted their mother, father, brother, sister, loved one to be remembered. As a way to honor them, I took a little time looking at each one. With each one, it became a little harder.

When I had finished, I turned from the photo wall and saw a bank of telephones. I approached the phones, not knowing their purpose. As I walked toward them, I could hear a voice coming from the phone held by a young woman, and it hit me immediately what it was. The phones allowed you to listen to the final words recorded by the passengers on Flight 93. These were the messages left behind for the people they treasured the most. The voice I heard coming from the phone was a mother's voice, and she was leaving a message for her children. I was overwhelmed and immediately left the museum.

I returned to Zorba and sat for a while, trying to gather myself before returning to the road. The history of September 11 was suddenly very real and not distant at all. I wanted to give my two daughters another hug as I did on that day, but that was not possible. I sat alone in the bus and looked out over the farmer's field, where Flight 93 ended. There is a walkway that takes you down to the point of impact, but I knew I was not strong enough to make that walk. I continued to sit in Zorba.

It was then that my cell phone rang. It was a reporter from the local paper back in Newburyport and he wanted to do a story about the journey I had embarked on and wondered if this was a good time to talk. It wasn't, but knowing I would be on the road for the rest of the day and unavailable, I gathered myself and said, "Sure."

I can't remember most of the questions he asked, but the words "adventure," "freedom," and "open road" kept coming up. He had his notion of what the trip would be like, and he kept leading the witness. However, at the time, the "joy of the open road" he referenced seemed a little out of reach for me. It was hot, I was tired, and the Flight 93 Memorial had drained all feelings of joy out of me. I did the best I could to recount my experiences so far, and the word I remember using the most was "challenge." I felt bad after we hung up and was certain he was disappointed in how I was describing my trip.

I saw the article online the next day. The headline was "A Dream, a VW bus and the Road to California." The accompanying picture, which Dianne provided him, showed me smiling and flashing the peace sign out the driver's window of the bus. So far, so good. As I read the article, I was relieved to see my fatigue and sadness did not seep into it, and he had found a way to use all those positive words of his. Any reader would assume I was living my dream, reveling in the freedom of the open road and traveling without a care in the world. And that was probably for the best.

V

*Life is trouble. Only death is not. To be alive
is to undo your belt and look for trouble.*

—Nikos Kazantzakis, *Zorba the Greek*

MOONSHINE

Zorba and I rolled out of Shanksville with the Flight 93 Memorial behind us. Within a few miles, it was time to depart the Lincoln Highway and head south on Route 281 toward West Virginia. Stopping for gas, I heard a voice call out from the other side of the pump, "I would recognize that sound anywhere. Nothing like a VW bus." Billy introduced himself and added, "I had one back in the day, a '76 bus."

"I'm trying to get to California in this one."

"Well, hell, those things will get you anywhere. I drove mine to godawful West Virginia once. The damn thing blew its engine, and I had to tow it home. Took me over ten hours."

West Virginia was only forty-five miles from where we stood, so Billy's comments did not strengthen my confidence. I concluded that a VW bus could get you anywhere, except "godawful West Virginia." Thanks for sharing, Billy.

I topped off the tank and headed for my fate in West Virginia. Just a mile before hitting the state line, I saw a sign advertising "Moonshine Tasting." Who could pass by that? Not this Kentucky boy, and since

Billy had convinced me my trip could end at any moment once I got to West Virginia, I decided to enjoy the moment I had.

I pulled into a gravel parking lot and entered a surprisingly civilized establishment called Tall Pines Distillery. They advertised themselves as "The first legal moonshine distillery in Somerset County, Pennsylvania, since prohibition." I wondered how many other moonshine distilleries had since cropped up, but in any case, I was glad to see that moonshine was making a comeback. I entered a small store where the distinct odor of corn mash greeted me. I was the only one there except for Mary Jo, who was tending bar. She gave me a warm welcome, and the tasting commenced.

So what defines moonshine? As the name implies, it was made illicitly and preferably at night when the Feds were not watching. It originated in Appalachia, where, given the narrow hollows and limited roadways, settlers found the corn they grew difficult to get to market. Growers realized that corn converted into whiskey was much easier to transport, and one horse could haul whiskey ten times the value of the corn. The moonshine trade is also credited with being the origin of NASCAR, as the good ole boys would supercharge their vehicles to outrun the Feds—which they did on most occasions. Moonshine wasn't legalized in the United States until 2010 and is defined as a "clear, un-aged whiskey" with corn mash as its primary ingredient.

Tall Pines had a wide variety of 'shine—Apple Pie, Forest Fire, Huckleberry, Pine Top, and Maple Rye, all got past my filter for acceptable moonshine flavors. I screened out Cafe Mocha, Pine Sap, and Bananas Foster. Really? Bananas Foster? Some poor moonshiner is turning over in his grave. I also passed on the Moonshine Margarita as the cultural clash was just too much for me. Mary Jo told me that they had been distilling since 2014 and added that no one had died yet. She said that with a smile, but it did cause me to cut back some on my sippin'. I bought a bottle of Pine Top for my sister Jeanette and her husband Mark, who were going to put me up when I got to my hometown of Louisville. Nothing gets you in the front door in Kentucky like a bottle of moonshine.

As I headed out the door, Mary Jo gave me one of their bumper stickers, which encouraged folks to "Support Your Local Moonshiner." Having done just that, I headed back to Zorba and the road to West Virginia. I fired up the engine, and the verse of a song titled "Moonshine" came to mind.

You can get it in a jug

You can get it in a jar

Run out of gas

You can put it in your car.

Zorba and I were properly braced for West Virginia.

Stopping for a sip

COAL COUNTRY

I crossed the state line into West Virginia and briefly held my breath as I waited for Billy's prediction to come true and Zorba's engine to implode. It didn't happen, and we rolled onto Interstate 68 heading west. My intent on this trip was to avoid the Interstate highways as much as possible, but on this occasion, I opted for I-68 since I was still trying to make up for the lost time in Bethlehem. And the hills of West Virginia had me worried.

From what my research told me about driving an air-cooled VW bus cross-country, overcoming the mountain ranges presented the biggest challenge. I had crossed the Berkshires just west of Boston on the Mass Pike, but they were more like rolling hills than mountains. I did encounter a sign proclaiming a particular crest to be the "Highest Point on I-90 East of South Dakota," but I think that was more a testament to the flatness of the Midwest than anything else. Crossing the Rockies was several weeks ahead of me, and I saw the Southern Appalachians in West Virginia as a good first test. The Interstate would modify the inclines some, and Zorba and I were okay with that.

I left Interstate 68 just outside of Morgantown and headed south on Interstate 79. Even on the Interstate, the hills became increasingly challenging, and there were a few occasions when I had to shift down into third gear to ascend them successfully. I was moving at a speed that was illegally slow, and I put my flashers on to warn the traffic coming up behind me. No one rear-ended me, but I got some looks—and they weren't the "How nice to see a VW bus" kind of look.

I passed the exit for Stonewall Jackson State Park, and it gave me pause. West Virginia seceded from the state of Virginia during the Civil War in 1863 as a result of an internal dispute over slavery and the Union. Up until that time, a new state could not be created from an existing state—that would be allowing secession. However, when

Virginia seceded from the Union, the door opened for the pro-Union residents in the western part of the state to then secede from Virginia. Hard for Virginia to argue against secession at that point.

The original name proposed for West Virginia was the State of Kanawha after the river that runs through it and the Native American tribe that once inhabited the region. But some legislators had trouble letting go and wanted the name to reflect their history as part of Virginia. So they added "West," and the Union had a new state. But why would a state with this pro-Union history name a state park after a Civil War Confederate General? The first answer to that is Jackson was born in nearby Clarksburg and was a native son. The second was the large number of Confederate battle flags I saw as I drove the back roads of the state. It became apparent to this casual observer that the hearts and minds of many West Virginia residents still reside in Confederate Virginia.

I pulled into a rest stop on I-79, which looked like a good spot for the night. The rules vary by state regarding how long you can "rest" in a rest stop. Some states have no objection to overnight parking, while others put a limit of anywhere from two to four hours. West Virginia just states "no overnight parking" but does not specify the maximum amount of time before you have worn out your welcome. I decided to test their patience and see what would happen, parking as far as I could from the restrooms and the constant foot traffic. I felt less guilty than I did staying in the Marriott parking lot and drinking their lobby coffee.

Waking in the morning, after an undisturbed night, and no Marriott lobby nearby, I set about making my coffee. I discovered early in the trip that the current generated by the auxiliary battery was insufficient to operate the small coffee maker I had brought. I learned to improvise by heating water on my propane stove and then pouring the hot water onto the coffee grounds in my coffee maker. As I sipped my cup of what I called my "hillbilly coffee," Jim and his boy came up to the bus and asked if they could take a picture with Zorba. I stepped aside since I was not invited into the picture, and they got their photo. Jim's wife, Becky, then joined us.

"Where you goin' in that old thing?" she inquired.

"California."

"You shouda taken a plane."

I considered whether I should stop telling people where I was heading.

Looking at my map, I decided to abandon the Interstate at the first opportunity and take Route 19 down to Beckley. I had read about a coal mine tour there, and after seeing all the roadside signs proclaiming, "Coal is King," "Support Coal," "Coal Keeps the Lights On," and "Proud of Our Coal Miners," I felt compelled to enter a mine. The closest I had ever gotten to coal was when I lived in Salem, Massachusetts, near a coal-powered electric plant. Depending on which way the wind was blowing during the night, I would often find a thin layer of coal ash from the plant covering my car in the morning. I always wondered what it was doing to my lungs. On the other hand, the lights stayed on.

During the Presidential election the previous year, Donald J. Trump had his widest margin of victory in West Virginia. He had made several campaign appearances in the state and always promised the people of West Virginia that he would bring back coal, and the mines would reopen. This comment would reliably elicit a roar of approval from the crowd, and I recall in particular the time he donned a coal miner's helmet and mimed shoveling coal. The image of a multi-million-dollar New York real estate guy and reality TV star pretending to shovel coal didn't convince me. Still, the vast majority of the people of West Virginia were won over. Trump won 68 percent of the vote to Clinton's 26 percent, a margin of 42 percent.

I wound my way through the streets of Beckley and pulled into the parking lot of the Beckley Exhibition Coal Mine. A bluegrass band was playing outside, and, as it was a Saturday, there were many families having picnics and enjoying themselves on the grounds. All this gave me the impression that the mine was lacking in some authenticity. But it was the only opportunity I had to enter a coal mine, so I bought my ticket and got in line, along with a gaggle of giggling children, for the vehicle that would take us below the earth. It was definitely feeling like an amusement park ride.

I grabbed a brochure in hopes of educating myself while I waited for the experience to begin. The name of this particular mine was the Phillips-Sprague Mine. It opened in 1889 and was operated as a drift mine, which means they tunneled horizontally into the side of a hill, and the shaft would follow the coal vein. They pulled coal from this particular vein until 1953 when operations ceased, and the mine was sold to the City of Beckley. In 1962, the city opened it as an exhibition mine, which is now solely dedicated to educating the public about coal mining.

Standing in line, I stared at the dark opening of the mine ahead and began doing some math in my head. The Phillips-Sprague Mine is now over 125 years old. The mine's age is either testament to its durability or evidence that it is running on borrowed time. I, of course, concluded the latter. A small mine conveyor, resembling a short, squat train, clattered to a stop, and we climbed into the cars for our trip underground. The families with the young children had embraced the amusement park ride approach fully, and while I considered pointing out to them the age of the mine, I decided the parents would likely appreciate my keeping that to myself.

The contraption we rode in noisily entered the mine shaft, and, as we passed the wooden timbers that braced the ceiling every few feet, I dodged the water dripping from the roof of the mine. Earl, our guide for the day, stopped the little train at various locations to point out assorted mining tools displayed in the shaft while explaining their uses. Earl had worked in coal mines for over thirty years, and while he did a great job engaging us, one got the sense that he preferred digging coal to dealing with tourists. He got particular satisfaction in turning off the lights so we could experience total darkness deep in the mine. The children squealed. I was unnerved.

After we exited the mine, I corralled Earl, and we talked a bit more about his experiences mining coal. He was kind enough to share a few stories, and then I gingerly asked him the question I already knew the answer to.

"The President says coal is going to make a comeback. What do you think?"

"People are feeling very hopeful."

"Do you see some of the mines that closed reopening?" I tried to ask in a way that projected an open mind on the subject.

"I do. I really do."

I thanked him for his time, and I noted to myself, his last answer was the one time in the conversation Earl did not look me in the eye.

Exiting the exhibition mine, I stopped outside by the table promoting tourism in West Virginia that was staffed by two young college students doing their part to lure people to West Virginia. Not an easy job. Jimmy and Susie were heading back to college in a few weeks, and both were Mountaineers at West Virginia University in Morgantown. I shared my plans for driving across the country in an old VW bus, thus establishing my lack of sense, and then asked if the people of West Virginia believed coal was making a comeback, testing their senses. They both shook their heads and said people knew better.

"As much as the environmental issues are an obstacle, the economics of digging coal is an even bigger obstacle. Natural gas is easier to extract and much cheaper to bring to market." Susie knew her stuff.

I walked away impressed with the education they were getting at WVU. I also walked away impressed with the miners who for so long worked in the dark, wet shafts, risking their lives to, in fact, keep the lights on in America. When you travel through New England, you find that nearly every town has a Civil War statue prominently standing in the town green, and often the names of the men who perished fighting to preserve the Union are inscribed upon them. In West Virginia, nearly every town has a memorial in the town center to the miners who died in that county. The lists are stunningly long. In Beckley, a historical marker lists a few of the worst mine disasters in the history of Raleigh County. Among them:

Five miles west at Eccles, on April 28, 1914, a gas explosion in No. 5 Mine in the Beckley seam killed 174 miners; another nine died in No. 6 Mine above from blackdamp.

It notes that from 1891 to 1991, mining accidents claimed the lives of 2,121 miners. That is in just one county in West Virginia. According to the Department of Labor Statistics, during the early twentieth century, an average of over 1,500 miners were killed every year. The worst year in history was 1907, when 3,242 miners died—the cost of keeping the lights on.

I made one more stop before leaving Beckley, and it was quite by chance. I passed a sculpture that caught my eye and pulled over to take a closer look. It was a six-foot-tall bronze figure of a man who appeared to be smelling his armpit—strangest thing I had ever seen. It was entitled *Mortality* and was the work of West Virginia sculptor Bill Hopen. The statue stood outside the Tamarak Art & Craft Exposition

Center and, eager to learn more, I entered the Center where a young woman behind the reception desk greeted me.

"Can you please tell me about that sculpture out front?" I asked.

She laughed. "I sure get a lot of people coming in the door because of that statue. It's a memorial to some miners who died digging a tunnel east of here. The figure is a miner trying not to inhale dust. Google it. It's called Hawks Nest." She turned with her smile to greet another visitor.

I did as she told me. The Hawks Nest tunnel is three miles long and was dug in 1930. Its purpose is to divert the New River to a hydroelectric plant downstream operated by Union Carbide. The tunneling pierced rock that had high levels of silica, a substance that can be fatal if inhaled. They used a dry tunneling technique that released a large amount of dust into the air. Due to the lack of ventilation and safety precautions of any kind, the miners inhaled large amounts of silica, exiting the tunnel covered in white dust at the end of their day. Union Carbide assured the miners there was no risk to their health; however, whenever the Union Carbide management visited the tunnel, they always wore breathing masks. They knew. Of the 2,900 men who worked in the shaft during the excavation, it is estimated that nearly 1,000 died from silicosis.

The story takes an even darker turn when you learn that the majority of the miners were African Americans, and there were no burial plots nearby that would accept their remains. The cemeteries were "White Only," and apparently, the silica dust did not make them white enough. A funeral parlor located a farmer's field in the area, and they were buried there, later to be relocated when a roadway was expanded. It is uncertain now where these men lie. The tunnel is still in use today, producing electricity, and keeping the lights on—the steep price for that electricity, paid in 1930.

Earl in the Beckley Exhibition Mine   Mortality by Bill Hopper

COALWOOD

I had a route planned for this trip not based on any particular roads I wanted to travel but defined more by certain places that had piqued my interest over the years. Coalwood, a small town in the southern section of West Virginia with a listed population of 700, was one of those places. I followed Route 16 south out of Beckley, its path dictated by the steep hills and narrow hollows in the southern part of the state. Route 16 wound through many small towns, each looking increasingly desolate as I traveled farther from Beckley. Helen, Rhodell, Corrine, and Wolf Pen all had the same "all hope is lost here" look about them. Where there were side streets, I would abandon Route 16 in search of life and energy but found little. Deserted streets, abandoned houses, and the telltale signs of poverty were everywhere.

The town of Welch had bolder type on my map and was the hub of McDowell County. I was hoping I would find in Welch some sign of vibrancy, and if not, then at least people who still had a sense of purpose beyond surviving day to day. It was getting late in the day, and I also hoped it would provide a place to get a bite to eat and to park Zorba for the night.

Route 16 splits when it enters the center of Welch and becomes Wyoming Street in one direction and McDowell Street in the other. I rode down Wyoming then circled back on McDowell in search of a diner or any establishment that served food. Raymond's Restaurant at the end of McDowell Street looked promising, but I found that it closed at 5 pm, and it was fifteen minutes past. Around the corner was the Hot Dog Hutt, but that was closed as well. Over half of the buildings in the downtown stretch along Wyoming and McDowell were boarded up. It was Saturday night in Welch, and it resembled some of the ghost towns I had passed through in Arizona and Nevada—towns whose demise was also linked to a mining operation that had long ago ceased to produce ore.

The population of Welch reached its peak in 1950 at 98,887. Old photos show parades down McDowell Street, its sidewalks lined with smiling faces celebrating the Fourth of July and honoring the heroes of World War II. In the later part of the twentieth century, mine closures increased, and people began to leave in search of work and opportunity elsewhere. The current population of the entire county is now estimated at 18,456. Welch is what a county seat looks like when you have lost 80 percent of your people.

I had enough provisions in Zorba to make dinner, and I found a small park alongside Elkhorn Creek which flowed through the center of town. When I pulled to a stop, the view of the buildings comprising the heart of Welch filled Zorba's big bay window. The heart of Welch was barely pulsing, and the feeling that overcame me as I gazed on it convinced me I had to move on. It wasn't just what I saw in Welch that brought on that feeling, but rather a residual feeling from all the little towns I passed through on my way there. I had spent my career as a social worker and been in every neighborhood in Boston that was considered "poor" by some economic standard, but I had never witnessed what I saw on the back roads of West Virginia. I don't believe that hopelessness is contagious, but I wasn't going to risk it. Feeling I couldn't stay there for the night, and with Coalwood only five miles down the road, I decided I had enough light to make it there and see what I wanted to see.

Zorba and I sputtered back onto Route 16, and with the silence of Welch behind us, my thoughts went back to my days working at the Charlestown Boys & Girls Club. Charlestown had historically been a working-class Irish community, but that was changing rapidly. It was becoming increasingly gentrified, which created unrest among the "Townies" as white-collar professionals began buying up properties. Also, the federal courts had mandated integration of the previously all-white housing development, the largest in the City of Boston's system.

At the Boys & Girls Club, we knew it was important to find ways to welcome the families of color moving into the community and send the message the Club was there for every child in the community. During our early efforts in this regard, a clique of young Hispanic boys of twelve to fourteen began attending the Club regularly. The energy they brought to the Club was boundless and welcomed but did not always stay within the prescribed boundaries as they increasingly challenged the rules of the Club. The staff was getting frustrated, and in our debates on the situation, we considered expelling some of our newest members. Having made inroads into engaging the families of color who were new to Charlestown, expulsions would be a disappointing step backward.

In my youth, I enjoyed building and launching rockets and remembered the excitement I felt seeing them scream into the sky. It was the early '60s, and I felt I was participating in the race with the

Soviets into space. I decided to form a Rocket Club targeting the group of rowdy boys who needed a place to channel their energy. Surely things that have the potential to explode could capture their attention.

I coaxed this group of energetic Latinos into participating, and we started meeting twice a week building rockets. I also taught them the history of rocketry—from the first rockets built by the Chinese, to Robert Goddard, who launched the first liquid-fueled rocket only sixty-five miles from Charlestown, and on up through NASA and the space program. I promised them that if they were successful in launching and recovering their rockets and could pass a test on the history lessons, we would take a trip to the Air and Space Museum in Washington, D.C., where they could see real rockets.

The whole experience was not without its challenges, including the local community college asking us to move our launch location as they were tired of retrieving rockets from their roof. But in the end, it was a success. The young men adapted to the routine of the Club, and the opportunity to travel to Washington, D.C. provided enough of an incentive that they all succeeded in learning such obscure things as the name of the first dog in space—Laika, a stray mongrel that had been wandering the streets of Moscow. More importantly the Boys & Girls Club over time was successful in becoming a place where every child in the community felt welcomed. I continued offering the Rocket Club each year until the time I departed the Club ten years later.

During this time, the movie *October Sky*, starring Jake Gyllenhaal and Chris Cooper, came out. The movie is based on the nonfiction book *Rocket Boys*, which tells the story of seven boys attending high school in Coalwood, West Virginia. While a few Coalwood boys would escape the coal mines with a football scholarship, the future for the rest was underground with its accompanying dangers. The launch of Sputnik in 1957 caught the imagination of these seven boys, and they started a rocket club, calling themselves the Big Creek Missile Agency, and their launch location Cape Coalwood.

These Coalwood rocket boys overcame impossible odds, won the National Science Fair in 1960, and secured college scholarships and a path forward in life outside the coal mines. I found it inspiring in many ways, and it resonated with my youthful desire to separate from my childhood home in Kentucky. As part of the graduation celebration for the Rocket Club at the Boys & Girls Club, we would make popcorn and watch the movie together. The scenes of the Coalwood boys' rockets exploding or failing in other ways always brought laughter to the group as we had shared the same experiences.

Rocket Boys was written by one of the boys from Coalwood, Homer Hickam Jr., played by Jake Gyllenhaal in the movie. While all the rocket boys went on to successful careers, it was Homer who went on to work for NASA to train astronauts. Chris Cooper, who played Homer's father, lives just outside of Boston, and I had the opportunity to meet him once at a reception raising money to support public Shakespeare performances on the Boston Common.

Unfortunately for Cooper, I cornered him and began chattering about the movie and its impact on me and the members of my little rocket club at the Boys & Girls Club. I also asked more questions than are customarily considered courteous at a charitable event. Eventually, Cooper slowly backed away and said something about needing another beverage from the bar. I got the hint and let him escape.

I had seen the movie perhaps a dozen times and wanted to make Coalwood a stop on my trip, as it had lived in my head for many years. Heading south out of Welch, I continued on Route 16 as it wound its way through the narrow and steep hills carved out of the West Virginia landscape. Coalwood is too small to be officially incorporated as a town, and after the Olga Coal Company ceased operations in 1961, it shrunk in size. Route 16 took me to the center of town, which was no more than a small collection of houses and a gas station.

I took a right onto Frog Level Road, where there are still some abandoned mine buildings, including the machine shop where the workers sometimes helped Homer and his friends build their rockets. The high school the rocket boys attended, Big Creek High School, was located in War, six miles away. It closed in 2010 due to low attendance, and in 2015, the week before it was scheduled to be demolished, caught fire and burned to the ground—just another odd footnote in this depressed region of West Virginia.

The Rocket Boys' launch site, which they had christened Cape Coalwood, is just off Frog Level Road, and I followed the gravel road to the open area where the Coalwood Seven launched themselves beyond the coal mines. The field is a slag heap where various mines in the area had dumped their refuse, and it is shrinking along with Coalwood as the forest grows into it. On the edge of the field stands a replica of the blockhouse they used during launches to protect themselves.

I had seen what I hoped to see in Coalwood and ready to move on when I passed some people sitting on their back porch. I saw this as an opportunity to learn a little more and hoped it would go better than my close encounter with Chris Cooper. Pulling Zorba onto a narrow side street, I parked off to the side and approached the gate to their backyard. I gave a wave, and they waved back, which I chose to interpret as an invitation into their yard. More importantly, their dog did not object.

Stepping onto their back porch, I introduced myself, leaving out the part about driving to California. I did not want to make a bad first impression. I started the conversation by asking if they knew where Homer Hickam had lived.

"Rat hare," they responded.

"I know he's from Coalwood, but I wondered if you could point me in the direction of his house."

"Rat hare," they repeated.

I thought maybe my Boston accent was the obstacle, minimal though it is, and was about to ask in another way when they stopped me and said, "You is standing on his back porch."

I realized by "rat hare" they meant "rat hare!" Dim-witted Northerner.

"You parked your van on Homer Hickham Lane," they pointed out.

After a little small talk about Coalwood, I ventured to ask, "What did you all think of the movie?"

"'Twas fine," they responded, but there was some hesitation in the words. Betty, who seemed to be the matriarch of the group, added, "The movie company changed everyone's names so's no one got paid."

I'm not sure how these things work, but my Coalwood friends were under the impression there would be some compensation if they were represented in the movie, which they felt they were.

"Does Homer ever come back to town?"

"Used to. Thar used to be an annual Rocket Boys Festival held in town, but now they do it in Beckley. 'Parently, sixty miles is too fur for Homer to drive, so's we don't see him anymore."

Having just driven the sixty miles of winding, narrow roads that connected Coalwood to Beckley, I sympathized with Homer—but kept that to myself.

"Do you mind if I take a picture of the house?" I asked.

"Go rat ahead, but you probably wants to walk 'round front and take the picture thar."

I took the hint and left their back porch. It seems they did not want to be in my travel photos, and I can't say that I blame them. I got my shot of the house, and as I was saying goodbye, they warned me about the stretch of Route 16 I was about to drive.

"You be careful now. It's steep an' tricky an' someone dies on it more than you wanna know."

"I appreciate the heads-up."

I gave Zorba an encouraging pat on the dash as I climbed in, and turned off Homer Hickham Lane and back onto Route 16 heading south. Barring death on the road, I hoped to make it to Tazewell, Virginia, thirty-one miles away, and spend the night there. When I drove out of town, I passed a sign that said, "Welcome to Coalwood, West Virginia—Home of the Rocket Boys." The paint was peeling, and with the "C" completely gone, the name of the town had become "Oalwood". Maintaining the sign seemed pretty low on everyone's to-do list, and I wasn't surprised. After all, they changed all the names, and no one got paid.

Welcome to Coalwood sign

TAZEWELL

The good people I met in Coalwood did not exaggerate about that stretch of Route 16. It was a narrow and steep roller coaster of a ride with an endless number of blind curves. Some inclines were so steep I had to put Zorba into second gear to climb them, while the downhill curves required repeated downshifting and frequent reminders to myself not to ride the brakes. The blind curves were extreme and elicited a silent prayer from me that every other driver on the road was being just as cautious. It only takes one for two to die.

Route 16 finally settled down when I got to the Virginia border, and as I entered Tazewell at dusk, I found a display of antique autos lined up along Main Street. There were street vendors and live music, and people were strolling about enjoying the warm summer evening. I was tempted to park Zorba among the other vintage automobiles but decided it would be bad form given that we had not been invited. Besides, I was more interested in the steakhouse I saw on Main Street than the red '65 Mustang convertible or the turquoise '57 Chevy parked next to it. Following the smell of grilled steak, I entered the establishment and grabbed a seat at the bar.

My priority was a cold beer followed with an order of a rib eye, rare, and a baked potato with all the fixings. I looked out the window at the live music, the bustling street, and at the packed restaurant around me. I thought back to Welch an hour behind me, where the only restaurant in town closed at 5 pm, and the streets were not just deserted, but forsaken. It was only thirty-five miles down Route 16 but it seemed a world away.

Towns are like people sometimes. Hard to figure why some get by and others don't. Bethlehem, PA, had lost its steel plant, but the people managed to reinvent themselves and carry on. Did it have something to do with the isolation created by the West Virginia hills?

Does despair get trapped in the narrow hollows, and the limited sunlight prevent hope from taking root? An answer did not come readily to me, so I asked the bartender for another beer and dug into my steak and baked potato.

After my meal, I needed a place to park Zorba for the night. He had earned a well-deserved rest after successfully navigating the curves on Route 16—the steak being my reward. Driving through Tazewell, I was having trouble identifying a suitable spot. Generally, in a small town I could find a park or town green where I could discreetly park and sleep undisturbed—not that this strategy always turns out well.

The best example of how poorly this can play out occurred on a road trip I took in the Province of Ontario, Canada, several years back. I was traveling in my 2003 Saab with my bicycle hanging on the back of the car. On these trips, I would often travel light with no camping gear. When it was time to sleep, I would pull down the back seat of the Saab and stretch a sleeping bag into the exposed trunk space. It provided just enough space for me to stretch out, and I could get a good night's sleep with no one ever knowing there was someone in the car. By comparison, a VW bus is quite luxurious.

On one particular night, I rolled into the lovely little town of Niagara-on-the-Lake in Ontario, Canada. I believed I had found a suitable night-time spot next to a small park overlooking Lake Ontario. The evening light was fading as I parked along the edge of the picnic grounds and squeezed myself into the back end of my car. Just as I settled in, a car pulled up and parked directly in front of me, and a young couple emerged. I made myself small as they walked holding hands over to a nearby picnic table. In their rush to get to the picnic table, they failed to set the emergency brake correctly, and their car rolled back, thumping up against my Saab.

I thought this would prompt a return to their vehicle, but their focus was already on other matters. As they got to know each other better—not sure how else to say it—I lay in my car wondering how to extract myself from this situation. My first instinct was to wait it out. Eventually, they would know everything they needed to know about each other, at least for that night, and would return to their car and drive off. These young lovers had not seen me when they parked, and I assumed they would not see me when they returned. In my defense here, I would like to say that not every person sleeping in a car is a creeper. Some. But not all.

I was comfortable with this plan until the situation evolved. The evolution had to do with my bladder and my sudden and urgent need to relieve myself. My attempt to wait it out became more difficult as things had evolved for them also. They were getting very busy on that picnic table. As much as I tried to assure myself otherwise, the longer I stayed, the more the "creeper" label fit. My self-respect compelled me to escape the situation, and my bladder was equally insistent. Slowly and quietly, I crawled from the back seat into the driver's seat.

I had two concerns before starting the engine. First, I did not want to startle the young couple too severely. The whole episode had the potential to leave a lasting mark on them and perhaps limit their ability to further explore their relationship in the future. Second, their car had rolled into mine. Once I moved, their vehicle would inevitably begin rolling down the incline where we were parked. Would they be able to catch it in time before any serious harm was done? I had no good solution to either of those problems. I just knew I had to relieve myself, and no one likes a creeper. Time to go. I started the engine, threw the car into reverse, and then accelerated away fleeing the scene. I got away unscathed. I hope they—and their car—did too.

Now in Tazewell, after completing a circuit of the town's streets, I could not find a suitable park or town square, but I did find the parking lot of the Presbyterian church. It was away from foot traffic, and I was confident I could be up and gone by the time church services started at 9 am. As a plus, I noted there were no picnic tables nearby. I tucked Zorba into a cozy spot under some trees and crawled into the back for some reading and then sleep. Thankfully, it was an uneventful night.

BONNY BLUE HOLLOW

I woke up with Kentucky on my mind. I was 115 miles from the state line, and since I was not sticking around for church services, it was time to free up my spot for some God-fearing Presbyterian. Zorba and I jumped onto Route 19 west and, with little traffic on a Sunday morning, made good time. We exited Route 19 at Pennington Gap and took Route 421 west, the Coal Heritage Trail, which would take us to the Kentucky state line. Passing an intersection, I saw a hitchhiker by the road and recalling my pledge to pay it forward, I pulled over. He had a tired look about him, said his name was Tim, and asked if I could take him home. Knowing Kentucky could wait, I told him to show me the way. As I drove, Tim told me his story.

He was a coal miner—or used to be. He was injured in the mines fifteen years ago when a slab of coal fell on him and cracked several vertebrae in his back. Tim said he was out of work eight weeks, and the vertebrae never healed, but he returned to the mine as the bills were piling up. He worked another ten years until the company decided they had gotten all the work out of him they could. They informed him he was impaired and cut him loose. Shortly after that, the doctors piled on and told Tim he had black lung disease. When I picked him up that morning, he was coming back from a medical appointment.

"Imma one a d'lucky ones," he shared. "I gots my black lung benefits and can 'ford my medical care."

He added that many others he knew hadn't been approved for the benefits and could not afford what little treatment there was for something incurable. Tim's great-grandfather on down to his father had all been miners, and he never thought about doing anything else. He had lived his whole life in St. Charles, population 117, up Bonny Blue Hollow, and assured me he would die there.

"Tried living in Roanoke once whar thar was some work, but they's too much concrete. Came back to the holler."

As we drove, Tim pointed out the small trails that led from the backs of some of the homes into the hills behind them. He said some people had their personal mine up in the mountain where they could dig out a little coal to heat their home. A little more work involved than my act of turning up the thermostat back home.

I mentioned my coal mine tour back in Beckley, and Tim laughed at my experience but not in a demeaning way. But for him, there was no doubt that it was an amusement park ride. He shared some stories of his time in the mine, which left me feeling relieved the Beckley experience was not more authentic.

"Did they tell ye about the rats?"

I shook my head, "No."

"The rats were the best friends yuh had. They always know'd when somethin' bad's 'bout to happen long 'fore you did. If you seen them rats runnin' for the opening, you drops what's you doin' and takes your hind end with 'em."

"Thanks. I hope I never have to use that information."

I decided to give Tim the last word on the coal debate. "Do you think the mines are going to make a comeback? The President keeps saying so."

Tim shook his head. "People know'd better. But they likes to hear the talk. Makes 'em feel respected."

I dropped Tim off and thanked him for sharing his story and for his service in the mines, and he thanked me for the ride.

It occurred to me that Tim might be the closest person to Zorba the Greek I would meet on this trip. The Zorba in Kazantzakis's novel was based on a coal miner turned monk named Georgios Zorbas. Zorbas did some mining in Greece before running off with the owner's daughter and starting a new life. After much tragedy and the death of his wife, he retreated to a monastery on Mount Athos, and it was there that Kazantzakis met him and a friendship ensued. Kazantzakis convinced Zorbas to return to coal mining in Mani, a southern peninsula in Greece, and their shared experience there is the basis for much of the novel. Zorbas and Kazantzakis remained lifelong friends and exchanged letters until Zorbas died in 1941. Given the risks of mining and the dance they do with death whenever they enter the mines, it is not surprising that a coal miner would become the literary model for one who lives solely in the present.

After dropping Tim off, I followed Bonny Blue Hollow Road up to the end of the hollow to see what I could find. I passed a house where several people were sitting on the front porch, and they gave me a wave. The narrow road wound its way up to the small town of Bonny Bell, which is unincorporated with only a handful of people still living there. The houses didn't even qualify to be called "fixer-uppers" but were more teetering on the edge of condemnation. The last paint job was not in this century, and the front porches appeared more precarious and dangerous than the mine I had toured in Beckley. The Bonny Blue mine at the end of the hollow closed in 1946, and the last post office in town closed in 1962. Another lost community on the backroads of America. I did a U-turn at the chained-off entrance to the mine and headed back down the hollow.

When I returned to the house where I had received the friendly wave, Jimmy was standing by the road waiting for me. Jimmy was in his late twenties, and while his smile showed the need for some dental work, it was so inviting you had to smile back. He knew the only way out of the hollow was to return by way of his house, so he had waited for me.

"Welcome to Bonny Blue Holler. I sure do loves your van. What the heck you doin' back hare?" Jimmy pronounced it as "holler,"—as Tim did, and like most of the people who live in them do—not "hollow." A hollow, by definition, is an elongated lowland between two ranges of mountains, hills, or other uplands, but "holler" is acceptable in what linguists refer to as Appalachian English. And that is the only English they speak in these parts.

"I gave a guy a ride—Tim. Just wanted to see where the road took me after I dropped him off."

"Tim's a good man. Thanks fer helpn' him out."

"Happy to do it. He shared some good stories."

"I really do love this here van. I gots a dune buggy out back. You wouldn't consider a trade woudya? I betcha my buggy goes a lot faster than what you got here."

"Everything goes a lot faster than what I got here."

Roger laughed. "Ah 'magine so. Where you goin' from here?"

"California."

"Shoot. I hopes to get thar some day. But so fur I haven't left the state of Virginia." I appreciated that Jimmy didn't laugh at the idea of me getting to California or suggest I had a few marbles loose. Then Jimmy asked, "Are you on Facebook?"

I did not see that coming and replied, "Not much, but I'm there occasionally."

Jimmy gave me his full name and asked me to connect with him the next time I was online. I said I would look for him and concluded that Facebook can cease all marketing efforts as their reach is now total—Bonny Blue Hollow is connected.

"Thanks for flaggn' me down. Reckon I should get goin'. I need to get to Kentucky today." The holler was creeping into my speech, just as my Kentucky accent does when I am on the phone for any length of time with friends or relatives back in Kentucky.

As he turned toward his house, I called out to Jimmy, "I hope you get to California. You would have some fun with your dune buggy on the beaches there." With that, Zorba and I coasted down out of Bonny Blue Hollow, leaving the isolation behind us, something I "hopes" Jimmy will do one day.

Tim in Bonny Blue Hollow

Happy the youth who believes that his duty is to remake the world and bring it more in accord with virtue and justice, more in accord with his own heart. Woe to whoever commences his life without lunacy.

—Nikos Kazantzakis, *Report to Greco*

HARLAN COUNTY

I arrived at the state line and crossed over into Harlan County, Kentucky. It has been over forty years since I called Kentucky home, but the feeling that comes over me whenever I return never changes. There is a sudden and immediate familiarity that welcomes me every time. The smell of the grass, the sounds of the birds and cicadas, even the dirt has a unique smell and reminds me of my youth. Wherever I am in the state, the horizon has a familiar look. It always feels like home.

This was my very first visit to Harlan County, and while there might be some discussion among Kentuckians as to which county— there are 120 of them—best represents the state, in my mind, it has always been Harlan. Certainly not Jefferson County, where Louisville, the largest city in the state resides, and where I grew up. Louisville, with its progressive ways, always seems to be at odds with the rest of the state. Fayette County, in the heart of the state, with the beautiful horse farms around Lexington, could make a case, but it's just a little too fancy and somewhat elitist. Franklin County, where the state capital

Frankfort sits, is out of the question as that's where the "guv'ment" is, and no one wants the guv'ment to represent you—even though that's what we elect them to do.

No, because so much of the character of Kentucky flows out of the Appalachian Mountains—the grit, the orneriness, the desire to live independently, but also the willingness to get along with others often evidenced in border states—the chosen one has to be in Appalachia. I choose Harlan County.

Harlan County is in the heart of Appalachia, tucked up against Virginia in the southeast corner of the state. It is one of those places that you never pass through even on your way to somewhere else—it is too much off the beaten path. No interstate highways dissect the county, and the cities of Cumberland and Harlan compete to be the largest towns, each having just over 1,500 residents. The county is what is commonly referred to as "moist," as opposed to a "dry" county where no alcoholic beverages are sold. In a moist county, alcohol can be purchased in only one town, and Cumberland owns that right in Harlan County. You can be sure on Friday and Saturday nights that the number of inhabitants in Cumberland spikes well above Harlan's.

The county is named after Silas Harlan, who was born in Virginia and often traveled to the region of Kentucky as a scout and hunter. He later became a major in the Continental Army and died at the Battle of Blue Licks near present-day Mount Olivet, Kentucky, in 1782. It was one of the last battles waged in the Revolutionary War and fought a full ten months after the British Commander General Charles Cornwallis surrendered in the East at Yorktown. While the war effectively ended in the East at Yorktown, it was still being waged on the Western frontier by some stubborn loyalists to the Crown. Fighting alongside Silas was Daniel Boone who survived the battle, lived a long and adventurous life, and is buried, well, that is a "whole 'nother story" as we Kentuckians say, which I will get to later.

Harlan is popular in both literature and music, and numerous country music artists originated there, most notably Jerry Chestnut, whose songs were performed by Elvis, Dolly Parton, Waylon Jennings, Tammy Wynette, and Jerry Lee Lewis. The most popular song written about Harlan County might be "You'll Never Leave Harlan Alive," which I can happily say was one of the two wedding songs selected when Dianne and I tied the knot. Written and performed by Darrell Scott, there is something in the lyrics Dianne never warmed up to as a wedding song. The recurring refrain speaks of filling your cup "with whatever bitter brew you're drinking"….and spending the rest of your life "just thinking how to get away." There is some romance in the song as well, but one can understand why Dianne insisted on a second wedding song.

The most well-known person to Kentuckians to ever come out of Harlan County is Cawood Ledford, the voice of Kentucky basketball for thirty-nine years. Many Kentuckians in my generation learned to mimic his legendary play-by-play call of the games. His last game as an announcer was the 1992 NCAA East Regional Final, won by Duke in overtime, 104-103, on a last-second shot by Christian Laettner. Universally considered to be one of the greatest college basketball games ever played, it made the Laettner name a curse word in the state. But nobody blames Cawood. He was just the messenger.

And of course, coal runs through the veins of Harlan County. It has been mined and fought over for the past hundred years. The coal wars of the 1930s were particularly violent as the county earned the name Bloody Harlan. The strife over whether the miners would be allowed to organize and improve their wages and working conditions included pitched battles, executions, and bombings. It has not been definitively determined how many people died during the conflict, which lasted from 1931 to 1939. Like the making of moonshine, many incidents happened in the dark of night. Eventually, the Governor called in the National Guard to put down the strike, but the miners got their union.

Another death occurred during a miners' strike in 1973, and the ensuing documentary *Harlan County, USA* received the Academy Award for Best Documentary in 1976. Miners still go underground, tunneling through the mountains surrounding Harlan, and to date, more than 700 miners have lost their lives in the county—most recently Hubert Grubbs, age twenty-nine, on March 28, 2018. Mr. Grubbs was splicing a conveyor belt when it started unexpectedly, and he became entangled. The price of keeping the lights on continues to rise.

The most recent treatment of Harlan County is the television show *Justified* which ran six seasons, stretching from 2010 to 2015. The show is based on the writings of Elmore Leonard and portrays US Marshal Raylan Givens who returns to his roots in Harlan County and attempts to curtail the production and distribution of crystal meth by the Lexington Mafia. Many of the characters in the show are based on actual residents of the county, and my favorite is Mags.

In *Justified*, it is Mags Bennett, but in real life, it was Mags Bailey who operated a small country store outside Harlan where she sold vital provisions to the people of Harlan—the most vital of all being her moonshine. Mags did time in federal prison but generally was able to avoid the law through bribes and other means, passing away in 2005. Dianne and I became avid watchers of the show, and Dianne's most frequent comment as we watched an avalanche of bad Kentucky behavior was, "These are your peeps." I would just nod. Never deny your people.

Zorba and I rolled into Harlan on a Sunday afternoon, hoping to talk to some of the locals and gauge their impression of *Justified*. There were very few people visible, but I did spot three individuals lounging under an elm tree on the grounds of the county courthouse in the center of town. I strode up to them and was greeted with a "You livin' in that?" as they pointed to the bus.

"I do for now," I replied.

I introduced myself to Jimmy, Donna, and Billy Bob—not making that one up. The first topic of conversation was the weather. They had settled in underneath the shade of the elm, but it wasn't helping much. The air was thick with the heat and humidity of a Kentucky summer.

Billy Bob offered, "It's so dang hot I just saw a hound dog chasn' a rabbit—and they were both walking."

I laughed pretty hard at that, which Billy Bob appreciated. You just don't get that kind of humor in Boston. After some complaints about the "damn politicians"—no one in particular, just the lot of them—I worked the conversation around to *Justified*. Both Jimmy and Donna had seen parts of it, but not Billy Bob.

"It paints a pretty dark picture of Harlan. Did that upset you at all?" I asked.

"Naw. They pretty much got it right," Donna said.

That surprised me, since the show leaves you with the impression that just about everyone in Harlan is either making crystal meth, selling crystal meth, or using crystal meth—and if not meth, then moonshine and marijuana. When I pointed that out, Donna just said "Yep" and took a long draw on her cigarette—hopefully, one made with Kentucky tobacco.

It took me a while to figure out that my new acquaintances were not just lounging under the elm tree but were, in fact, homeless. I told them I left Boston nine days ago and was heading toward my hometown of Louisville, then on to California.

"I spent a month in Luavull once, living underneath a bridge. Didn't like it much." Donna said.

I wasn't sure if she meant the "living under the bridge" part or the City of Louisville, but I didn't pursue it.

Since Mags and her store had played such a prominent role in *Justified*, I asked if Mags's store was still in the county as I'd like to drive by and pay my respects. Donna, the most talkative in the group, answered, "Nope. Torn down. But her house is still here."

"Well, that will have to do then. Can you tell me how to get there?"

Without taking the cigarette out of her mouth, Donna waved in the general direction east of Harlan, "Take a left, and it's a blue house."

I pressed for a few more details, but all I got was, "You'll find it. Just don't miss the left."

Thanking them for their time and the directions, I went in search of Mags's "historic" homestead. Heading in the general direction that Donna had waved her hand, I found a lot of lefts and several blue houses. I suppose I saw Mags's house, but I can't be sure. I decided to declare victory and headed back into Harlan. Passing the courthouse again, I waved to Billy Bob, Jimmy, and Donna, who were still sitting in the shade of their elm tree. They were good people on hard times, but I think they felt sorry for me, the one who had to live in an old bus. I believe they would have shared anything they had with me if I asked—except maybe good directions. I was lucky to meet them.

PINEVILLE

From Harlan, I headed west on Route 119. A state park in Pineville looked promising as a place to spend the night. Stopping at the junction of Route 119 and Route 25E, I filled up at a gas station and succumbed to one of my weaknesses, Arby's. If you think Dianne shakes her head at the bad Kentucky behavior on *Justified*, you should see her reaction when I mention Arby's. But, she was 1,000 miles away, and I was feeling bold and reckless.

"Make that two roast beef sandwiches, Ma'am."

After filling up myself and Zorba, I went searching for Pine Mountain State Park. It did not seem to be where the map said it was. Not wanting to venture another attempt at directions from my fellow Kentuckians, I kept wandering. Eventually, I stumbled on it, the sign hidden by both a hanging limb and a truck parked along the road. Guiding Zorba up the winding road, which led to the top of Pine Mountain, I found several trailheads where I could park the bus for the night. I selected the one where I could pull in and be unseen by passersby. The two roast beef sandwiches were having the effect that fast food always has on me, a combination of feeling bloated, dissatisfied, and guilty, but that won't stop me from repeating the experience down the road. Mags had her moonshine—I've got my Arby's.

The next morning, after a jolt of coffee and some scrambled eggs with ham, I continued the drive to the top of Pine Mountain, which overlooks the town of Pineville in the valley below. A short hike from the mountain top parking lot took me to a large boulder that looms precariously over Pineville's homes and businesses. It is so precarious that many years ago, the people of Pineville became increasingly worried that the boulder could break loose and create considerable destruction in the town. Not wanting to leave their homes' fate dependent on the stability of the boulder, they decided to do something about it. In 1933, using a mule team, they dragged a large chain from a wrecked steam shovel up the mountain and secured it to the boulder, thus ensuring Pineville's future. I was impressed with the strength and weight of the chain and concluded the townspeople of Pineville could sleep well at night.

There is, however, another version of the story which involves the local Kiwanis. In this version, the Kiwanis Club saw the boulder as an opportunity of sorts. They decided a chained rock overlooking their town, and a corresponding tale of impending doom, would draw interest and attract visitors. The scheming Kiwanians, along with the local boy scout troop and conservation corps, secured the chain to the boulder knowing full well the boulder perched above the town was actually part of the mountain and never moving.

So take your pick of stories. As for me, I say, "Well played, Kiwanis." Here I am, standing on top of Pine Mountain and spending money at the Arby's in your town. Atop the securely chained boulder, I gazed down at Pineville and wondered what badge the scout troop received for their participation in this deception. All scouts pledge to do their "duty to God and country" and keep themselves "morally straight." These scouts may have fudged a bit on the "morally straight" part. In any case, I'm sure the badge they earned had a boulder and chain on it, and no other troop had one.

Hiking back to Zorba, I passed a woman sitting on a bench with her dog waiting patiently at her side. After a friendly hello, she asked if I could do her a favor. She wanted me to look for an elderly gentleman in the parking lot with two young girls and tell them, "The glasses are in the glove compartment." It sounded like a code for something, but I readily agreed and asked for her name so I would have some credibility.

"My name is Joyce, but they know me as Grandma."

When I got to the parking lot, I could see no one who fit the description she had given me, so the message stayed with me. Zorba and I drove on down the mountain, but the undelivered message left me feeling unsettled—more so than even the Arby's. Knowing the town's history for deception, had Grandma been left behind? I hope not. Pineville has enough to answer for.

Chained boulder overlooking Pineville

IMAGINE

Kentucky is known for many things, and you could get quite an argument among its residents over which is the crown jewel of the state. The tradition of thoroughbred horse racing would be in the conversation as Man O'War and American Pharoah are just a few of the horses bred in Kentucky that went on to greatness. And, the Kentucky Derby is commonly referred to as "the most exciting two minutes in sports." On Derby Day, Churchill Downs is a gathering spot for celebrities of all ilks, along with thousands of college students who gather in the infield, consume large numbers of mint juleps, and never see a horse—and could care less. I speak from experience.

Kentucky is also the birthplace of bourbon, which is always in the discussion of what most distinguishes the state—even though it's illegal to sell it in a third of the counties. In fact, just to have this discussion, or pretty much any debate, most Kentuckians would need to open a bottle to wake up the brain cells. Kentuckians find a myriad of ways to consume bourbon, and there is a limitless number of dishes that call for it as an ingredient. Burgoo, also known as "roadkill stew," is the most famous of these, frequently served at Kentucky Derby parties. The ingredients have evolved from possum, squirrel, and raccoon to more civilized pork, beef, and lamb, but bourbon remains a constant and essential addition.

Bourbon is America's only native spirit, and while it does not have to be made in Kentucky to be called bourbon—a general misconception—there is not a God-fearing Kentuckian who would drink a bourbon made out of state. Thankfully such a breach of etiquette is hard to do, since 95 percent of all bourbon is made in Kentucky.

Let's add to this crown jewel discussion the Louisville Slugger. Wielded by Babe Ruth, Lou Gehrig, and Mickey Mantle, this iconic bat continues to be the preferred instrument of many major league baseball players. Originally ash was the wood of choice, but maple has gradually taken its place, as it is less likely to splinter. Barry Bonds used a maple Louisville Slugger, and perhaps a little help from another source, to hit seventy-three home runs in 2001.

But I would like to make a case for Berea College, located in idyllic Berea, Kentucky, as being the real crown jewel of Kentucky. Founded in 1855, it was the first southern college to be both coeducational and integrated—Oberlin College in Ohio holds that distinction in the north. The abolitionist John Gregg Fee founded Berea College on land donated by a fellow abolitionist, Cassius Marcellus Clay—former namesake of Muhammed Ali. In 1859, a group of armed white men, not ready for change, attacked Berea College and gave the abolitionists ten days to leave the state. Forced to abandon the College, they fled to Ohio, and John Fee's son, who was ill from diphtheria, died during the exodus.

The ordeal strengthened Fee's resolve, and he returned to Berea at the conclusion of the Civil War to restart the college. In 1866, 187 students enrolled, with half being recently freed slaves. For the rest of the 1800s, enrollment continued to be evenly split between black and white students and continued to be coeducational. Unfortunately, the school's approach to equal education for all made some Kentuckians uncomfortable. One "uncomfortable" moment occurred in 1904 when a state legislator passed through town on a train and observed two young women—one white and one black—embracing each other. Shortly after that, he introduced legislation in the Kentucky House of Representatives that made integrated schools illegal with a stiff fine imposed on any school that dared to enroll students of different races.

The 1904 Kentucky law was challenged but ultimately upheld by the Supreme Court of the United States, with the one dissenting voice being John Marshall Harlan, a Kentucky native and nephew of Silas Harlan. (John Marshall Harlan was also the lone dissenter in *Plessy vs. Ferguson*, the case which legalized the "separate but equal" principle applied throughout the Jim Crow South.) While Berea had to step away from a core part of its mission and stop enrolling black students, it returned to it in 1950 when the 1904 law was amended to allow integration for schools above the secondary level in the state. Berea was quick to expand enrollment of black students further after the *Brown* vs. *Board of Education* ruling in 1955, and today the College continues to be a beacon for diversity in the state.

While leading the fight for integration distinguishes Berea College among educational institutions in the South, what distinguishes it even more is the decision made in 1892 that all students attending Berea would attend tuition-free. The tuition bill is paid internally by the college, and all students are engaged in jobs, both on- and off-campus, which cover the bulk of their room and board. The College's mission focuses on educating the poor youth of Appalachia, and even the small number of international students who enroll must be considered low-income in their home country. *Washington Monthly,* which ranks schools based on their "contribution to the public good," perennially rates Berea College as the top Liberal Arts School in the country. In their rankings of schools by the percentage of students accepted who subsequently enroll, Berea is surpassed only by Harvard and Stanford. It is a jewel whose value is widely recognized.

Sometimes you take a wrong turn in life, and you feel fortunate you did. That happened to me on my way to Berea. My wrong turn took me onto a dead-end street, and being disoriented, I pulled over to check my map, the GPS on my phone, and whatever other celestial guidance I could get. I sat in a parking lot next to one of the innumerable Baptist churches you pass traveling through Kentucky and studied the map trying to figure out how to get back on track to Berea. Ira was cutting the grass for the church, and he startled me a bit when he pulled up on his riding mower to Zorba's driver's side door. Introducing himself, he pointed to his riding mower, smiled, and described himself as "the Forrest Gump of Berea."

Ira had retired from his custodian job at Eastern Kentucky University the previous year, and shortly after, he decided to take on a few mowing jobs for a little extra money—and respect his wife's suggestion that he get out of the house more. The one or two jobs he took on grew into twelve, and now he spends almost every day on his mower. Ira happily gave me some excellent directions that would get me back on course to Berea, and I concluded that my friends back in Harlan could learn a thing or two from him. Seeing Ira as a wise sage in the mold of Forrest Gump, I asked him if he thought the old bus would get me to California. His answer reflected wisdom gained over a lifetime of fixing things: "Of course it will—if you have enough money." We laughed at that, and I encouraged Ira to get back to being retired.

I planned for my stop in Berea to be a short one. I wanted to get something to eat at the historic Boone Tavern and move on after taking a look at the Berea College campus. All that changed when I got there. I discovered it was the first day in the Fall semester, and the campus had that energy unique to young people who believe all their dreams are ahead of them, and anything is possible. I parked in a lot near one of the dorms where there was very little foot traffic and started cleaning and organizing Zorba, a constant activity on the trip. Soon the students began to find me.

Maria was the first to stop by. She was born in Mexico but had lived most of her life in Spain and Morocco. Her friends had alerted her to the presence of an old VW hippie van on campus, which had prompted her to come find me.

"I've got an old van myself, a Ford Econoline. Once I get it fixed and set up for living in, I'm going to hit the road. But I need to graduate first. My friends think I'm a little nuts."

"I know that feeling," I said with a smile. "The part about your friends thinking you are a little crazy. I've got several in that category, not to mention a wife."

"Secretly, I think they might be a little jealous," Maria said.

"Maybe. Or maybe they just know better than us," I countered.

Maria and I laughed at that.

"I tried a road trip right after I graduated from college. I didn't get far. I'm sure yours will turn out better. What do you hope to do if you survive your road trip?" I asked.

"I want to return to Mexico, attend dental school there, then provide free care to the people who need it most."

Miranda and her mom stopped by after Maria. Mom was dropping her off for the start of the school year and seemed reluctant to let go and return to their home state of Tennessee.

"I saw your van and just had to see it up close. I hope you don't mind," Miranda said.

"Happy to show it off. Are you happy to be back at school?"

"I am. I worked too hard this summer!"

Miranda shared that she had spent the summer working on a farm in rural Tennessee, and the experience had changed her perspective on many things and taught her the importance of working with the soil. Even though she described it as the hardest work she had ever done, she was changing her major to Agriculture and Natural

Resources. She planned to commit herself to sustainable farming—attuned to the ecosystem, and minimizing any negative impact on the environment.

"My first job out of college was picking corn and cucumbers on a farm in South Alabama. I can attest to the hard work. Had the opposite effect on me. Convinced me to never be a farmer!"

Miranda laughed and said her real dream was to do what I was doing. "Before I take on farming I want to wander the country in an old VW bus." I caught her mom rolling her eyes at this, but to mom's credit, she didn't utter a discouraging word.

"I thought that was a dream particular to my generation, but I am beginning to think otherwise. If that is what you dream of doing, then I am sure you will do it."

And then there was Connor. I immediately had hair envy when I saw him; his locks were full and dark and reached down to his shoulders. Connor would have been welcomed with open arms at Hector's Inn back in Bethel, New York.

"Are you living in the bus?" he asked.

"For now, I am. I do have a perfectly fine house back in Massachusetts," assuring Connor that it was my choice to do so.

Of course, Connor thought living in an old VW bus just might be the ultimate goal in life, so I would have made a better impression by leaving out the house part. I noticed he had a wooden medallion hanging from his neck. It was a VW emblem.

"What model VW do you drive?" I asked.

"Don't have one. One day I will own an old bus like this. I made the medallion to remind me of what I have to look forward to. School is not really my thing."

Where does Berea College find these kids? Or do these kids find Berea College?

Around the campus, I saw many symbols and signs that reminded me of the idealism I had once held onto as a college student in the '60s.

Love thy neighbor as yourself

is not followed by the word

"UNLESS."

And...

This could be the place

Welcoming ALL.

No Kidding.

No Exceptions.

Then there was the T-shirt that Connor was wearing. I believe it spoke for all the students at Berea.

WE ARE THE

COURAGEOUS

WE ARE THE

PASSIONATE

WE ARE THE

DETERMINED

WE ARE HOPE

Right on, Connor!

After absorbing the jolt of energy I received from the students who stopped by the bus, I walked over to Boone Tavern, built in 1909 to provide lodging for visitors to the college. The "tavern" portion of the name refers to the word's original meaning, which was "public lodging for travelers." Boone Tavern did not begin serving alcohol until 2014. Berea is in a moist county, and until that time, alcohol sales were allowed only in the town of Richmond, eighteen miles up the road. An exception was made for Boone Tavern given its historic prominence in the county. I fear things are getting a little loose in Raleigh County.

What Boone Tavern is most known for, and what brings travelers from far away, is its southern cuisine—most notably its spoonbread. It is what it says it is—bread that you eat with a spoon from the cast iron dish it is baked in. James Beard described it as a "heavy soufflé," and it is also called "cornbread's fancy cousin"—eggy, buttery, tender, and moist. It complements any meal, and I call it delicious and mouth-watering.

I paired the spoonbread with the Blue Ribbon Pork Chops and took advantage of their relatively new liquor license by sipping some fine Kentucky bourbon. Afterward, I decided to linger a while longer in Berea and spend the night. The bourbon I sipped may have had something to do with that. While most of the parking lots on campus required a parking sticker, the lot near the Admissions Office did not, so I found a lovely tulip tree—the state tree of Kentucky—and parked under it on the edge of the lot. Like the worn-out traveler that I was, I slept well, and the bourbon may get some credit for that too.

Waking in the morning, I was in no hurry to leave Berea as it was the day of "The Great Solar Eclipse" as it came to be called, and I decided to experience it there. Berea was just outside the "zone of totality," and an eclipse of 95 percent was expected. I wandered back over to Boone Tavern, knowing if the world was going to end that day, as predicted by some, I would be near one last helping of spoonbread.

As the anticipated time drew close, I gathered with others lingering near Boone Tavern and stumbled onto Jim, who had set up his telescope for viewing. I did not have the special eclipse glasses that someone made a lot of money selling that week, but Jim assured me

I would not melt my retina by peering through his telescope. Sure enough, I got a great view of the solar eclipse, and while it didn't get as dark as I hoped—no crickets came out—I enjoyed sharing the experience with the good people of Berea. After full sunlight returned, I passed on more bourbon at Boone Tavern and returned to Zorba. I was ready to hit the road and hoped to get to Louisville that night. As a tribute to the Berea College students, I listened to John Lennon's "Imagine" as I rolled out of town.

Ira - The Forrest Gump of Berea

Connor of Berea College

RICK'S WHITE LIGHT DINER

Because I had passed on more southern cuisine at Boone Tavern, I needed to find a lunch spot along the way to Louisville. Back in Boston, I had read about a diner in Frankfort, Kentucky—featured on *Guy Fieri's Diners, Drive-Ins, and Dives*—Rick's White Light Diner. It specializes in Cajun cooking, which is not particularly common in Kentucky given its distance from New Orleans and Cajun country.

From the article, it sounded like my kind of place, and since it had been a while since I visited the state capital, I headed for Frankfort.

As best as I could recall, the last time I had set foot in Frankfort I was protesting the Vietnam War during my college years, my only public protest against the war. The march led to the Capitol grounds where we laid on the lawn, each holding a cross representing a soldier from Kentucky who had died in Vietnam. I had seen a notice for the march on a bulletin board at college, and it was one more thing I talked my friend Art into doing with me. We did the march, laid on the lawn, then drove home to our sheltered environment in the seminary, risking very little.

I pulled into Frankfort, found Rick's White Light Diner without too much wandering, and from its appearance, it qualified as both a diner and a dive. I concluded the food would be delicious. In truth, the owner, Rick Paul, has some serious street cred among chefs—he graduated from the Culinary Institute of America in Hyde Park, New York.

Entering, I found a seat at the counter where Hannah, Rick's daughter, welcomed me. Behind Hannah was a collection of souvenirs and various artifacts from Rick's travels and other tokens left by previous diners. There were also some political stickers and signs which reflected a Democratic leaning, which surprised me, since I thought all the Democrats lived in the big city of Louisville. There was even a Hillary Clinton bumper sticker, and she lost the state by 30 percentage points.

The Hillary sticker was next to a Jesus action figure with "glow in the dark" hands, and, being unaware of that particular miracle, I already considered my visit a success. And since they specialized in Cajun food, there was the obligatory preserved alligator head, even though alligators did not make it onto the White Light menu. Directly behind Hannah, there was a prominent sign promoting their grits, and next to that, an autographed picture of Waylon Jennings, who vouched for the food at the White Light.

But my favorite sign of all might have been the one that asked the philosophical question: "If going to church makes you a Christian, does going to the garage make you a car?"

I'm sure Jesus, with the "glow in the dark" hands, knew the answer to that one.

I studied the menu, and the choice was obvious—crawfish pie. Hannah shouted my order back to Jennifer, who was doing all the cooking that day, and as Jennifer prepared my pie in the back, Hannah told me about the time they were visited by the Food Network and Guy Fieri. She brought out a photo album, and as I thumbed through the pictures, Hannah gave me a play-by- play of what the day was like. You could see it was a proud moment for the diner, and she had nothing but good things to say about Guy Fieri, who also had the crawfish pie. I was in good company.

At one point, I began a shouting conversation with Jennifer as she worked the grill and juggled the multitude of tasks that short order grill cooks always have to manage. The conversation didn't slow her down.

"I've worked here twenty years, more or less. That's not countn' the times I either quit or got fired." She shared that she and Rick have had some monumental clashes in the diner, which because of its compact size and close quarters, I'm sure were felt by everyone there.

"But Rick and Hannah are like family for me, so I always come back."

I got a clear picture that Jennifer didn't back down from anyone, and there would be more monumental clashes in the future. The crawfish pie did not disappoint—though I did find myself longing for some spoonbread to go with it. But I was more than satisfied and bid my farewell to the folks at the White Light Diner.

Before heading back on the road, I swung by the state Capitol Building to revisit the spot on the lawn where I had made my horizontal statement about the Vietnam War. Unfortunately, the foolishness that frequently occurs in the State Capitol, going back to the Berea College decisions, has continued throughout the years. Every state has its quirky laws, but Kentucky seems to have more than its fair share. I offer as examples:

> By law, anyone who has been drinking is *"sober"* until he or she *"cannot hold onto the ground."* (Contrary to my experience, which is, you are most drunk when desperately holding onto the ground.)

> *"Every citizen of Kentucky is required to take a shower once a year."* (Don't set the bar too high for my fellow Kentuckians.)

> *Cats may not molest cars.* (No argument with that one.)

> *One cannot legally trade horses after dark.* (Hell no!)

But then there are the laws that, instead of eliciting a chuckle, make you wonder what the hell they are trying to hold onto—besides the ground. I share with some sadness that the Kentucky State Legislature did not ratify the 13th Amendment to the Constitution, banning the institution of slavery, until 1976. Only Mississippi was slower, ratifying the amendment in 1995 and not certifying the vote until 2013. Thank you, Mississippi. Good to know my home state was not last in endorsing the elimination of slavery.

As I stepped onto the lawn at the State Capitol, it appeared smaller than in my memories, and I walked up the steps and entered the massive front door—the one that doesn't keep all the foolishness out. Standing in the center of the rotunda under the dome is a four-teen-foot statue of the state's most favorite son, Abraham Lincoln. He is surrounded by statues of other sons of Kentucky—no daughters—and there I received a jarring reminder of Kentucky's history as a slave state with emotional ties to the Confederacy—although it never seceded from the Union. To Lincoln's left stood Kentucky's unfortunate son, Jefferson Davis, the one and only president of the Confederacy. His statue stood a foot taller than Lincoln's—a fact that irritated me—but even more grating was the plaque at the foot of the statue which read:

PATRIOT - HERO - STATESMAN

I was baffled how someone who led a rebellion against his country could be termed a "Patriot" and was tempted to go back out and lie on the lawn again. Instead, I just let out a sigh and said a quiet prayer for my state that it would do a better job of coming to terms with its history. That was the extent of my protest. It turns out I am no braver now than I was in my twenties.

My final stop in Frankfort was the burial site of someone Kentucky has always held in high esteem and is seen as the founding father of the state, Daniel Boone. Kentucky is not the only state that has a claim on Boone, as he was born in Eastern Pennsylvania and spent his childhood at the Boone Homestead in Birdsboro. The Boone family then moved to North Carolina, where he lived for twenty-one years; if you go to Mocksville in the state you can hike the Boone Heritage Trail. Boone explored and hunted in Kentucky, then a part of Virginia, before bringing his family west and establishing Boonesborough in 1775, the first permanent white settlement in the state.

There are probably more things in Kentucky named after Boone than any other personage. This shows Kentuckians did not hold a grudge when he subsequently moved to Missouri, saying Kentucky was getting too crowded. He lived out his final years with his wife, Rebecca, on their homestead in St. Charles just outside St. Louis. Boone passed on to the great hunting grounds in the sky in 1820 and was buried next to Rebecca on the grounds of their Missouri estate. However, no one got around to marking the gravesite until ten years later in 1830, which contributed to the strange events that ensued several years later.

In 1845, some Kentuckians, including one of Boone's sons, showed up at the Boone Homestead in Missouri and laid claim to his remains. These future members of the Kentucky Chamber of Commerce disinterred him and moved him to what they felt was his proper resting grounds in Frankfort, Kentucky, hoping they could attract visitors. The people of Missouri were not happy with the situation, and the story arose that the Kentuckians had taken the wrong remains back to Frankfort. According to the story, when they finally got around to putting a marker on Boone's grave in Missouri, they erred in its location. Some of the family descendants in Missouri were aware of the mistake but chose not to tell the Kentuckians when they started digging. It seems you can't trust the good people of the "Show Me State" to correctly show you anything.

Questions about the actual location of Boone's burial site lingered until 1983 when a forensic anthropologist examined a crude plaster cast of Boone's skull, made before his Kentucky burial. He determined it to be that of an African American, and in fact, slaves had been buried near the Boone site in Missouri, which gave his determination some credence. The anthropologist then backtracked some—after I'm sure some persuasion from the current members of the Kentucky Chamber of Commerce—and said he wasn't 100 percent certain. But doubt had been sown, which was good enough for the people back in Missouri. They promptly erected a new marker near the old gravesite in Missouri and began inviting people to visit. So if you want to visit Daniel Boone's grave, you can take your pick as there are two of them. I, of course, chose Kentucky and paid my respects in Frankfort.

Jennifer at Rick's White Light Diner

HOMETOWN

I had been on the road for ten days when I rolled into Louisville, but it felt much longer than that. Zorba needed a thorough internal cleaning and reorganization, as I had not entirely developed a proper system for keeping everything in its place. There was an odor that hung in the air inside the bus, but I was pretty confident that it was me and not the bus itself. I was looking forward to my first hot shower since leaving Boston, and with my bottle of moonshine in hand, I showed up at my sister Jeanette's door. Jeanette has a dog-grooming business, and I hoped she had seen worse than me come through her door. She led me to my room—and the shower.

I planned to spend three days in Louisville, and had a short to-do list that I needed to work through while I was there. For myself, I needed a real bed for a few days and some good home cooking. For Zorba, I needed to address the heat issue along with a problem that had arisen with the sliding side door. The door required several attempts before it would catch. As it worsened, I stopped trying altogether and began using a bungee cord to keep it shut as I drove. Zorba was also due for an oil change.

According to Samba, the online site listing mechanics proficient on air-cooled engines, the options for air-cooled mechanics in Louisville are limited, but then I only needed one. I called AirKooled Motorwerks, which looked the most promising, and left a message. My brother-in-law Mark put some bourbon-soaked steaks on the grill, and we tried the Pine Top moonshine. Not bourbon, but not bad. It felt good to be back in my hometown.

The following day I got a call from Jeff at AirKooled Motorwerks. He told me that working on air-cooled vehicles was not his day job but his night job. His shop was in an old brick warehouse near south-central Louisville, and if I could get Zorba over there, he could work on it that night. My friend Art swung by, and we headed out. It took some looking around, but we eventually found Jeff and AirKooled Inc. tucked back in an alley with no sign advertising the shop.

Jeff looked a bit young to be an accomplished air-cooled mechanic, but his shop had a collection of air-cooled vehicles in various states of repair and reminded me of Dave's shop back in Bethlehem. That gave me confidence I had found the right guy, and I handed over the keys. Art and I returned to my sister's place, where we skipped the moonshine and went right to the bourbon.

Bourbon has a special capacity for eliciting memories, and Art and I commenced reminiscing about our ill-fated trip that ended in Warrior, Alabama. Art expressed some regret about not being on my current journey with me. I assured him that while the bus was larger than the Beetle we had headed out in forty-five years ago, it was still too small for both of us to live in and only one of us would exit alive. However, we made plans to rendezvous on my return leg and spend some time exploring the back roads of Louisiana and Mississippi together. We sealed the deal with more bourbon and went back to discussing our days on the road together in '72.

The following day I returned to see Jeff at AirKooled Motorwerks. Zorba had gotten an oil change, his sliding door was buttery smooth, and Jeff showed me where he had closed off the heating vents so they no longer directed hot air into the bus. Asking what I owed him, he waved me off, saying "You're living the dream, man. Just get back on the road."

I was taken aback by his generosity, and he repeatedly refused to take any compensation from me for the work he had done. I told him he was a good man, and he gave me an "AirKooled Motorwerks" sticker to put on *Zorba*. I had found another mechanic with a generous heart and an appreciation for a good road trip. They were starting to add up on this trip.

As I turned to walk away, I stopped and asked him the question posed to a lot of people along the way, especially the mechanics: "Do you think I will make it?"

"You are ballsier than I am!" he said with a smile.

I liked that—although I didn't necessarily take it as a vote of confidence.

On my last night in Louisville, I stopped by my nephew Jonny's house to spend some time with him and his wife, Ashley. I timed my visit perfectly as their two beautiful children, Lila and Evan, had just settled into bed. My visit, of course, interrupted the entire bedtime process. I took full advantage of it, taking the kids out to Zorba so they could see what their Great-Uncle Jerry had been traveling in. Much to their parents' dismay, I told Lila and Evan that if they worked hard and lived a good life, they too could live in a van one day. I believe I planted a seed that no amount of good parenting could ever uproot.

The next day, I set aside time for two stops before leaving Louisville. The first was the place I had lived and worked in my senior year of college, Boys Haven. During my junior year, I had been living at home with my parents and two younger sisters while working at a YMCA after school program in a nearby middle school. Knowing I wanted a career in youth work, I looked for a deeper and more intense experience and took the opportunity to work at Boys Haven, a residential program for teens.

Boys Haven was founded in 1950 by Father James Maloney, a Catholic priest, and Father Maloney was still directing it when I joined the staff in 1971. Hired to be a live-in counselor, I spent my senior year of college residing with the high school boys for whom Boys Haven was their refuge. Many had transitioned from the local Catholic orphanage where they had "aged out" and were considered "un-adoptable." Others were court-involved and had become wards of the state. My younger sisters, Jeanette and Sally, did not seem upset to see me move out of the house and relocate to Boys Haven. I'm pretty sure they considered me aged-out and un-adoptable as well.

The position required that I reside in one of the dorms on the campus. In return for payment of my college tuition, I would provide daily supervision of the residents' activities and some impromptu counseling, which I was ill-equipped to do. I shared the dorm responsibilities with a "House Mother," Miss Louise, and together we tried to create a supportive environment for the boys while they, in turn, tried to drive us crazy.

Not surprisingly, the boys were better at their job than I was at mine. My day would start by waking everyone up and, after breakfast made by Miss Louise, drive them to the local high school in the old yellow school bus owned by the Haven. I then had approximately six hours to squeeze in my college classes at the University of Louisville before returning in time to organize the afternoon recreation program—supervise dinner made by Miss Louise—oversee study time for the residents—then enforce bedtime (always an adventure). After everyone settled in, I could finally begin the work I needed to do for my college classes. I wanted something more intense, and I got it. My college tuition was only $500 a semester at the time, which made it a good deal for Boys Haven, but I got an even better deal by learning so much from the young men in my charge. The lessons they taught me served me well throughout my forty-five-year career in youth work.

After I graduated college in the spring of 1972, I left Boys Haven and embarked on my failed road trip with Art. This visit was my first time returning to the grounds. Father Maloney passed away in 1998, but the program continues to thrive, and when I drove through the front entrance, I was pleased to see the name was now Boys & Girls Haven. I found my way to the administrative offices intending to make a small donation—a much delayed thank you for the experience I had received there.

As I made out the check, I mentioned my experience as a live-in counselor and asked if I could take a walk around the grounds. Stacey, who oversees the independent living program, offered to show me around. Most of my memories were of the small dorm I lived in with the boys—referred to as House 2—and Stacey and I headed in that direction. My room was located in the back of the house, and it's where I had spent so many late nights studying and making my inexperienced and often fumbling attempts at providing counseling and support to the teens residing in the house. It had a special place in my memory. And as we walked the hallway towards the back of the house, I recalled the many times I had knocked on doors and herded the boys to break-fast, dinner, or out to the playing fields.

When we got to my old room, Stacey mentioned she didn't think it was still used as a counselor's room. Sure enough, as she unlocked the door, a well-organized storage space was revealed. To be clear, I was not expecting a commemorative plaque on the door, but still, some disappointment rose up in me at seeing my memory converted to a storage closet. I laughed and commented that it was much cleaner than when I had lived in it. Thanking Stacey for her time, I headed back to Zorba and took one last glimpse at Boys & Girls Haven in my rearview mirror as I rolled away. I hoped I had helped those boys as much as they helped me.

My second stop that day before leaving Louisville and continuing my journey west was the University of Louisville. After leaving the seminary following my sophomore year of college, I had a choice as to where to finish my studies: enroll at the local Catholic college, Bellarmine, which was affiliated with the seminary, or the larger and very secular University of Louisville. Most of my seminary classmates, those not continuing in their studies for the priesthood, chose Bellarmine. It was the safe and comfortable choice. But after six years of living in the bubble of the seminary, the last thing I needed was more "safe and comfortable." I became a UofL Cardinal. My many nephews who attended UofL's rival, the University of Kentucky, will tell you this is the worst decision anyone could make in their life, but it turned out well. The world opened up to me, and my perspective broadened in immeasurable ways.

Having shared my plans for my cross-country road trip in an old VW bus with the University's Alumni Office, they had been kind enough to highlight it in the alumni newsletter. My UofK nephews' comments were along the lines of "Anytime a UofL alum has a van to live in, they should absolutely celebrate that." Funny guys.

I walked around the campus a bit, not recognizing much. Before leaving the campus, I ate lunch in the student union and reflected on my final days at the school prior to my first attempt at a cross country journey in 1972. Some of those questions that we ponder in the later years of our life crept into my head. *Was I happy with the path my life had taken? Did I have regrets? Would I change anything if I could? And why the hell did I feel compelled to attempt another cross-country journey in an old VW!?* And finally—*Did I learn anything along the way in life that better prepared me for the trip?*

I didn't come up with a lot of answers, and I wasn't sure I was any wiser than my 1972 self, but I did possess something I did not have when I was fresh out of college—credit cards. And according to my friend Ira, the Forrest Gump of Berea, that would make all the difference.

After three days of rest and recuperation, that comfort I feel whenever in my home state was starting to settle in. Fearing I could not pull myself away if I stayed any longer, I knew it was time to hit the road. I swung by my sister Jeanette's house to thank her for her hospitality, and she sent me off with some homemade pesto. It's good to have family watching your back.

Jeff and Jerry at AirKooled Motorwerks

VII

*To think things out properly and fairly, a fellow's got
to be calm and old and toothless. When you're an old
gaffer with no teeth, it's easy to say: 'Damn it boys, you
mustn't bite!' But, when you've got all thirty-two teeth....*

—Nikos Kazantzakis, *Zorba the Greek*

GO WEST, YOUNG MAN

Meriwether Lewis and William Clark undertook the first "road trip" west from May 1804 to September 1806. President Thomas Jefferson commissioned the expedition to explore the newly acquired Louisiana Purchase and identify the best route west. While mapping the territory, they also studied the area's plants, animal life, and geography, and established trade with the native Americans. It was an epic journey, and I consider every road trip west to be a nod to Lewis & Clark.

While their official journey started in St. Louis, a year earlier in Louisville, Kentucky, they recruited nine young men whom they enlisted into their Corps of Discovery. This Corps traveled together to St. Louis, so in my mind, the whole thing started in my hometown. My other connection to this fabled expedition is that I grew up next to George Rogers Clark Park, where I spent most of my childhood exploring the woods and playing with friends.

George Rogers Clark was not on the expedition but was William Clark's older brother. While he had some early success leading the Kentucky militia throughout most of the Revolutionary War, George was eventually forced to resign his commission in disgrace, having been accused of being drunk while on duty. He spent the final decades of his life evading creditors while living in poverty and obscurity. George also traveled west on occasion but for very different reasons than his brother William. He just needed a little distance from the bankers. I love the park that bears his name and gave me refuge as a child, but I will look more to William than George for inspiration on this journey.

The expression "Go West, Young Man" is often credited to newspaper editor Horace Greeley, although the evidence he ever used the phrase is a little shaky. He did write an editorial in 1865 urging Civil War veterans to take advantage of the 1862 Homestead Act and go west to colonize the public lands. How the lands which tribes of Native Americans called home became "public" is a shameful chapter of American history. The "Go West" phrase is also associated with the popular concept of Manifest Destiny, which is, of course, a load of buffalo poop used to justify endless atrocities. But Americans most certainly did go west, and the urge for anyone living east of the Mississippi to explore the broad expanse of lands that stretched to the Pacific Ocean lingered well into the twentieth century.

Another migration west occurred as recently as 1967; it was called the Summer of Love. This social phenomenon propelled as many as 100,000 young people embracing the hippie culture to head to the Haight Ashbury neighborhood of San Francisco. The prelude to the Summer of Love was a Human Be-In at Golden Gate Park in January of that year, and it was there that Dr. Timothy Leary encouraged people to "turn on, tune in, drop out." In May of that year, Scott McKenzie's song "San Francisco (Be Sure to Wear Flowers In Your Hair)" was released, and the exodus to the West Coast began. With the song ringing in my ears as I walked the halls of my high school, I desperately wanted to be a part of it all. But I stayed in school, just as two years later, I did not join the migration to Woodstock. I was not a risk-taker.

The Summer of Love was as chaotic and out of control as Woodstock, and San Francisco was ill-prepared to provide essential services for the thousands now living on the streets and finding refuge wherever they could. Thanks to a group calling themselves the Council for the Summer of Love, a free clinic was organized to provide housing, food, sanitation, along with music and the opportunity for free expression. By the end of the summer, most of the young people retreated from the scene, returning to school or a job, with some staying in California and joining the Back to the Land Movement of the late '60s.

A mock funeral entitled "Death of the Hippie" was staged on October 6, 1967, signifying the end of the Summer of Love. The organizer, Mary Kasper, delivered the eulogy: "This is the end of it, stay where you are, bring the revolution to where you live and don't come here because it's over and done with."

And take your damn flowers with you!

Okay, she didn't say that last part... although she kind of did.

So as I prepared to head west from Louisville, the starting point for my failed trip in 1972, I had many sources of inspiration to draw on: the epic journey of Lewis & Clark, the words of Horace Greeley, and it was the fiftieth anniversary of the Summer of Love. No shortage of things to reflect on and motivate me as I made my way to California. But in truth, I wasn't thinking about any of that as I crossed the Ohio River on the Sherman Minton Bridge just downriver from the Falls of the Ohio and turned onto Route 150 heading west. I was thinking about my dad.

My dad was born in Great Bend, Kansas, and was raised on the vast American prairie that stretches from the Mississippi River to the foothills of the Rockies. He was a chemist and spent his entire adult career working for one company, Seagram. Dad was in charge of the gin formula at the plant, and he ensured that the distilled quality of the product was pure and consistent. I have one photo of him at work, and he is in his white lab coat supervising a group of tasters. Dad did his tasting when he got home after a long day of work. Dedication. As for me, thanks to Seagram's products, I was able to navigate my way through college and receive my degree in political science. And you can take that any way you want.

Seagram gave Dad two weeks' paid vacation every year, and there was never any discussion as to how we would spend that time. Every summer, our family of seven (Seagram's 7?) loaded into our 1957 Ford station wagon and, always starting before dawn, headed west to Kansas. It is just over 700 miles from Louisville to Wichita, where my Kansas relatives lived, and in the days when there were no interstates, that was a full two-day drive. The before-dawn start was essential if we were to get to the halfway point, the Missouri state line, on the first day where we would stay in a roadside motel. Dad drove. Mom supervised the kids. By nightfall the following day, we were rolling into the driveway of a relative, my mom usually more exhausted than my dad thanks to the five of us in the back seats. I have never seen Kansas on the top ten list of vacation spots, but I could not have been more excited about this annual road trip with my family. My place was in the back seat directly behind my mom with my face planted against the window as I took in the countryside rolling past.

Of all the things I looked for, the Burma Shave signs gave me the most joy. Burma Shave, introduced in 1925, was a brushless shaving cream, considered a significant advancement over the shaving soap and brush set. In the beginning, sales were slow, and the company resorted to an advertising campaign based on roadside signs. Typically, six consecutive signs would be lined up along the road, and they delivered a poetic message that always ended with "Burma Shave." The first set of road signs appeared along US Highway 65 near Lakeville, Minnesota, then spread throughout the country along with the growing highway system.

The signs were always red and white, except for South Dakota, which reserved the color red for official warning signs—blue and white there. They appeared in every state except New Mexico, Arizona, Nevada, and Massachusetts. The traffic in the western states was deemed insufficient to justify placement, and Massachusetts was left out because of the high cost of the land rental, and the roadside foliage was deemed to be too distracting. I can vouch for the fact that everything is still too expensive in Massachusetts, and the roadside foliage continues to be very distracting.

Initially, the signs were just promoting the product:

Shave the modern way/No brush/No Lather/No rub-in/Big tube 35 cents/Burma-Shave

As they became popular with motorists they added some wit:

Every shaver/Now can snore/Six more minutes/Than before/By using/Burma-Shave

And:

Does your husband/Misbehave/Grunt and grumble/Rant and rave/Shoot the brute some/Burma-Shave

Then in the late 1930s, the signs took on a public service bent with safety messages:

Hardly a driver/Is now alive/Who passed/On hills/At 75/ Burma-Shave

And:

Past/ Schoolhouses/Take it Slow/Let the little/Shavers grow/ Burma-Shave

The demise of the Burma Shave campaign was caused by the same thing which eliminated a lot of the joy of road tripping—the Interstate Highway System. As Interstates expanded in the late 1950s and road speeds increased, there was no time to read a ditty strung out along the road on small signs. The last of the signs were officially removed in 1963, although you still occasionally stumble across one on an old back road. Slow down and absorb the message if you do— assuming you are not looking at your GPS and miss it altogether.

These road trips with my family planted the seed for all my future road trips. Every trip I take is an attempt to re-experience the joy I would feel climbing into the back seat of the 1957 Ford station wagon and backing down the driveway for a new adventure. I don't know how my dad felt about them. Did he eagerly anticipate time away from work and a reconnection with his family? Did he do it out of a sense of obligation to visit his parents and siblings in Kansas? Did my mom, also from Kansas, talk him into it so she could visit her family back home? Like many things regarding my dad, it remains a mystery, and I am okay with that. Whatever motivated him, he introduced me to the road more than Jack Kerouac, John Steinbeck, or Nikos Kazantzakis ever could, and I thank him for that.

THE ACCIDENT

As a nod to my dad, I wanted my journey west from Louisville to trace the route that the family always took on those summer trips to Kansas. However, not remembering the roads we took, and with both of my parents deceased, I tried to determine the route by piecing together the best recollections of my three sisters and one brother. My two younger sisters barely had memories of the trips at all, my brother wondered why I cared, but my older sister, Mary Lee, gave it a shot and offered a few clues. Not having much success, I decided to purchase Shell Oil road maps of Indiana, Illinois, and Missouri from 1957, which

I located on eBay. Once they arrived, I spread them out on my dining room table and reached down inside to summon my inner dad.

With two adults and five children packed into a station wagon, I asked myself, what is the most direct, the quickest, and the most painless way to get from Louisville to Wichita using the roads that existed in the '50s? Today's maps tell you to hop onto Interstate 64, and you will get to the Missouri state line in under four hours. The 1957 maps told me that dad would take two-lane US Highway 150 from Louisville to Vincennes, Indiana, then hop on historic Route 50, also two lanes, which crossed Southern Illinois. After crossing the Mississippi River at St. Louis, the family station wagon would continue on Route 50 with ten miles of four-lane traffic, until it converted back to two lanes for the remainder of Missouri.

I had another clue regarding the route the family took. Whenever anyone in the family referred to "the accident," we knew what they were referring to. It occurred in the summer of 1957 on our way to Kansas, when I was seven years old. We were traveling west on the first day of our journey, and as dad approached a sharp turn in the road, an oncoming car took the turn too wide and forced us off the road.

The brand new '57 Ford station wagon struck the soft shoulder of the roadway causing it to swerve back onto the road and into the path of an oncoming car. (Now is probably a good time to note that dad, being a frugal man, had passed on purchasing seatbelts, which were an "option" on cars at the time. Seatbelts were not required in vehicles until 1968, and then whether you wore them or not was completely up to you.) A collision occurred, and our bodies went flying. Mom got the worst of it. Thrown from the car, it required some time for Dad to locate her, as she was lying underneath the carriage of the station wagon. I was next in terms of the seriousness of my injuries. My arm had shattered the rear window through which I viewed the passing world, and an artery was severed near my shoulder. Dad and the rest of my siblings were thrown about in the car but escaped pretty much unscathed.

I still remember sitting by the side of the road and seeing the blood running down my right arm. To my good fortune, the accident occurred directly in front of a farmhouse where an Eagle Scout lived. Hearing the sounds of the accident, he ran out to the road, and seeing that I was bleeding out, used his T-shirt as a compress on my wound. He was able to stem the flow of blood, and I was still conscious when the ambulances arrived to gather us all up and take us to the nearest hospital.

At a later date—this being my siblings' favorite part of the story—my parents sent the Eagle Scout a reward for saving my life—$7. It's hard to put a financial value on any one life, but in my case, the value was definitively established in 1957. You may think my parents lowballed it a bit, but in their defense, and having checked the inflationary tables, the scout's reward is the equivalent of $63 in today's dollars—the price of a high-end bottle of bourbon. Sounds about right.

I knew that the location of the accident could be the biggest clue in determining the route my dad took. I asked Mary Lee, who was nine at the time of the accident, to dig a little deeper into her memory banks. Better yet, she began digging through the old family photo albums and our mom's letters for clues. She discovered an old photo of a hospital. Written on it in Mom's distinctive handwriting was "St. Joseph's, Highland, Illinois." We surmised that the only reason Mom would have a photo of a hospital in Illinois is that it is where the ambulances took us after the accident. The town of Highland is nine miles north of Route 50. That was the confirmation I needed. I had correctly determined the route dad took to Kansas.

All this got me reflecting on the accident that almost terminated my life at age seven, and the scout who is credited with saving my life. *Could I find the accident site? Could the scout still live on the old family farm? Would anyone recall the accident and the events of that day?* I knew it was a long shot, but I wanted to search these things out, and Mary Lee and her husband, Allen, agreed to join me in the quest for the answers. I include Allen because he came along, but his interest was more along the lines of just how foolish were Mary Lee and I willing to look in our pursuit of some lost family history.

Before I departed Louisville, we agreed to rendezvous at a Walmart parking lot along Route 50 just outside of Odin, Illinois, and begin the search there. Mary Lee and Allen gave me a day's head start, and I left Louisville on a Friday morning, tracing the route my father took to Kansas along Highway 150 in Indiana. They planned to hop onto I-64 West the following day and catch up, pulling their teardrop trailer behind them.

Traveling on Route 150, I felt, for the first time since I left Boston, that I had escaped the congestion of the East Coast. The land was open and flat, and the distance between towns increased the farther I headed west. Traffic was light, and no one seemed to be in a particular hurry to get anywhere. Even Zorba seemed a little bigger, and his speed fit in with the other vehicles heading west on 150. Thanks to Jeff at AirKooled Motorwerks in Louisville, the heating vents were closed. For the first time, I felt relaxed and comfortable driving Zorba.

Just outside of Montgomery, Indiana, I began looking for a lunch spot. I was well provisioned having just left Louisville, and just wanted a shady area where I could make a sandwich, when I came upon Redbones. Redbones didn't look like much, but the sign said they had the best fried chicken in Indiana. I put the idea of a cold sandwich aside and headed for the back door of Redbones, the only way to enter. Finding a spot at the bar, I was all set to order the fried chicken when I saw a plate of fried frog legs go by. Figuring the opportunities for fried chicken would be more frequent than frog legs, I called an audible and asked my bartender Dorothy for a plate of frogs. She nodded, said I made the right choice, shouted back at the kitchen, then brought me a cold beer.

Looking around Redbones, it was clear that everyone knew everyone else. The conversation and the friendly ribbings happening around me were loud, and I thought of Indiana native John Mellencamp and his song "Small Town." It all seemed to fit. I told Dorothy I was driving an old VW bus and was looking for a place to spend the night. She suggested I drive up to Fred's house. She was certain he would let me park in his yard and gave me directions. "Tell him Dorothy sent you." Small towns are like that.

After I got my fill of frog legs—and yes, they tasted like chicken—I headed out to Zorba and looked at my map. Wanting to put some more miles behind me before stopping for the night, I decided to pass on Fred's. I'm sure I missed an opportunity, but I was feeling something else in Redbones that surprised me. I loved the sense of community that flowed around me, but as I sat at the bar, I felt disconnected. I was an outsider. The sense of belonging we all strive for was absent for me in the cozy community bar.

The feeling may have been a reaction to having just left the friendly confines of Louisville and my family, but it was one of those times on the trip where I felt alone, isolated. I chose to escape that feeling by heading farther down the road, which made me wonder how many times in my life I had dealt with discomfort in one environment by moving on to another. Is wanderlust motivated more by wondering what's around the next bend in the road, or a desire to leave something behind? Zorba and I jumped back onto Route 150 and headed west, looking for my comfort zone.

As I traveled, I always kept an eye out for signs indicating where there were fresh eggs available, and not far from Montgomery I sped past one, partially hidden in the tall grass around it. I almost concluded it was not worth the trouble it took to turn around, but the appeal of fresh eggs won out. I reversed direction and pulled onto a partially paved road heading north. The route back to the farm was unclear, and I passed several more "fresh eggs" signs, all of them partially hidden by grass as well. The road became a combination of dirt and gravel, and I saw a jeep with its own trail of dust approaching from the distance. We both slowed as we approached each other and stopped to exchange greetings.

"Wow! Love that old van of yours." A common greeting I received, but one I never got tired of. The two young women in the jeep, one blonde and one brunette, with the top-down and the dust from the road in their hair and on their faces, were the perfect image of carefree youth.

I returned the compliment. "I love your jeep. My first car was a jeep, and I'd consider a trade. I'd get where I'm going a lot quicker."

"Where you heading?"

"California. I've got a ways to go."

"You'll get there."

I was beginning to realize there was a correlation between the age of the observer and their level of confidence that I would make it to the West Coast. We lose a lot of things as we get older. It appears that the belief we can overcome any challenge might be one of them. Perhaps we are worn down by the many calamities and failures we inevitably experience along the way. Doubt takes up permanent residence in our minds. Or maybe we just get tired.

"I'm looking for fresh eggs, and these damn signs have me feeling I'm going in circles."

"You're on the right track. Take the next two rights, and the eggs are there."

"Thanks. And do me a favor. Stay young."

"We're planning on it!" the driver with the untamed blonde hair shouted back, and with that, they sped off in their jeep kicking up some gravel onto Zorba. I didn't mind.

After taking two rights, I pulled onto the dirt driveway that led to a farmhouse where I saw a multitude of chickens filling the yard—a good sign. I also counted six dogs. Ida came out to greet me, and after giving Zorba a once-over and hearing about my plans, she was considerably less confident than the young women in the jeep. But Ida was not just older but a farmer as well, and I think when you farm, you come to expect the worst because you have usually experienced it.

She went to the barn to fetch me a half dozen eggs and, when she returned, she refused to take any money for them. She repeatedly wished me luck, and I got the feeling she thought her eggs were the last I would ever eat. I thanked her, and Zorba and I weaved our way back to Route 150 hoping I would encounter the hopeful young women in the jeep again because Ida had left me feeling like I needed another boost in confidence. But I appreciated her generosity.

Not long after leaving Ida's farm, I crossed the state line and entered Illinois with Indiana receding in my rearview mirror. I had crossed an entire state, though a very narrow part of it, in one day. Zorba was humming. We were now on historic Route 50, and I enjoyed the view knowing it was not much different than what I saw out the window on my family vacations—minus the Burma Shave signs. I set my sights on Red Hills State Park just outside of Sumner, Illinois, seventeen miles beyond the state line. It wouldn't be as homey as Fred's yard, but it would have to do.

Pulling into the park, I found it surprisingly deserted for a day in late August. I could not locate a ranger's station, and there was no apparent place to pay a camp fee for the night. The parking lot at one of the campgrounds was empty, with no tents or campers in view. It looked like a good place to spend the night as it gave me access to a picnic table, and if they wanted a camp fee, I was confident they would find me. They never did, and waking the next morning I exited the park feeling like I probably owed the State of Illinois some money. Despite that, I had gotten a good night's sleep.

I drove into the center of Sumner, with a listed population of just over 3,000, in my Rand McNally, but as with the State Park, there was no traffic and no one to be seen on the street. Driving through Sumner, I was skeptical that over 3,000 people lived there, which caused me to wonder if there had recently been a dramatic exodus of people from the area. It turns out it was just the opposite. The population of Sumner was only 1,022 in the year 2000, which is only one more person than it had in 1880. Having a steady population for more than 100 years, how did this small hamlet in the middle of nowhere triple in size in only seven years?

The explanation was a simple one. The State of Illinois selected the outskirts of Sumner as the site for a new medium-security prison with a capacity of 2,458 men. Sumner now promotes itself as having a higher ratio of men to women than any other American town, 9:1. Any woman who moves to Sumner thinking that it expands her selection options is in for some disappointment—unless she wants to make frequent trips to the new "housing development" west of town.

There was a small MIA/POW memorial in the center of Sumner, and I parked Zorba there. I planned to participate in a thirty-mile ALS Ride when I arrived in California, but the hills of West Virginia and Kentucky had discouraged me from getting on my bike and doing any training. Looking at the flat cornfields surrounding Sumner, I had run out of excuses and pulled my bike down off its rack. Every road heading out of town was long and flat, and I picked the one heading south, State Road 250E, for no particular reason. My ride remained flat, and other than cornfields, the only thing of note was the abandoned Red Hill Racetrack.

The gate was open, and I wandered in climbing up into the stands, a risky exercise as several wooden planks were missing in the steps. In its heyday, Red Hill could accommodate as many as 5,000 spectators, but the dirt track below was being reclaimed by grass and tall weeds, the roar of the engines having long receded into the past. It was a quarter-mile track, and you could sense the excitement it must have held on Friday nights for the people of Sumner and the surrounding farm families. The silence gave me a sad feeling as if I also had lost something, so I moved on.

Shortly after I returned to Zorba, I finally saw some traffic in Sumner, and it was someone on his bike heading my way. His bike was a simple one-speed, and he must have looked at my eighteen-speed bike and wondered why I needed all those gears when the nearest incline was over fifty miles away.

"Everything okay?" he asked.

"Well, it's too damn hot, and there's no shade. Can you help with that?"

"No, sir, I can't. I'm Jess. That's quite a vehicle you got. What year?"

"1973."

"Well, it's a lot younger than me," Jess offered as he straddled his bike.

Jess was welcoming and easy to talk to, and piece by piece, we shared our stories. He had grown up in Sumner, married his high school sweetheart, and never left. They took a vacation in Florida once, but that was it. All his family lived nearby, and while he listened patiently to my odyssey of life, I could tell he in no way felt he had missed anything by staying in Sumner. I'm sure he knew every individual in town—no anonymity allowed in small-town America.

And in truth, he appeared to be one of the happiest and most content people I met on my entire journey. I can't explain why some people feel the need to wander and others to stay put. I just know for me the curiosity of what's around the next bend in the road always got the better of me, and over my lifetime, I have lived in nine different cities and towns and made countless road trips to get away from those. As much as I sometimes envy the familiarity that Jess has in his life, I know it was never in me to do that.

A pickup truck pulled up to us, and the driver stuck his head out the window directing his question to me. "Is this local harassing you?" It was Jess's brother Bill. Bill stepped out of his pickup, and as both checked out the interior of Zorba, they were happy to see I had some cold beers in my cooler to help me along my way. There were three less by the time the conversation ended.

Ready to hit the road, I thanked Jess and Bill for checking in on me, and Jess wrote his phone number on a scrap of paper for me in the event I ran into any problems and needed help. However, he added the offer only extended out for twenty miles, and after that, I was on my own. I knew that radius had existed for Jess for a long time, and I shouldn't test it. As I drove west from Sumner for the next twenty miles, I had not a worry in the world. After that, I threw Jess's number away. In the event anything happened, I did not want the temptation to test his limits.

DEAD MAN'S CURVE

Sixty miles west of Sumner on Route 50, I rendezvoused with Mary Lee and Allen in the parking lot of a Walmart. They had given me a twenty-four-hour head start but arrived an hour before me. How embarrassing for Zorba. In any case, the search for the infamous crash site was on. Most of Route 50 over the years has been repaved and much has been relocated. Still, directly south of Highland, Illinois, where St.

Joseph's Hospital was located, there was a twenty-mile stretch of old Route 50 that was undisturbed from 1957, the year of the accident. We agreed to concentrate our search there.

Based on family lore, our car was heading west and encountered a significant left-hand bend in the road. Given how straight roads were in this part of the state, we set off on old Route 50, looking for that curve to the left. Mary Lee, who was nine years old at the time of the accident, and having revisited the site with our parents in her teens, claimed to have some recollection of what it looked like. I was skeptical of her recall skills. It had been exactly sixty years since the accident and fifty years since she last saw it. I know things change more slowly in rural America, but that much time would impact any place—for instance, the Walmart parking lot we had just left behind us.

As expected, the road was a straight line, and for the first fifteen miles, we did not encounter any curves that appeared severe enough to create an accident. Just after the fifteen-mile mark, we saw some yellow warning signs ahead. As we approached, the signs alerted us to an imminent bend in the road, a sharp turn to the left, which fit with the description of the accident site. Arriving at the curve, we pulled off the road and surveyed the scene.

I looked for the home of the Eagle Scout who had saved my life and eyed a white farmhouse with a few outbuildings, set back nearly a hundred yards from the road. In my eyes, it looked like the kind of all-American farm that would produce a life-saving Eagle Scout. I pictured him running down the long dirt driveway, stunned by the carnage of the accident spread along the road, then singling me out and putting his first aid training to use.

"I think we need to talk to the people in that farmhouse," I proposed to Mary Lee.

"Okay. But this doesn't feel right to me."

"It doesn't feel right knocking on their door?"

"No, it's just not how I remember the accident site."

"That was fifty years ago. Let's go knock on their door."

"Okay. Just sayn'... not as I remember it."

"I'll stay here and keep an eye on the curve just in case there is another accident," Allen offered. Allen's humor is as dry as the wind that blows across the American prairie.

Leaving Allen with our vehicles, Mary Lee and I walked up to the house. There were some vehicles next to one of the outbuildings, but otherwise no other indication there was anyone home. Hoping the farm had stayed in family hands, I used the time it took to walk up the long dusty driveway to think about what I would say to the now elderly Eagle Scout who had saved my life.

A few raps on the door was all it took to create a ruckus among the dogs on the other side. They sounded very large and very eager to see who was outside their door. A husky man in his late fifties arrived at the door, shouted at his dogs to settle down, then turned his attention to us. Since I had initiated this quest, I felt it was on me to begin the conversation. After brief introductions were exchanged, I dove right in.

"This might seem a little strange... in fact, a lot strange... but my sister and I are following up on some old family history. Our family suffered a bad accident while traveling to Kansas on Route 50, and we think it was in front of your house. Can I ask how long you have lived here?"

Bill pretended not to think it as odd for us to show up on his doorstep and replied, "We bought the house in 2001."

"Do you know anything about the previous owners?" I ventured.

"Nope. It was a foreclosure. Bought it from the bank. Never met them."

Bill's wife, Maggie, joined him at this point and shouted at the dogs some more, since they never stopped when Bill asked them to. The dogs took Maggie more seriously and finally quieted down.

"It's about an accident they had," Bill offered as a form of explanation to Maggie.

"What accident?!" Maggie asked with some alarm in her voice.

"A long time ago, before we lived here," Bill assured her, and this calmed Maggie a bit.

I figured I better jump into the conversation again as Maggie still looked at us like we might be from some insurance company and were considering filing a claim of some sort. I shared the story of the accident, how I almost died sitting on the side of the road in front of their house, and the story of the Eagle Scout who saved my life. Maggie seemed relieved and offered, "There are a lot of accidents on that curve. That's why the county put all those signs up."

But as for what happened in front of their farmhouse in 1957, they couldn't be much help. Not willing to leave it there, I asked if they knew any neighbors who might have lived in the area at the time. Maggie thought for a bit, looked at Bill, shouted at the dogs one more time, then said more to Bill than to us, "Don and Ann have lived in the area a long time. Maybe them?"

Bill agreed, "They're your best bet. They're both in their eighties and live just a half-mile from here. Take your next left, and it's the second house on the left. Don't know the exact address. They might not be home, though. There's a church picnic this afternoon, and I know they plan to be there."

We thanked them, and as we turned to retreat down their driveway, Bill proudly added, "You know, my son is an Eagle Scout." I smiled and thanked him again as the thought of another Eagle Scout, living in the iconic American farmhouse, on a dangerous curve, made me feel the travelers on old Route 50 would be a little safer.

Allen was waiting for us at the end of the driveway and pretended to be shocked when we told him the residents at the house did not remember this epochal event in our family history. We followed the directions to Don and Ann's house and were happy to see they were in their driveway standing by their car. The trunk was open, and they were loading enough food for a good thirty people into it. With his gray hair and wrinkled brow, Don looked the part of the local historian, and once again, I found a way to start a rather peculiar conversation.

Don eagerly took to the task. "That curve is treacherous. It even has a name, Ablinger Curve. It's named after a local priest who was coming home after administering the last rites to someone at St. Joseph's Hospital and took the curve too fast." Don added that no one got there in time for Father Ablinger to receive his last rites. I wondered where Bill's Eagle Scout was but kept that to myself.

Somehow, from there, the conversation veered into basketball as Don had been the coach at the local high school for over thirty years. As images of Gene Hackman in *Hoosiers* came into my mind, Don explained his approach to the game and gave a detailed description of the state semis his team had played in over forty years ago. I was impressed with his ability to recall long-past details, which made me hopeful for when I could eventually steer the conversation back to Ablinger Curve. You could tell Ann had heard all his basketball stories a thousand times and had learned to be patient and wait him out. Not having Ann's patience, I jumped in with a question that swerved the conversation back to the curve.

"How long have you both lived here?"

"Moved here in 1964. From Pinckneyville, forty miles south of here."

That shut the door on our search, as 1964 was seven years after the crash and forty miles was too far away to have heard of an accident on Route 50. We asked if they knew anyone who had lived in the area longer than them, and they both shook their heads. At this point, we had talked for a good fifteen minutes, and I was concerned the food they had prepared for the Church picnic was going to wreak havoc among the congregation if it sat out in the hot August sun much longer. Not wanting to be responsible for food poisoning at the First United Methodist Church, Mary Lee and I thanked Don and Ann for their time and headed back to Allen, who had wisely waited in the air-conditioned car, keeping his distance from this quixotic expedition.

Allen sensed our disappointment and was a little kinder this time and probably relieved that the search had ended. It was then that Mary Lee and I had our own collision on old Route 50. I was convinced we had found the spot. The curve was on old Route 50, the 1957 route to Kansas, and was only ten miles from St. Joseph's Hospital. The curve was notorious for accidents, to the extent that the State of Illinois had heavily invested in road signs, and for god's sake, it even had a name. Only the deadliest curves get names.

Also, we could not find any other curves on that stretch of old Route 50, as it made a straight line across an open farmland for long distances in both directions. I was fully prepared to declare victory. Mary Lee just said, "It's not how I remember it."

I mumbled something about how old she was and continued to feel confident I had revisited the site of my near death. Allen wisely stayed out of the way of the careening siblings. As we drove through the curve one last time, I felt my gratitude toward the Eagle Scout and expressed my hope that he got something nice for himself with the $7—maybe a new T-shirt to replace the one I had ruined.

TOUR DE BRATS

We spent the night at Eldon Hazlet State Park, where I pulled my fishing rod from Zorba and spent some time lazily casting and catching nothing. Having visited the crash site where, thanks to the actions of others, I was able to live past age seven, I was in a self-reflective mood. This trip for me had many moments where I had the opportunity to think back on my life and the road I had taken, and this was one of them.

I am not a big believer in regrets. There are certain things I could have done better or would have liked to have done differently, but changing any of them would also mean I wouldn't be where I am now with the people in my life who love and care about me. Changing one thing changes everything—the "butterfly effect"—the belief that the simple act of a butterfly flapping its wings creates a ripple that affects the entire universe. If my failures and missteps contributed to my arrival at the place I am now, I accept them because I am at peace where I am—halfway across the country in an old VW bus. After my navel-gazing, I returned to Mary Lee and Allen at the campsite and made peace with Mary Lee's doubts regarding our success that day. We all create our own reality; I just liked mine better.

One of the occurrences that lifted my mood that afternoon was the visit Zorba and I received from a group of fellow campers. Four close friends—Chris, Lindsey, Paul, and Phil—were having a weekend getaway. They had grown up together in the town of Greenville, thirty miles south, and I could tell they made these getaways frequently. They were drawn to my campsite by Zorba and wanted to stop by and check him out. Paul's uncle had a VW bus back in the day, and he shared his memories of trips they would take to the lake with his cousins packed into the bus. I was surprised how many people I met along the way who had a connection to an old VW bus. I loved hearing their stories.

Like Jess, back in Sumner, none of the four had strayed far from home. I found there is less mobility, or wanderlust, in what we on the coasts call the Fly-Over States. And I suspect the change they encounter in their daily lives is less rapid than what occurs on the coasts. Does that make them suspicious or at least more cautious about change? Maybe. I just know the four boys from Greenville could not have been friendlier or more welcoming. I imagined them as teens visiting the same lake, and I knew the friendly jousting they engaged in had been going on their entire lives. They promised to follow my blog if I put their picture on it, and I said I would in exchange for a beer. A deal was made.

That evening, Mary Lee, Allen, and I drove into Highland, Illinois, to meet our cousin Pat and his wife, Karen, at St. Paul's Catholic Church, which was hosting a Kiirchenfest (German for church festival). After we nearly OD'd on a feast of German food including bratwursts, spaetzle, bratkartoffeln, sauerbraten, leberkase, and of course schnitzel, Allen and I were inspired to sign up for the Tour de Brats Bike Race the following day. The twenty-five-mile race takes you into the countryside around Highland, and while you don't have to eat brats while you ride, when you finish, you receive a one-minute credit on your time for each bratwurst you can consume. After an evening of devouring everything in sight at Kirchenfest, Allen and I felt well prepared for the race.

I had not seen Pat since my teen years during visits to Kansas, and we caught up on our pasts and the various roads we had taken along the way. Karen shared stories of her father, Karl Heinz, whose journey started in Nazi Germany. Raised on a farm in Germany, he was conscripted into the German Army toward the end of WWII, at the age of fifteen. Captured by the Russian military as it moved into Germany, he was sent to a gulag in Siberia, where he performed forced labor on a farm. While he flirted with death on several occasions, he was one of the very few who survived the gulags. When the Russians felt they had drained all the work possible out of him, he was put on a train and sent back to East Germany. His family had fled to West Germany, and at sixteen, he found his way across the border undetected and was reunited with his family on his mother's birthday. The story was a good reminder of how simple and blessed my life had been.

Allen and I survived the Tour de Brats bike ride the following day, although our training the night before proved to be insufficient as we could each consume only one bratwurst after we finished. We earned a T-shirt showing a bratwurst riding a bike, which pretty much describes how I felt the entire twenty-five miles. Before leaving town, we drove by the location of the old St. Joseph's Hospital, which took us in and healed us in 1957. The hospital had been torn down in 2014, and a group of kids were playing in the large field of grass where it once stood. They looked to be about the age Mary Lee and I were when the ambulances brought us there in 1957. We smiled at that and then continued our journey west.

The Greenville Boys at Eldon Hazlet State Park

NEW RHINELAND

In the 1830s, Germans who had settled in the Philadelphia area became increasingly concerned about how quickly their countrymen who migrated to the United States were being assimilated into American society. They dreamed of creating a new Rhineland in the western region of the United States, where German culture could be celebrated and preserved. Calling themselves the German Settlement Society of Philadelphia, they sent a scout, George Bayer, west to find land suitable for farming and a location for what would become the capital of the new Rhineland.

George proceeded to purchase 11,000 acres of the steepest, most rugged terrain to be found anywhere along the Missouri River. Meanwhile, back in Philadelphia, members of the German Settlement Society were planning the streets of the new Rhineland's capital, which they named "Hermann" after the Germanic warrior who had defeated three Roman legions in the Battle of the Teutoburg Forest in the year 9 AD. In their minds, and on paper, the town of Hermann was flat, and their design of the capital of the new Rhineland reflected that with spacious market squares and a broad main boulevard ten feet wider than Broad Street in Philadelphia. They were thinking big—and flat.

In 1837, the first settlers disembarked from a steamboat on the Missouri River at the location of Hermann. They had purchased lots on the very flat plot map shown to them by the German Settlement Society and they found what could be best described as "vertical acreage." While one of them described it as a "howling wilderness," still, they decided to make the best of it. The reality was they had little choice as they had just stepped off the last steamboat to or from St. Louis until the following spring. The steep hills reminded them of the wine-growing regions of Germany, so they decided to plant vineyards and sustain themselves by making wine. Within ten years, people were arriving from St. Louis for the very first Weinfest, and by the turn of the century, the Missouri Valley in the new Rhineland was the largest wine-producing region in the country.

In fact, at one time, vines along the Missouri River planted by the Germans in the 1800s were called upon to save the entire French wine industry. In 1868, a disease was ravaging the vineyards of France. Upon closer inspection, the French realized that a tiny aphid, phylloxera, had infested the vines, and the louse was causing the grapevines to rot from the inside out. By 1883 nearly 40 percent of the vines in France had been destroyed.

Back in Missouri, Charles Riley, the Missouri state entomologist, recognized the symptoms and knew the American vines had developed a resistance to the aphids. Riley offered to assist the French but was dismissed. With their centuries of winemaking history, the French doubted they could learn anything from an American wine producer. Riley persisted, however, and in their desperation, they opened up to receiving help from an American. He demonstrated that by grafting French vines onto American rootstock, the resistance could be transferred to the French vines.

Riley sent nearly 400,000 vine cuttings to France, and what the French called "La Defense" was put in action. Today the rootstock in France, with few exceptions, can resist phylloxera. If you ever visit the town of Montpellier in France, in a small park, you will find a statue thanking a group of German wine producers from Missouri for saving the entire French wine industry. I'm sure the list of things the French feel they need to thank Germans for is a pretty short list—but this would be on it.

Once the new Rhineland was established along the banks of the Missouri River, the German Settlement Society of Philadelphia began encouraging emigrant Germans to move west and be a part of a new Germanic beginning in the West. In addition to encouraging

Germans who had already migrated to the United States, they reached back to Germany and encouraged Germans in the Fatherland to come and settle in Missouri. My great-great-grandfather, Hubertus Steimel, got caught up in the excitement. He also wished to avoid the universal military conscription that existed in Germany in the nineteenth century. In 1853, he boarded a steamship for America and, at the age of twenty-seven, found his way to the new Rhineland in Missouri.

Hubertus opted not to invest in "vertical acreage" but found some rich farmland in Tipton, Missouri, eighty-five miles further west. There the acreage was horizontal. He settled there, working the land, having lots of kids—ten—and when the Civil War began, he did what he hoped to avoid in Germany and enlisted to help preserve the Union. As a member of the Missouri Home Guard, he fought in one significant engagement, the Battle of Wilson's Creek, in the southwest corner of Missouri. It was a Rebel victory, and I assume Hubertus fled with the rest of the Missouri Home Guard and Union regulars back to the protection of Springfield, the state capital. The rest of his military record is a bit murky, but family lore tells us he returned at the end of the war, and many of his children did not recognize him when he walked through the front door of his farmhouse. I assume his wife Catharina did, as he did not get shot when he came through the door.

I did a little research on Tipton before starting the journey with Zorba and could not find any Steimels listed living in the community. What I did discover was that there is a Steimel Road. It is outside of town, and I deduced, although I could find no way to verify it, it is where Hubertus had established his homestead. I convinced Mary Lee and Allen to accompany me further west, and we crossed the Mississippi River just north of St. Louis on Interstate 70 and rendezvoused at Graham Cave State Park just north of Hermann.

Zorba experienced a flat tire in the park, and after mounting the spare, we drove to Scheidegger's Service Center in Hermann.

Doug Scheidegger welcomed me to the shop, and as he addressed the problem with the tire, he shared how his father started the business in 1945 after returning from fighting Germans in the European Theatre. Participating in the war was the Scheidegger way to visit their ancestral roots. Doug charged me $10 for the repair. Clearly, I was a long way from Boston.

I shared with Doug our purpose for being in the area, and he mentioned that he thought some Steimels lived in Hermann. Mary Lee and I went in search of them even though I knew we were testing Allen's patience at this point with our wanderings through family history. Doug had mentioned a real estate office where we could possibly find a distant relative, but it turns out she was not a Steimel but a Steinle. We decided the best way to massage our disappointment was to consume more bratwurst, and luckily next door was the Hermann Wurst Haus.

We did a bratwurst tasting, a true gastronomical challenge, and met the Haus's owner and preeminent bratwurst maker, Michael Sloan. If you have never heard of Michael, it's because you are not familiar with the "Cured Meats Hall of Fame." Michael was inducted in 2016 at the American Association of Meat Processors 77th Annual Convention in Omaha, Nebraska. At the convention, Michael's German-style bologna was Grand Champion and finished in the top five for Best in Show. Michael proudly pointed out there were over forty-five different flavors of brats at the Wurst Haus, and we barely made a dent in our tasting. Afterward, we walked over to the Lager House and did a beer tasting. Everyone describes what would be a "perfect day" differently, but this one came pretty damn close for me.

After a second night at Graham Cave State Park, our party headed west to Tipton in search of Steimel Road and perhaps the Steimel Homestead built in the 1850s. I envisioned Steimel Road as an impressive thoroughfare and hopefully one that ended at a large Ponderosa style ranch where long-lost relatives might reside. What we discovered when we arrived was a one-lane dirt road that led to a ranch, but it was more the '70s style ranch house that is ubiquitous in this country. Mary Lee and I attempted a knock on the door—Allen kept his distance and the car motor running—in hopes they would know the story behind the road they lived on. No one answered. We tried one other house that was set back from the road, with the same result. I surveyed the land from the porch and imagined my great-great-grandfather clearing the fields that stretched off into the distance. It was good land, and he had chosen wisely, but it sure looked like a lot of work.

Our final stop was at the library in Tipton. Tipton has a small one-room library and one very friendly librarian, Susan. She patiently listened as we explained our purpose and responded, "I knew some Steimels, but they are all dead now."

"Well, I guess we got here too late then," I said with a smile. I added, "You know there is a Steimel Road just outside of town," hoping that would impress upon her the vital role my family had played in the history of her town.

"Never heard of it," Susan said, clearly unimpressed.

"I've got a book that might be helpful, though," and Susan moved from behind the simple front desk of the library with the "Checkout Limit is Four Books" sign prominently displayed, and led us to a back corner—the small reference section of the room.

"Here. Take a look through this," she said, handing me *The Collected History of Tipton.*

Mary Lee and I huddled over it. It was everything anyone would ever want to know about the history of Tipton, Missouri, even though it wasn't a substantial volume. Several chapters into the book, we found the roster of Company H of the Missouri Home Guard, and among the list of names was "Hubert Steinell." That had to be our Hubertus, and I credit the misspelling to sloppy penmanship, a family trait that even the strict nuns who taught me at St. Stephen Martyr in Louisville could not drill out of me. My dad was even worse and took to printing everything he wrote, giving up on cursive entirely.

The book confirmed for me that Hubertus was a good Union man, and Mary Lee and I mercifully—Allen's word—concluded our ancestral search. After one more meal of German meats, my sister and her patient husband headed toward the Interstate and their route home. I climbed into Zorba and continued west on Route 50, a solo traveler again.

Doug at Scheidegger's Service Center, Hermann, Missouri

Steimel Road

VIII

*God changes his appearance every second. Blessed is
the man who can recognize him in all his disguises.*

—Nikos Kazantzakis, *Zorba the Greek*

BLEEDING KANSAS

Normally, time and distance from a subject give us the ability to
properly sort it out, and with a broader and longer perspective,
we are able to reconcile a person's proper place in history. The memory
and actions of John Brown, a white abolitionist, have resisted that.
An ardent preacher against the evils of slavery, he was no Gandhi or
Martin Luther King, and he despised the pacifism of the organized
anti-slavery movement.

He is remembered most for his attack on the armory at Harper's
Ferry in 1860. There, Brown hoped to arm Virginia's slaves with rifles
captured from the arsenal and begin a violent insurrection similar to
Nat Turner's actions in North Carolina in 1831. The raid was a failure,
and Brown and his surviving men were surrounded and captured by
troops under the command of Robert E. Lee, then a Colonel in the
United States Army. Hastily tried, Brown became the first person
convicted of treason in the history of this country and was hanged on
December 2, 1859, in now Charles Town, West Virginia.

John Brown's violent opposition to slavery ended at Harper's
Ferry, but it began in the eastern counties of Kansas. Born in 1800 in
Connecticut, Brown grew up in the progressive northeast section of

Ohio, where anti-slavery feelings ran strong, and he later established a homestead in upstate New York. He was drawn to Kansas along with other free state settlers in 1855, hoping to prevent Kansas from entering the Union as a slave state. The Kansas–Nebraska Act, passed in 1854, established that the status of slavery in a new state would be based on "popular sovereignty." The residents of the newly formed state of Kansas would determine by vote whether or not slavery would be allowed, taking the decision out of the hands of the federal government. The elected representatives in Washington had decided to pass the buck.

The pro-slavery forces in Kansas were particularly violent, and in May 1856, they sacked the town of Lawrenceville, destroying the offices of the local newspaper which professed abolitionist views. Brown viewed most of his fellow free state settlers as cowards and was determined to take action and exact revenge on the pro-slavery ruffians.

On the night of May 24, Brown, along with four of his sons and two other free state settlers, went to the house of James P. Doyle and ordered him and two of his sons out into the darkness of Doyle's yard. A third son was left in the house with Doyle's wife as she pleaded for his life and professed that he was not a member of the pro-slavery group in the area. After a brief interrogation in the yard, Doyle and his two sons were hacked to death with broadswords. Brown and his party then went to the house of Allen Wilkinson, where a similar scene occurred, leaving Wilkinson dead. Lastly, the party arrived at the home of James Harris, where William Sherman, brother of Henry Sherman, a militant pro-slavery activist, was visiting. Sherman met the same fate, hacked to death by broadswords. This night of terror resulted in five men being killed in a brutal manner. It became known as the Pottawatomie Massacre, named after the gentle creek that flowed nearby.

In the two years prior to this night of killings, there had been eight deaths in Kansas attributed to the politics of slavery. Brown had killed five in one night and ignited a period of retaliation over the next three months that resulted in twenty-nine deaths and earned Kansas the moniker "Bleeding Kansas." Whether Kansas would enter the Union as a free or slave state was settled in 1859 at the ballot box, three years after the massacre, when free state settlers carried the day. The state constitution banning slavery was passed by a 2-1 margin. Some chose to overlook his butchery and credited John Brown's passion and advocacy with attracting an increasing number of free state settlers to the territory with the resulting blow to slavery.

Crossing the border from Missouri to Kansas, I headed south on Route 169 toward Osawatomie, where John Brown had carried out the massacre in 1856. John Brown Park and Memorial is located in the town, and I found Cheryl greeting visitors—I was the only one—at a replica of John Brown's cabin. The debate on John Brown centers on whether he was a martyr or violent lunatic, and I queried Cheryl about that.

"You know, Cheryl, a lot of people think Brown was a violent madman. You have an opinion on that?"

"I sure do. Because of Brown, Kansas became a free state. I'm on the side of anyone who fought against slavery."

"He was no Gandhi."

"Well, neither were the Union soldiers who fought the Civil War and killed thousands, but we choose to honor them. Brown just got a head start on the killing. I'm okay with that." I concluded that Cheryl, like Brown, is not one to mess with.

Cheryl added, "I went to Harper's Ferry once. I shared my view with the tour guide, and he seemed a little put off by it. They need to do a better job of educating the tour guides is what I think. Anyway, I kind of kept my opinions to myself after that." I sensed that it was not easy for Cheryl.

"Do most people around here share your view?"

"Well, why do you think we have a park named after him?"

Stupid question, I guess.

I enjoyed my give and take with Cheryl, and when I was leaving the park, I stopped at the statue of Brown near the entrance. The statue depicts a figure standing proud with a rifle slung over his shoulder. The sculptor chose not to include a broadsword. As Cheryl had mentioned to me, she regrettably found that there are no statues of John Brown at Harper's Ferry. The only other statues of John Brown that I could discover are in Kansas City, and Lake Placid, New York. The statue in Kansas City is frequently the target of vandalism with swastikas and racial epithets the most common acts.

As for history, it still doesn't quite know what to do with Brown. Since his hanging in 1859, the literature has fluctuated in its assessment of his life. Initially, he attained the martyr status he had hoped for, and many Union soldiers huskily sang the tune John Brown's Body as they marched off to war. Many black leaders of the time, including Frederick Douglas and Harriet Tubman, knew and respected Brown, and black businesses across the north closed out of respect on the day of his hanging. With time, particularly as the Lost Cause narrative propagated by the South took rise, Brown was more commonly portrayed as a madman. Recently, however, the pendulum has swung back a bit, and historians take a less hostile view of Brown, noting his idealism and noble motives. My favorite perspective, however, is that of Malcolm X. When challenged about the prohibition against allowing white people to join his black nationalist Organization of Afro-Unity, he replied, "If John Brown were alive, we might accept him."

Leaving the park, I passed a house that proudly flew the stars and stripes but pointedly also flew two Confederate battle flags. Two seemed like a bit of an overstatement, and I assumed the owner wanted to make a counterstatement to Cheryl's point of view. Duly noted.

When I began this journey across the country, I was very tuned in to the divisions that existed in the country this first year of the Trump presidency. It was hard not to feel a little pessimistic about the direction the country was headed. The trip was having an impact on that. I encountered many people who lifted my spirits from Tim, the coal miner in Virginia, to the students at Berea College, and the mechanics who had generously worked on Zorba. The divisions seemed smaller, and the common ground we all share was taking up more and more space in my mind.

However, driving away from the Brown Memorial, I felt the negative feelings creeping back into my psyche. John Brown's history is very distant, but it seems to be resonating now in some way. The question of whether we could ever come together again as a people with a shared destiny and with collective hopes and dreams weighed on me.

Then a small occurrence broke through my negative thoughts. Having just left the boundaries of Osawatomie, heading west on the John Brown Highway, I passed a farmer on his tractor, out in his field turning the corn field he had recently harvested back into the soil. He saw the old VW bus approaching, and a smile came across his face. He flashed me a peace sign. That was all it took. A little bounce came back into the Peace Out Road Trip as I returned the smile and sent some peace back his way. The open road felt a little more hopeful. There are too many good people in this country for us not to find our way forward as one.

CLOSE ENCOUNTER OF THE STRANGE KIND

By the time I departed the scene of the Pottawatomie Massacre, it was late in the day. With the stories of the John Brown massacre dancing in my head, I sought a safe space for myself and Zorba before the sun set on the horizon. There were no state parks nearby, and the largest town ahead was Ottawa, population 12,649. I hoped to find a city park there or perhaps another Presbyterian parking lot that would accommodate me for the night. As I approached Ottawa on Highway 59, I saw a Walmart just outside the city limits. I made a mental note. Walmart generously allows campers to spend the night in their lots, but that was something I had vowed to avoid on this trip. The immense parking lot of a store that many believe is slowly depriving small towns of their character was low on my list of overnight options. Still, I knew on some nights, it might be my only option.

Shortly after the Walmart, I saw a park on my left. Entering the lot, I was pleased to discover it was a trailhead for the Prairie Spirit Rail Trail. The lot was empty, and trailheads, whether for hiking or biking, are often prime locations for parking a vehicle overnight. One is seldom disturbed.

I parked Zorba and placed the solar panel onto the roof, hoping to build up the charge on the auxiliary battery with what little daylight remained. Then I began to think about dinner. Not wanting to fire up the stove, I prepared one of my, increasingly frequent, Cobb Salads with some ham and a hard-boiled egg. The Cobb Salad originated at the Hollywood Brown Derby restaurant. Legend has it that the owner, Robert Howard Cobb, was looking for a meal late one night and threw everything leftover from the day's meals into a bowl. That would describe a lot of the meals I ate on this trip, or at home for that matter, but as of yet, none of them have been named after me.

As the sun slowly disappeared and after I cleaned up my dishes, I pulled out my laptop and began to write an entry in my blog describing my day's experience in Bleeding Kansas. Just after darkness settled in, another vehicle entered the trailhead parking lot. I was a little surprised when the driver pulled into the spot immediately to the left of Zorba. The lot was reasonably large with approximately fifty parking spaces, and only Zorba and I had claimed a place for the night. It was peculiar and a bit unnerving that he had chosen to park immediately next to us with so many other options available.

My antennae were up, and I closed the interior curtains in the bus, hopefully sending a message to my new neighbor. I guessed it would be a quick stop for him, but after ten minutes my neighbor remained; I peeked through the curtains to catch a glimpse of any activity taking place next to me. The vehicle was an older sedan, and the gentleman behind the wheel seemed to be rearranging some papers on the passenger seat and occasionally looking at his phone. He never looked in my direction or showed any interest in the old VW bus whose personal space he had invaded. His back seat was cluttered and full—not a good sign.

After another twenty minutes of doing very little while he sat in his car, he stepped out and approached the garbage barrel directly in front of his car. He began to pick through the trash in an orderly way as if he were looking for something in particular. I could no longer ignore the warning bells going off in my head and decided it was time for Zorba and me to move on. As quickly as possible, I slipped into the driver's seat, turned the ignition, and backed Zorba out of the space and headed for the exit from the lot. If our neighbor was startled by the old VW bus coming to life, he did not show it and continued on his mission of sorting through the garbage barrel at the trailhead. It was too dark to look for another suitable place for the night, and remembering the Walmart parking lot, I reluctantly returned to America's ubiquitous store.

Aside from one RV parked in a far corner, there were no other vehicles, and I had my choice of over 400 vacant parking spaces. I did not choose the one right next to the RV, as someone in a midsized, older sedan might do, but one in the opposite corner of the lot. I was relieved to see no garbage receptacles in view. Every twenty parking spaces or so, Walmart had placed a light pole, and the glow from the artificial heavens made me realize that darkness would never come to the lot. There was some litter being blown about by the prairie wind and my view of this bleak, semi-urban landscape, and the knowledge that I had failed in my attempt to avoid Walmart's clutches, gave me a lonely, abandoned feeling.

I knew when I embarked on this journey that the potential for occasional lonely moments loomed ahead of me, but so far, the sense of adventure and the open road had kept it at bay. It settled on me in full force at that moment. I realized if I stayed in that parking lot, the feeling might take hold in a more permanent way. The urge to vacate the Walmart lot trumped the impulse to avoid creepers in the night, and I decided to return to the trailhead. I had noticed a secondary parking area fifty yards from where my nighttime visitor had placed himself and decided to park there in hopes he would keep his distance. I had a semi-restful night, rising up occasionally to peek through the curtains to check on my surroundings.

In the morning, I awoke to a terrible realization. In my haste to flee my close encounter the night before, I had forgotten to remove the solar panel from the roof of Zorba. The panel was thin and flexible, and I had duct-taped large magnets along its edge to hold it in place. The magnets were strong enough to keep the panel in place if there was ever a gust of wind while parked but insufficient to keep it in place if I ever drove with it on the roof. I stepped up onto Zorba's bumper and gazing at my roof, confirmed that the panel was gone.

Cursing myself under my breath, and without much hope of locating it, I decided to drive back to Walmart and see if it was along the road somewhere. Between the trailhead and the Walmart, Highway 56 becomes a four-lane road with a wide grassy median. To my surprise, I spied the solar panel resting comfortably in the grassy strip dividing the highway. Pulling Zorba onto the gravel edge of the road, I dodged traffic and retrieved the panel from the grass. I happily discovered it had managed to detach itself without damaging the cables that fed solar power to the auxiliary battery. Dumb luck had saved me again.

When I drove back to the trailhead and saw that the gentleman who had caused me to flee the night before was no longer present, I returned to my original spot where I enjoyed coffee and breakfast. I took a quick glance at the trash barrel but did not inspect it further. I trusted whatever he was looking for had been found. My intentions were to travel to the town of Council Grove that day and revisit some childhood memories, and since it was only seventy miles away, I had time to do some cycling on the Prairie Spirit Bike Trail.

While pulling my bike off the rack, a man with long gray hair and a distinctive goatee rode up on his bike and whistled at Zorba.

"I saw a lot of those when I went to a Grateful Dead concert in Denver. I think it was 1973."

If ever there was a place for VW buses to gather, it would be a Grateful Dead concert.

"If this bus was there, then it would have just rolled off the line. I'm Jerry, and this is Zorba."

"Nice to meet you, my friend. I'm Roger."

It turned out that Roger was a bit of an expert on old vehicles, and he restored them in his spare time. The one he was most proud of was a "Woodie" station wagon, and he pulled a picture from his wallet just like any proud father would. A Woodie is a type of station wagon whose rear paneling is wooden construction. Popular in the '30s and '40s, they were eventually supplanted by bodies constructed of steel for reasons of strength, cost, safety, and durability. That pretty much checks all the boxes for what you want in a vehicle, but the Woodies trumped all of that with their beauty.

"I bought it from a local farmer after I found it sitting in his barn. Paid him $150 for it. He was reluctant to let it go and made me promise to bring him a picture of it when I finished restoring it. It took me eight months and $12,000, but you can see how it turned out."

"And did you take a picture to the farmer?"

"Hell, I did better than that! I drove down there and took him and his wife out to dinner in it."

The Prairie Spirit Bike Trail runs north and south from the Ottawa trailhead, and since Roger was on a bike, I asked which direction he recommended I take.

"Go south to the town of Princeton. But you'll be peddlin' all the way."

I looked in that direction and seeing the flatness of the land, which you see in every direction in Kansas, I was a bit confused. "Are there any hills between here and Princeton?" I inquired.

"No, which is why you will be peddlin' the whole way."

Ah, the wisdom of the plains.

I took Roger's advice and cycled the ten miles to Princeton, where thankfully, there were no Walmarts, but there was Angie Moore and her little house on the prairie with the sign:

Moore — Stuff

Antiques — Collectibles — More

Angie welcomed me when I stepped through the front door and said she got a number of bikers wandering in on occasion. As I looked around, I concluded she had most definitely cornered the market on "stuff" in Princeton. Walking through the store was like walking through the home of a hoarder, except very well organized. I told her about my journey and how Zorba tends to attract people and good conversation just like her store. I mentioned Roger as an example. Angie knew him quite well.

"I know Roger. He married someone from my hometown. It didn't work out, though. He's a bit of a pest, but he's okay. I suppose he showed you his cars?"

She seemed to have Roger's number, and I sensed she was blaming Roger for the marriage not succeeding, but I can't be sure. She described him as an "old hippie," but not in a negative way. At least this old hippie didn't take it that way.

My favorite item in Angie's store was a lovely stitched tapestry that read:

HOME

Where you can poop

Long as you want

There were two sunflowers in each corner of the tapestry, which made sense, Kansas being the Sunflower State, and they added a bit of cheeriness to the proverb on pooping. I longed to purchase it, but failing to think of any place in our home where Dianne would let me hang it, I decided to leave it for someone who could display it prominently in their home. I returned to the bike trail without my souvenir and traced my route back toward Zorba at the trailhead. Roger could not have been more correct. I peddled the whole way.

Roger

Angie's Proverb

THE GEOGRAPHIC CENTER

The geographic center of the contiguous United States, also known as the Lower 48, is just outside Lebanon, Kansas. Lebanon was several miles north of my route, but as I moved deeper into Kansas, I felt some satisfaction in knowing I had reached the midpoint of my journey. While I wanted this to be a solo trip, it would have been a lonely and more empty experience without the people I met along the way. Every encounter deepened my comprehension of what binds us all together, and I was gaining insight into my own inner compass. These interactions, no matter how brief, recharged my batteries and kept me anxious to see what or who was around the next bend in the road. Not a bad way to approach life, and it certainly had a Zorba-like feel to it.

Almost as a way to drive home this point, I was traveling north on Highway 31 in Osage County when I saw sitting alongside the road the oddest looking vehicle I had seen on my journey yet. It was a dark-gray 1957 Chevy station wagon and hitched to it was what appeared to be the rusted rear body of a mid-1940s Ford sedan. The hood was up on the station wagon, and as I drove past I saw a couple sitting in the front seat. I looked for a place to turn around to see if I could provide any assistance, but honestly, I also wanted to get a closer look at their vehicle. I was used to turning heads with Zorba as we motored down the road, but their vehicle had to have caused some severe cases of whiplash.

Pulling up alongside, I met Hank and Lucy; their two kids were crunched down in the back seat. Hank and Lucy had left Eugene, Oregon, on August 13, the exact date I had departed Newburyport, Massachusetts, to begin my journey. Since I was still east of the geographic center, I had to accept that Hank and Lucy had traveled farther east on their journey than Zorba and I had traveled west despite the contraption they were driving. I cast Zorba some shade.

"Looks like you're having some trouble. Can I help in any way?" I offered.

"Naw. We got some family in the area, and they're on their way. We were on our way to Ottawa, just down the road, and this thing decided to quit."

"Glad you're all set. Can I ask you a favor?"

"Sure."

"I'd love to take a picture of your vehicle."

"Go right ahead."

I knew taking a picture of their car was probably bad form, since they were broken down at the time, but I couldn't resist capturing the image of these two odd vehicles mating. Hank did get out to put the hood down, protecting the dignity of his car as best he could. None of this seemed to faze the two preteens who sat quietly in the back seat. It did not take much for me to imagine the reaction this kind of attention would have elicited from my two daughters if I were in Hank's shoes. Forgiveness would have taken years.

Hank and Lucy's vehicle

THE ADULT IN THE BOAT

In 1964, at the age of fourteen, I left home to attend St. Thomas Catholic Seminary just east of Louisville. If you grew up in a devout Catholic family in the '50s and '60s and attended a Catholic elementary school as I did, the question was frequently raised by the nuns and the priests of the parish as to whether you had a "calling." A calling demanded you devote your life to Christ and commit yourself to a life of service to the Church and your fellow man. The Baltimore Catechism (a collection of Catholic doctrine used to instruct children) used at the school showed a devoted father surrounded by his family at dinner with the caption indicating, "This is good." Next to that, it showed a priest celebrating Mass with the caption, "This is better." Not very subtle.

What influenced me even more was that my Uncle Charles, my father's younger brother, was an ordained priest; he had a charismatic personality when it came to his nephews and nieces. We all loved hanging with Father Charles, and he played with us in a way that most dads in the 1950s didn't. Plus, he drove a Ford Mustang, not the family station wagon my father piloted.

In the early 1960s, my teenage years, Father Charles served as pastor of Saint Rose of Lima Church in Council Grove, Kansas. Council Grove's name originates from an agreement made between settlers and the Osage Nation, which allowed wagon trains to pass through the area. The population of Council Grove is currently 2,182, which is twenty-nine fewer people than in 1890. During the intervening 125 years, the town never had less than 2,000 residents and never more than 3,000—a population as steady and constant as the wind that blows across the open prairie of eastern Kansas where it sits.

Shortly after leaving Hank and Lucy sitting alongside Route 31, I made a left onto Route 56 West, the old Santa Fe Trail, which took me to Council Grove. Westward-bound pioneers would gather in a grove of trees along the Neosho River outside of town before banding together for the journey west. I liked the idea of banding with others for protection and a shared purpose, so I kept my eyes open for other VW buses as I drove into town.

My father's side of the family would meet in Council Grove every summer to reconnect and share stories from the previous year— the MacMullens from Colorado, the Jacksons from Wichita, and the Steimels from Kentucky. My Aunt Dorothy Ann had a small boat, and most warm summer days we spent on the town lake just outside of town. Our primary pastime was water skiing, but occasionally our focus would shift to other activities, many of which demonstrated the rather loose leash we were on while in Kansas.

One day, Father Charles told us tales of the giant catfish living in the lake that had always eluded the local fishermen. He described catfish measuring four feet between the eyes, and he knew from a good source that they lingered at the base of the dam which created the lake. Drawing on our inner Ahabs, my brother and I determined we would be the ones to famously capture one of these legendary behemoths.

Our first attempt employed both traditional and nontraditional fishing methods. Given the size of these monsters, we knew we needed a hook with some girth, so we went to a neighboring farm where the farmer's wife kindly loaned us two hay hooks. I do not believe we described the purpose, and she probably foolishly thought we had some hay to move. We tied the two hay hooks together, making an impressive two-pronged hook, and then secured them to the ropes we used for water skiing. Our plan was to troll along the base of the dam until we felt the tug of a catfish taking hold. But what to use for bait? We knew the bait would need to be as substantial as the hooks, so we set out a trout line to see what the lake would provide us.

When we returned in the morning, we found the only thing caught on the line was a large snapping turtle. Unfortunately for the turtle, we decided with a little trimming, or more accurately a little butchering, we could carve out enough meat to entice a monster catfish to take hold. Using my uncle's hatchet, we dismembered the turtle and attached his various limbs to the hay hooks. It wasn't pretty, and I feel guilty to this day, but the turtle did exact some revenge as he lurched and briefly got hold of the flesh on my left thumb moments before the hatchet came down on his neck. I carry the scar to this day as a reminder to treat our fellow creatures more kindly than I did in my youth.

With the deed done, we slowly motored the boat toward the dam, and tossing the hay hooks with attached turtle parts into the lake, began trolling. Father Charles was driving the boat, and given the reported size of these fish, he had brought along a sidearm. He assured us that once we pulled the catfish to the surface, he would plug it with the Colt pistol he had retained from his days in the Army. Mind you, this was the adult in the boat.

I am not sure how many passes we made along the base of the dam, but given the short attention span of your typical teenage boy, and given we were not getting even a nibble, we retreated to the dock. At the time, my brother and I both owned scuba gear and had brought our diving equipment to Kansas. ("Kansas— Diver's Paradise" is a tagline you will never see in any tourist brochure.) We altered our plans a bit, and as I murmured my regrets to the turtle that had died in vain, we removed the turtle meat from the hay hooks.

The situation called for a more direct approach. My brother and I would each take a ski rope with a hay hook attached and then, using our scuba gear, dive to the base of the dam. Once at the bottom, we would simply locate one of the immense catfish, insert the hay hook into its gills, and Father Charles upon feeling the yank on the line signaling the fish was secured, would gun the motor. I can't recall precisely where he would tow the catfish, but that would have required some forethought, and this plan apparently had no thought at all, so it didn't really matter.

My brother and I entered the warm waters of Council Grove Lake near the dam, and giving each other a thumbs up, we in unison dove below the surface in search of our prey. As is typical of most inland lakes, the visibility was minimal near the surface, and after you reached a depth of more than a few feet, visibility was nonexistent. It soon became pitch black, and I was unable to see my hand even as I pressed it against my face mask. The stupidity of feeling around in the dark for a giant catfish, and then stabbing him with a hay hook, became apparent very quickly. John and I surfaced at nearly the same time with our empty hay hooks in hand and looks of resignation that we would not be the ones to snag the catfish of lore. To this day, I feel lucky neither of us got plugged by my uncle's sidearm when we broke the surface.

Now, almost sixty years later, Zorba and I entered Council Grove and drove down the center of town on Main Street, passing a collection of brick-and-wooden storefronts spanning two blocks. Nothing looked familiar. I was sure this was more a function of my faulty memory than any radical change that has occurred in the town. Zorba got some friendly waves, but just as I did not recognize the town, no one recognized me either. Fair enough. I turned off Main Street onto Spencer Street and, after a few short blocks, came to Saint Rose of Lima Church. There was a small chapel, which I remembered from when my uncle was pastor, but a larger and more modern structure now sat next to it.

Even though it had been more than fifty years since my uncle was a pastor at the church, I was hoping to find someone who might have a memory of him. It was midday on a Wednesday, and Sharon was staffing the parish office alone. She welcomed some company as

I stuck my head in the door. Sharon's history of working in the parish office went back a scant thirty years, but she thought she had heard my uncle's name mentioned before.

"I think I know who could help you, though," and she reached for the Rolodex sitting on her desk. "Try calling Deb. She's in her late sixties and has been an active member of the parish her entire life."

"Thanks. It's probably not worth bothering her over," and I stuck the number Sharon had written on a scrap of paper into my pocket.

Sharon led me to the old chapel where I had served as an altar boy to my uncle during services whenever we visited. Sunday Mass is held in the modern structure adjacent to the chapel now, but Sharon said weddings are often performed in the chapel as it is smaller and more romantic. Constructed in 1883, it is one of the oldest churches in Kansas. The parish added a vestibule in 1943, the construction aided by German prisoners of war interned two miles west of Council Grove. While internment and forced labor are never pleasant, being stuck in the middle of Kansas and building a church had to be better than the Eastern Front for these German soldiers.

Sharon left me in the chapel, and I said a prayer for a safe journey while kneeling in one of the pews that had contained me as a teen and which felt comforting now. I also figured a prayer couldn't hurt. After returning to the office and thanking Sharon for her help, I decided to head out to the town lake and to pay a visit to the dam where we had trolled for giant catfish in our youth. Driving Zorba onto the dirt road that traversed the dam, I stopped to test my luck by swimming in the spot where I still believed the behemoths to be lurking just below the surface. The water was warm under the August sun and felt familiar, as opposed to the ocean back home. The things we experience in our youth have a way of leaving a lasting marker on us that forever bonds us with the younger version of ourselves. I enjoyed the swim undisturbed by any large fish.

As I was getting dressed after my swim, I discovered in my pocket the scrap of paper Sharon had given me. I opted to roll the dice and give Deb a call, possibly embarrassing myself on this trip one more time. The call was not without some risk on my part. While I always loved the family visits to Kansas and had great memories on the lake, over time I had begun to wonder about my gun-toting uncle, the priest. Was he a good shepherd to his flock? As I aged, the playfulness he showed with his nieces and nephews diminished in value compared to the steady hand my father provided in guiding his own flock of five children. Did Father Charles take a more serious approach to his responsibilities as a priest than he did as an uncle? And surely he didn't tote a gun while preaching, did he? Would calling Deb confirm my doubts and put my pleasant childhood memories in jeopardy? I took that leap of faith into my past and made the call, hoping Deb would be kind.

She seemed happy to get the call, and her voice was warm and inviting.

"I remember you. At least I remember Father Steimel's nieces and nephews taking over the parish for a few weeks every summer. You were a rowdy lot." I offered no defense.

Deb continued, "I was a teen myself at the time and always a little jealous of the time and attention you got from him. Of all the priests who have ever served at St. Rose of Lima, he was my favorite."

"It makes me happy that you remember him," I offered in return.

"It was a difficult time for me," Deb shared. "I was having what you would call a crisis in confidence. High school years can be difficult for some, and they were for me. Your uncle was there for me. Thanks to him, I received the Marian Award, which the Girl Scouts give out each year. It's for how you demonstrate your faith or something like that. I just know I got it because of your uncle. It's the only award I've ever gotten. I never thought I could go to college, but he convinced me I had the smarts and the courage to leave Council Grove and then helped me get some scholarship money, which made all the difference. And it wasn't just me. He took care of everybody. Best priest we ever had here. The parish cookouts he threw were the most fun. He was always in charge of roasting the pig. Gosh! This brings back a lot of great memories for me."

"Well, he never roasted a pig for us when we visited, so you got me there," I said.

Deb added, "It was a sad day for me when he was assigned to another parish west of here. We stayed in touch, but I felt I was on my own then." I could hear the loss she still felt in her voice.

Surprised at Deb's willingness to share so much, I told her how grateful I was for giving me such a vivid picture of the work my uncle had done as a priest. When I left the dam, the town lake, and St. Rose of Lima Parish behind me that day—thanks to Deb—I was feeling very proud of my uncle, Father Charles—the adult in the boat.

Zorba on the dam at Council Grove Lake

DAM LUCK

As Zorba and I drove off the dam at Council Grove Lake and continued our journey, I was thankful for Deb's memories. And I was thankful that my memories of those days on a lake in Kansas during my youth were not turned upside down. It can be a risky thing to peel back the layers of your memory. What you discover is not always what you hope for, and memories are sometimes better left alone. In any case, the swim felt good, and neither the legendary catfish nor the snapping turtles tried to exact any revenge for my youthful follies.

As I safely drove away, I reflected on a previous road trip and another dam experience that nearly discouraged me from all future road trips. At the time, I was working for Boys & Girls Clubs of Boston, and I needed to attend a conference in Seattle, Washington. Longing for a road trip, instead of booking a direct flight to Seattle, I flew into Salt Lake City and secured a one-way car rental to Seattle. The 900-mile drive would give me a chance to clear my head of the clutter collected during my daily routines.

The route I had planned took me west across the Bonneville Salt Flats in Utah, through Nevada, then into California. Once I made it to the Pacific Ocean, I would follow the coast up through Oregon and to the conference in Seattle. On my third or fourth day on the road, I was making my way across California on Route 89, one of those highways highlighted in the Rand McNally with little green dots, designating it as "scenic." As I came down out of the Sierra Nevada Mountains, I found myself driving over the dam that forms Lake Almanor. The vista of the blue water set against the hills in the distance was magnificent, and I felt compelled to capture it in a photograph. There was a small dirt pull-off near the center of the earthen dam, and I guided my rental car into it.

I had a single-lens reflex camera that required a little fidgeting to ensure the settings were proper for the shot I wanted. Grabbing the camera from the passenger seat, I made some adjustments for the light reflecting off the water as I sat behind the wheel. I was nervous about being parked on the dam—the "No Parking" signs were well displayed—so I wanted to take the shot quickly after exiting the car. Leaving the engine running so I could make an immediate escape, I hopped out with my camera to capture the panoramic scene. The sound I heard when I closed the driver-side door was initially odd and then horrifying. It was the sound of all the car doors locking. This particular model had the ingenious safety feature that automatically locked the doors for you while driving. The sound of the locks engaging brought home with sudden clarity the fact that I had never shifted the transmission into "Park."

As cars will do in "Drive," it started to slowly creep forward as I frantically ran around the vehicle trying every door, hoping that one had failed to lock. The engineers had done their job, and the doors were firmly secured, providing added safety to the occupants. In this case, the sole occupant was outside and feeling rather helpless. The car continued to creep forward, slowly heading for the edge of the dam. As I watched this slow-motion accident unfold, I began to form in my mind the conversation I would have with the rental car company as I directed them to the portion of the lake where they could retrieve their car.

Then, if possible, things took an even more harrowing turn. The car determined that no, it did not belong in the lake, but on the road. It started to slowly steer itself toward Highway 89. I immediately envisioned a family of five on a weekend drive encountering my rental car wandering into their path on the top of a dam with no avenue of escape. I had to do something to prevent this tragedy from happening.

I observed the beginning of a guard rail twenty yards ahead, and I calculated that if I could prevent the car from turning any farther to the left, it might catch the guardrail and halt its progress there. I crouched down and began pushing against the front left fender of the car, hoping this pressure would diminish its slow and steady bend to the left. I have no idea if my pushing had any effect at all, but the front bumper came to rest up against the guardrail with six inches to spare. Exhausted, I sat on the ground leaning against the front fender with the gentle hum of the engine behind me. Of course, at this point, it began to rain.

After resting some and congratulating myself for the five lives I had saved, I flagged down a passing car. It was a middle-aged couple, not a family of five. I concluded they must have left their three children at home.

"Thank you for stopping. I've got a little problem here as I've locked myself out of my car."

"Are you okay, son? Did you hit the guardrail?"

"I did. But very slowly." I knew that made no sense, but they didn't seem to mind.

"When you get to the next town, could you look for a gas station and send a tow truck my way?" I requested.

"I don't know if there is a gas station up ahead, but if we see one, we'll send them your way. You know it's raining. Do you want to hop in out of the rain and go with us?"

I didn't want to leave the car with the engine running unattended, but I didn't get into that with them. "No, I better stay with my car."

After close to an hour went by, with steady rain falling, I decided the couple had failed in their mission, and I flagged down a passing utility truck. The driver also promised to send help when he got to the next town. Thirty minutes later, a tow truck showed up, but I don't know who gets the credit for it.

As the tow truck driver climbed out of his cab, I decided to put all my cards on the table.

"I'm feeling pretty stupid right now."

"Don't worry about it. A lot of people lock themselves out of their cars."

"Yeah, but the engine is running, and it's in drive."

He didn't respond to that but proceeded to pop the locks for me. There was a smile on his face, and I'm sure he couldn't wait to get back to the garage and share his story. I did not mention that I had heroically saved a passing couple from their deaths, but he probably would have left out that part of the story anyway.

Relaying this story later, I had someone tell me that the smart move would have been to remove my shirt and stuff it into the tailpipe, thus stalling out the engine. I suppose that makes sense, but I like to think I solved the problem without ruining my shirt. The larger lesson I learned from all this is unclear. The obvious one to most is that I am a bit of a klutz and should never stray too far from home. But here I am, some 2,580 miles from home, getting farther by the day—and still bold enough to drive over dams.

INCIDENT AT DOHERTY FARM

From Council Grove, I headed southwest toward Oklahoma, bypassing Wichita and Hutchinson, the only cities of any size along the way. Zorba and I spent the night at Sand Hills State Park off Highway 61 east of Hutchinson. I have to say the "camping" area was only a slight improvement over a Walmart parking lot. It had the appearance of a new suburban subdivision—ones you see with the streets newly paved, the identical houses, and the trees and shrubs that seem to have been planted only the previous day. However, at Sand Hills, they had not built any homes or planted any trees or shrubs. The driveways where you could park your RV off the circular quarter-mile roadway were there, all spotless, each with an identical metal picnic table. Despite the unimaginative surroundings, I applaud the state of

Kansas for wanting to protect the sand dunes in the area, an unusual feature amid the endless fields of wheat and corn.

The campground hosts, Grace and Billy, were sitting beside their massive RV on a driveway at the park's entrance. I stopped by for a chat and for permission to stay the night. After the fee was paid, they told me I had my pick of the spots with only one other camper in the park. We then compared notes on our respective vehicles.

"I like your old van but it's too small for us," Billy chuckled.

"Do you have a bathroom?" was Grace's first question.

"It's getting too small for me too. I've been living in it for about four weeks now. And yes, it has a bathroom… of sorts." I didn't get into the details of my toilet.

Billy had retired two years prior, and they sold their home and invested in their house on wheels. They wanted a life on the road.

"After we traveled some, we thought it would be nice to hang out in one spot but still get to meet people. So we volunteered for this gig." I could sense the disappointment in Billy's voice. He continued, "The only problem is not many people come here. We got here in early July, and what you see is pretty typical."

Grace added, "Anyway, we kind of miss our house now. Our neighbors. Our garden. We may go back to that." You could tell that Grace had already made up her mind and just needed to work on Billy a little more. "The only time we talk to people is to collect their money or to tell them to quiet down."

"Well, you won't need to ask me to quiet down."

"You never know about you old hippies," Billy said with a laugh.

I hope Grace and Billy find a retirement path that works for them. It's not an easy thing to do. On the one hand, you know you don't have much time left, and on the other hand, with your workdays behind you, you now have all this time to fill up. Heaven knows I have the occasional doubts about the path I am on. I found my spot and watched a beautiful sunset with no trees blocking my view.

The following morning I pulled my bike off the rack and headed off on one of the perfectly straight and flat roads leading away from the park. My training for the thirty-mile ALS ride I planned in Napa, California, had so far consisted of rides on perfectly flat roads. Another day in Kansas and the ride was no different. I promised myself to increase the level of difficulty once I got past the Great American Prairie, although I was not in any hurry to do so.

My ride took me to the town of Buhler, population 1,327. When I saw the sign welcoming me to Buhler, Kansas, I immediately thought that the movie *Ferris Bueller's Day Off* must have been very popular there. (These are the things you find humorous when you spend most of your time talking only to yourself.) However, as I biked through town, I realized that there was no movie theater in Buhler. And given the many large grain silos I biked past, these residents had little opportunity for days off, or for a movie that celebrated one.

Many of the small towns in Kansas grew up around the massive grain silos that dominate the landscape, but Buhler's history was a little different. Buhler was settled by Mennonite families that had emigrated from Russia in the late 1800s. This quiet little hamlet was briefly in the news in 2012 when the mayor and city council received a notice from the Freedom from Religion Foundation that the city seal, which incorporated a cross, violated the principle of separation of church and state. After attorneys informed the town officials they would lose any legal fight which followed, they opted to redesign their seal without the cross. The high school sports teams, however, are still the Crusaders. Infidels beware. Being an infidel myself, I reversed my direction and did not linger in Buhler.

As I was departing Sand Hills later that afternoon, I waved goodbye to Billy and Grace sitting outside their RV and felt a twinge of guilt for abandoning them at their circular parking lot. At the time, there were no campers for them to host and no one for them to tell to "settle down." However, my destiny was to confront some history from my past on a small farm in Oklahoma, so I headed south.

Taking assorted county roads, I reached the state line, crossed over into Oklahoma, and pulled out the directions I had to my cousin Pete's farm. When I last stepped foot on the farm, I was twelve years old and the farm was in the hands of Pete's father, Ed. I have not visited the Doherty farm since the age of twelve, primarily due to distance and other circumstances, but what occurred during my last visit may have played a role as well. The "incident," as the family refers to it, happened during a family reunion in 1962.

My cousins and I were rampaging about with our trusted BB guns, a common activity for young boys on a farm. I'm not sure if mine was a Red Ryder Carbine-Action 200 Shot Range Model, which created havoc for Ralph in the movie *A Christmas Story*, but it offered the same level of excitement when I cocked and fired BBs into whatever I chose to target. We had spent much of the morning shooting frogs in the puddle behind the barn—another of God's creatures that I owe an apology to—and when our rifles ran out of BBs, we began pointing them at each other as a mock battle broke out.

I remember climbing onto the back of a flatbed truck in the barn, and my cousin Ernie foolishly making a frontal assault on my strong defensive position. It was ill-advised. I held the high ground just as General Meade and the Union Army had at Gettysburg, and Ernie's charge had just as much chance of success as Pickett's. As he began to climb onto the back of the flatbed, I took a bead and pulled the trigger on my Red Ryder. Suddenly, after dozens of empty discharges, the rifle found one last BB. One BB is all it took. My aim was true, and I planted the BB directly in the middle of Ernie's forehead.

I am not sure who was more shocked, Ernie or me, but I knew immediately that the consequence for me would be larger than the red lump growing on Ernie's forehead. The adults tended to Ernie while I put my gun away behind some boards in the barn. *What gun?* However, Ernie left no doubt as to who had played the role of John Wilkes Booth in this tragedy. My father and Uncle Ed, on whose farm this tragic assault had occurred, conferred regarding what they needed to do with me. The sentence was immediate and devastating. That night, a rabbit hunt was planned with .22 caliber rifles. My dad and Uncle Ed decided that if I could not be trusted with a BB gun, then I certainly couldn't be trusted with a .22 rifle.

On the one hand, I understood the logic used by the adults. My carelessness had almost resulted in Ernie losing an eye. On the other hand, where I come from, you don't keep your best horse out of the Kentucky Derby on the first Saturday in May. I had proven my aim was accurate, and the odds on the rabbits surviving, with me on the side-lines, had just expanded like the red welt growing on Ernie's forehead. Unarmed, I was told I could join the hunt, but forever banned from ever carrying a weapon of any kind on the Doherty Farm.

The hunt took place, and in truth, the rabbits could not have been safer from a group of marksmen. My well-armed cousins and I, about seven of us, were loaded onto the back of the same flatbed truck I had been defending from Ernie. In the dark of night, with only the truck's headlamps as illumination, we started out. Bouncing along, we proceeded to drive through an alfalfa field, firing away at anything that appeared in the headlights. I am sure the adults in the truck were having a good laugh, while I stayed low and out of the gun sights of my cousins... especially Ernie's.

Given all that had occurred nearly sixty years ago, I was approaching the farm with some trepidation. My directions delivered me to the outskirts of Alva, Oklahoma, where I made a right onto a long, straight dirt road. I passed a few of the ubiquitous oil pumps you see in fields throughout Oklahoma, rhythmically pumping up and down, pulling the oil from underground wells. On the way there, I pondered what Pete and his wife, Anita, would think of this long-lost cousin from the East showing up in an old VW bus. An earlier email had been very welcoming, but that may have been out of obligation to family, something that runs strong in these parts.

Would we recognize each other after almost sixty years? Would we have anything to talk about given the very different paths our lives had taken? Pete had lived on the farm his entire life, while I was a bit of a wandering soul. Liberal Boston versus Conservative Oklahoma. Social Worker versus Farmer. I seemed to be entering the vortex of the divide that seemed to define so much in our country these days. And finally, would they recall the "incident" or would it never be mentioned like a lot of old family stories that get hidden away and purposely forgotten? I pulled into the driveway and was greeted by three dogs, with only one taking on the responsibility for barking.

Stepping out of the bus, and as the dogs gathered around, the most important question was answered immediately. Pete appeared at the farmhouse door and shouted out to me, "You here to shoot Ernie again?"

All of my other questions were answered quickly as well. For two days, Pete and Anita took me in, and their farm was my refuge from the road. They fed me with home-cooked meals and stories of their life farming for the past forty years. We never discussed politics, and for all I know, they could be raging socialists. We often assume too much about people based on where they are from or the work they do. When I attended the University of Chicago, some classmates later told me that they had made some assumptions about me based on my southern accent. Assumptions seldom feel good when you are on the receiving end.

I found with Pete and Anita that our values could not have been more similar: put your children first, be loyal to your friends and community, work hard, and never let the hard times discourage you. The "working hard" part is one they invested in heavily, as is true with all small family farms. No matter the season, there is always something that needs to be tended to, and it's not something you can temporarily hand off to someone else while you wander off to explore the meaning of life. The meaning of life is clear—keep the farm afloat. In the forty years they had operated the farm, Pete and Anita had taken one vacation—a few days in Saint Louis.

Now in their 70s, Pete and Anita are pondering what is next for both them and the farm. Currently, they raise livestock, and with the income from allowing Exxon to place oil pumps on their property, they are getting by, and the farm survives. Pete's son, Jack, works the farm full-time, and soon Pete and Anita will hand the big house over to him and his family, along with all the responsibilities that come with it. They are avid Oklahoma State Cowboy fans but have never seen a game in person, so maybe that will be in their future one day.

I know that I have relied on people like Pete and Anita in a way that they have never relied on me. Their commitment to the land and their perseverance through hard times benefit all of us in this country in many unseen ways. I felt an immense debt of gratitude to their taking me in, the food they had helped put on my table back in Boston, and for the warm acceptance they extended to this wandering cousin from the East.

After doing my laundry and consuming as much of Anita's cooking as I could in two days, it was time to return to the road. As I folded and packed my clothes, a thought crossed my mind. Pete's father, Ed, had instituted the ban, forbidding me from ever holding a rifle again on the Doherty Farm. Ed had passed away in 1993, and Pete was now master of the domain. It occurred to me that it was in his power to lift the ban and to remove the stain on my pride, which I had carried throughout life. Could clemency be close at hand?

I loaded up Zorba, and Anita gave me enough farm fresh eggs to last me to the California state line along with some bacon from their freezer. I then took Pete aside, and with as much humility and contrition as I could muster, I raised the issue.

"You know, Pete, it was your dad who banned me from ever again holding a gun on the farm."

"Well, yes, he did. After all, you did shoot Ernie." I could see Pete was not going to make this easy.

"I did. I make no excuses for that. But seems to me, after what, fifty-five years, maybe I've paid my debt to society?"

"Well, it seems you didn't do any permanent damage to Ernie. What the hell… let's go get some guns!"

Pete ducked into the house and returned with two rifles in hand. We strode to the barn where I had shot Ernie so many years ago, and we struck a pose while Anita snapped a photo. The eternal power of forgiveness and redemption can be seen in my smile.

Redemption at Doherty Farm

CARRIE NATION

L eaving the farm and an embarrassing chapter in my life behind, and leaving the guns as well, I headed north back into Kansas. The first town I encountered over the border was Kiowa, which claimed to have more than 1,000 residents, but that number had to include the cattle I saw wandering into the road. If there is a gas station in Kiowa, I didn't see it, but I was more interested in the existence of any bars. It was not that I needed an early morning nip, but rather the historical marker just outside of town prompted the search.

In the early 1900s, Carrie Nation, the militant crusader against the evils of alcohol, had lived in Medicine Lodge, twenty-four miles north of Kiowa. She and her followers had managed to close all the bars in Medicine Lodge by holding prayer vigils on their premises, which was such a buzzkill, all the men in town stopped drinking there. Much to Carrie's surprise, however, she continued to discover men sleeping it off in the local jail. When she inquired where they were getting their liquor, she was told "Kiowa."

A voice told her to go to Kiowa, and forsaking her tactic of holding prayer vigils, Carrie opted to take a more direct course of action. Using stones, brickbats (a brick when used as a weapon), full malt bottles, and reportedly one billiard ball, she and her posse of sober women proceeded to Kiowa and smashed the three saloons in town. The local town officials were caught off guard, and the sheriff did not know how to respond, since the bars were all operating illegally.

Mission accomplished, Carrie and her fellow crusaders returned to Medicine Lodge. Her husband's response to her actions was to suggest that next time she use a hatchet for maximum damage, to which Carrie responded, "That is the most sensible thing you have said since I married you." A hatchet became her future calling card as she continued her crusade of smashing saloons across the country. In all, she was arrested over thirty times. Carrie Nation died peacefully in

1911 without her husband by her side. He left her in 1901 and for good reason after he had seen what she could do with a hatchet.

I wandered through Kiowa—it did not take long—and was pleased to find Dovie's Bar & Grill on Main Street. Too early in the day for Dovie's to be open, so I was unable to toss one back in Carrie Nation's memory. Still, I was relieved to see that Kiowa had recovered from the trauma it experienced in 1900 and was back providing its residents with basic sustenance. Knowing Kiowa was in Dovie's capable hands, I picked up Route 281, which took me directly north toward Medicine Lodge. I thought about Carrie Nation and her band of women caravanning south on the same road to cast out the demons in Kiowa. I doubt the view had changed much—flat farm fields in every direction. In my mind, the fields, and the work they required, would be hard to endure without a cold one now and then. Eager to get to Medicine Lodge, I was curious to see how they would choose to remember their favorite daughter and how many bars existed in her hometown.

I passed the customary "Welcome to Medicine Lodge" sign along the state road with no instructions to leave my libations at the town line. From there, other signs directed me to Carrie Nation's house, which is preserved, having been converted into a small museum. The small brick building, painted white, sat on the corner of South Oak and West Fowler Avenue. It was here that Carrie Nation received the message from God telling her, "Go to Kiowa." I found the parking lot behind the house, and Zorba had his pick of the spots as no one else appeared to be visiting the museum.

Entering the front door of the museum, I was greeted by Tami and her daughter, Aubrey, age nine, who were the volunteer guides for the day. Aubrey seemed particularly happy to welcome someone from the outside world and started the tour by pointing out the infamous hatchet encased in glass that Carrie had used to intimidate so many bartenders. Nation's typical greeting when entering bars was "Good morning, destroyer of men's souls." She got right to the point.

Also inside the house were various artifacts owned by Nation, and hanging throughout the museum were photos, both humorous and intimidating, of her and her fellow crusaders. In one photo, she sat holding her hatchet surrounded by nine very stern-looking women under the sign "Lips That Touch Liquor Shall Not Touch Ours." Personally, I refrain from kissing any woman holding a hatchet, whether I'm liquored up or not.

In the parlor, a life-size portrait of Nation was mounted on the wall, and she was holding both a bible and her hatchet. Instead of the harsh frown that appeared in all her other photos, in this portrait, there was an almost Mona Lisa–like smile on her lips. I asked Tami and Aubrey to pose for me in front of Nation's portrait and to give me their best Carrie Nation scowl. This was particularly hard for Aubrey to do. She is one of those young people who have a perpetual smile on her face, but she gave it her best shot. Her mom Tami did much better. Life will do that to you.

I then asked them to let loose with their best smiles, which came much more easily. As my warmhearted guide, Aubrey, escorted me to the front door, I asked her if she liked living in Medicine Lodge. She responded, "It's a good place to start—if you like history." Perfect.

Tami, Aubrey and Carrie Nation

WILMORE, KANSAS

Before departing Medicine Lodge, I circled around town and found several establishments that provided basic sustenance (liquor) to its inhabitants. Relieved, I headed west on Route 160 to my next destination, Wilmore, Kansas, the birthplace of my mother. Having been born in close proximity to Carrie Nation's home did not impact my mom too severely. She enjoyed an occasional glass of wine and, in her later years, would drink half a beer—if you consider Keystone Light to be beer—before bedtime, every night. Maybe if Carrie Nation had raised five kids, she would have been more enlightened about the need for spirits.

Wilmore was on the map, but there did not appear to be a road that would actually take me there. It just floated above Route 160 like a spectral ghost of a town sitting on the banks of Mule Creek in the northern part of Comanche County. However, since my mom had gotten out of there at a young age, I figured there had to be a way for Zorba and me to get in. Sure enough, I encountered a small sign alongside Route 160 indicating that a right turn down a rough and uneven road would get us to Wilmore. The view had not changed much since we had crossed the state line into Kansas. Miles of open prairie stretched out in every direction, but I did see a cluster of trees in the direction the road was taking us and figured that would be Wilmore.

The road that took me into town had been paved at one point, but the time for repaving had long come and gone. Once it reached the outskirts of Wilmore, the deteriorating pavement ended, and the streets that wove through town were hard-packed prairie dirt. Painted on the side of what appeared to be an abandoned business of some kind were the words "Welcome to Wilmore, Est. 1887, Population 50." My search commenced for the house in which my mother was born, and as I explored the five roads that comprised the thoroughfares of

Wilmore, I concluded that 50 was an exaggeration. Or perhaps they just rounded the number up.

I had brought an old photo of my mom standing in front of the house with two of my sisters to assist me in my search. The photo was taken in 1971 and recorded the first and only time she ever visited her birthplace after she left. The family moved to Wichita when she was just short of six years old and never looked back. The house was distinctive and not hard to find among the approximately twenty homes scattered among the trees along Mule Creek. It was well cared for, which I was happy to see, but when I knocked on the front door, there was no response.

I spied someone working on a lawnmower in the driveway next door and, walking over, introduced myself, and explained my reasons for being in Wilmore. If he thought it odd that someone came from as far away as Boston to see Wilmore, he did not say so.

"My mom was born in that house," I said as I pointed to his neighbor's home.

"That so."

"I'm on my way to California and just wanted to see it for myself."

"That so."

I realized I had better ask some direct questions if I wanted a more balanced dialogue. "Mind telling me who lives there now?"

"They live in Dodge City. They come to Wilmore to get away from it all."

"That so." I figured that might be Kansas code for "keep talking," and sure enough, he did.

"It's a nice family. Two kids. They take good care of the place. Dodge City just gets too congested, and they want their kids to have some time in the country."

It was hard for me to imagine that Dodge City, with a population of just over 28,000, gets too congested. But then I'm from the East Coast. I'm sure they set the bar for "congested" a little lower in these parts.

I thanked him for his time and returned to the house, leaving a note explaining why I had stopped by and informing them of the significance of their house in my family history. I never heard from them, but then they didn't report me to anyone either. I departed Wilmore the way I came in—the only way available—and noted that the only person I had seen in town was the neighbor to my mom's birthplace. They definitely rounded up.

Wilmore, Kansas

GREGG STEIMEL 1950–1970

When I set out on this journey, I knew my chances of making it to California were, at best, 50/50. I was confident the trip would last longer than my first cross-country attempt in 1972—one day—but beyond that, it was a roll of the dice. While I told everyone my goal was California, I knew the real goal for me was Wright, Kansas, a small town in western Kansas with a population of 163. Anything short of that would signify failure—anything beyond it, success. I had to get to Wright. How this became the case is another story.

I shared earlier that I had formed the Rocket Club during my days working at the Charlestown Boys & Girls Club. This Club would build rockets and terrorize both the residents of Charlestown and ourselves when we launched them. In the spring of each year, I would load the Rocket Club survivors into a fifteen-passenger van and travel to Washington, D.C., where they could see real rockets at the Air and Space Museum. During the week there, we would visit the Washington Monument, the Capitol, perhaps the White House, and always the Vietnam Memorial.

I wanted the Rocket Club members to see the incredible toll that the war took and to honor the people who sacrificed so much. It always made a lasting impression. Even for young teens, full of boundless energy and promise, it was a sobering experience, and the quiet peace one feels at the Wall would linger in the group for the remainder of the day.

At the Memorial there is a ledger, soiled and frayed by the thousands who have leafed through it looking for the names of loved ones. The ledger lists alphabetically every person whose name is inscribed on the Wall. I had taken this trip with the Boys & Girls Club members on eight separate occasions without looking at the ledger. I did not know anyone who had died in Vietnam, and since there was usually a line at the ledger, I always walked past it.

For some reason, in 2001, on what turned out to be my last trip to Washington, D.C., with the Rocket Club, I stopped at the ledger. I did what I often do when seeing names on a memorial, and I flipped through the pages to the Ss to see if there was anyone who shared my last name, Steimel. It had been an odd ritual and up until that day, a fruitless one. But on this day, that changed. Looking back at me was the name *Sgt. Gregg Francis Steimel.*

I was surprised, but it did not give me any great pause because, while not a common last name, I had encountered it on occasion and even knew of another Jerry Steimel who owned a farm in Iowa. Then I saw Gregg's birthdate, August 12, 1950, which followed my birthdate by only five days, and the ledger indicated that he was from Wright, Kansas. This captured my attention, since both of my parents were born and raised in Kansas. It all felt a little close to home.

I pulled the Air and Space Museum admission ticket from my pocket and scratched out the limited information in the ledger about Gregg. I sought out his name on the Wall. Not knowing if we were in any way related, I still felt a connection and made an etching of his name to take home with me. I promised myself that when I returned to Boston, I would try to get to know Gregg a little better.

The research I did, if you can call it that, was straightforward. My father, Jake, had compiled a very detailed genealogy dating back to my great-great-grandfather Hubertus. He had laid out every branch of the tree that had sprouted from the Hubertus trunk in the organized way that Jake, the chemist, did things. Finding the binder in the disorganized basement of Jerry, the social worker, was the hard part. Once I dug it out from an unlabeled cardboard box and dusted it off, it did not take me long to find Gregg listed under "Generation 4" on branch number 46. He was the son of Alfred and Evelyn Steimel and had seven siblings. Alfred and Evelyn lived in Wright, Kansas, where Gregg had grown up and from where he departed for the Army in 1969.

Gregg's tour of duty in Vietnam began on January 12, 1970, and he died as a result of hostile ground fire in the Tay Ninh Province on July 31 that same year, twelve days short of his twentieth birthday. His body was recovered and returned to his parents in Wright, Kansas, where he was buried in the local Catholic cemetery. After a brief search, I had Alfred and Evelyn's address, and I sat down to write them a letter. I had never written a letter to someone who had lost a child, and I don't recall much of what I said. I know I talked about my reasons for visiting the Wall each year and shared my feelings upon finding Gregg's name on it. I explained our connection through some distant relatives and expressed my sorrow at their loss, which had occurred over thirty years prior to my letter. I did not know if I would hear back from them.

The letter I received from Evelyn the following week was simple, touching, and reflected the loss she still felt so deeply. She expressed her gratitude for my pausing at the Wall to honor Gregg and for taking the time to reach out to them. Evelyn and I began corresponding regularly, and I learned she was the accomplished writer I had always dreamed of being. She was a reporter for the Dodge City newspaper and, after Gregg's death, wrote a book about his life, entitled *A Letter to Gregg*, a copy of which she signed and mailed to me. Her inscription read:

> *To Jerry, whose diligent search united us as cousins and his respect and homage made to our Gregg at the Wall brought us together.*
>
> —*Peace, Evelyn*

Evelyn was a pacifist even before the war, and after Gregg's death, she became an activist with Pax Christi, an international Catholic peace movement. She wrote letters to other mothers who lost children, and she visited women whose loved ones were POWs in Vietnam. One of her articles protesting the war appeared in *Newsweek* magazine, and another article, defending the soldiers who fought in Vietnam, was published in *U.S. News and World Report*.

Shortly after beginning my correspondence with Evelyn, I went to the Virtual Wall, the online version of the Vietnam Memorial, and left a message honoring both Gregg and his parents, Evelyn and Alfred. A few months went by before I received an email from Ron Hughes, who was employed by the State of Texas in the highway department. Ron had been in Gregg's platoon and in his email described his heroism. Gregg had sacrificed himself on that July day in the Tay Ninh

Province so that Ron and others could escape to the helicopter that was taking them out of a hot zone. Ron wrote:

> *Gregg gave his life that day so I and others could live. I'm 54 years old, been married for 33 years, have three children and seven grandchildren. If Gregg hadn't done what he did that day, none of this would have been possible. I owe him everything that I am and have today.*

Ron asked if I knew how to reach Gregg's parents—he had been trying to find them— and I shared their address with him. I received a powerful response.

> *Thank you, thank you so much. I can't believe that this is all happening for me at this time. I've been searching on the net for two years now trying to get some information on Gregg's family, and by God's graces he sent me to you. I just can't hardly believe this. I am in tears right now trying to write this email to you. You don't know what this means to me. I can't really express how I feel right now, so I will email you Monday. Thank you again and again!!!*
>
> —*Your friend for life, Ron Hughes.*

A few months later, I received a letter from Evelyn. She shared how Ron and other members of Gregg's platoon had come to visit her in Wright, Kansas. It was an emotional experience for everyone. The men who served with Gregg over thirty years ago gathered at his gravesite to pay their respects both to him and to Alfred and Evelyn. The Talmud says: "Whoever saves one life saves the entire world." I know the men in Gregg's platoon felt he saved many worlds.

Evelyn and I continued to exchange Christmas cards for several years but one year they stopped, and I did not hear from her again. I searched for information and found that Alfred had passed away in 2012. I could find no information on Evelyn or whether she still lived in

Wright. I knew as part of this trip, if possible, I wanted to visit Evelyn. I also wanted to stand at Gregg's gravesite, as the survivors of his platoon did, to honor him and the parents who raised him.

From Wilmore, I followed several lightly traveled state roads until I returned to historic Route 50, which took me to Wright. I exited Route 50 onto Jewell Road and headed to the center of town. The grain silo in Wright was the largest I had seen on my travels and dwarfed every other structure in town. Gregg had worked at the Alliance Ag & Grain Silo part-time—where everyone called his dad "Boss"—the physical work keeping him in shape for baseball and football at St. Mary of the Plains High School. He was an undersized lineman on the football team, but his teammates could not recall anyone ever getting the better of him. He was competitive but always had a strong sense of fair play.

Gregg attended one year of college at Dodge City Community College and planned to work with youth in the recreation field, hoping to be a coach. He could have avoided the war with a college deferment, as I did, but when he saw friends from Wright going to Vietnam, his sense of fair play told him he could not stay behind. Evelyn was distraught when he enlisted, and she even called his recruiter to see if she could stop him. Gregg was determined and left for the army in the Fall of 1969.

There were a lot of things he did not like about the army. His friend Martin wrote:

> *You run into all kinds of things in the Army. Gregg and I wrote and talked together about this. Prejudice was really bad. We had a lot of good friends in high school who were Hispanic, our teammates and friends. Now we saw them really mistreated. That was something we couldn't get used to.*

Again, Gregg's sense of fair play came out.

When Gregg was in Vietnam, another young man from Wright, Richard Conrardy, a medic, was killed. When this happened, Gregg wrote to Richard's parents:

Maybe some day all the sorrow and lives that are lost every day over here will show people that there is nothing to come out of war and there will be peace.

Gregg was killed three weeks later.

I had Evelyn's address from the last letter I received from her, and as I drove through Wright in search of her house, I hoped my quest would be as simple as knocking on her door and introducing myself. With a population of just over 150, it did not take long to navigate through the quiet streets to the house on Doll Street. The small ranch-style home painted a pale yellow was within sight of Saint Andrew's Catholic Church, which Gregg had attended, and across the street from the house was the church cemetery. In her book, Evelyn had mentioned that Gregg was buried in a spot where she could see his stone marker from the large bay window on the front of her house. Later in life, she began to regret this. It was so hard on Alfred seeing Gregg's gravestone every day from their living room.

I pulled into the driveway, paused, and collected myself before I climbed out of Zorba and walked to the side door. I was not surprised to see a small ramp leading up to the door since Evelyn would now be ninety-four years old. I felt disappointment after several knocks elicited no response. I returned to Zorba, where I retrieved a piece of notepaper and scratched out a short note to Evelyn. I reintroduced myself as the man from Boston who had reached out to her fifteen years ago. I hoped she would remember. I also hoped it was still her home.

My attempt to meet Evelyn called for more than a mere note on the door. Since it was Saturday night, I decided to stay in the area and attend St. Andrew's services in the morning. I deduced if Evelyn was still living in Wright and able, she would attend Church services in the morning. I drove to the outskirts of Dodge City, eight miles away, where I stayed at a small hotel on Wyatt Earp Boulevard. A hotel for the night seemed like a wise choice, since having a shower in the morning before attending Mass at Saint Andrew's would significantly enhance the odds of Evelyn, or anyone else, talking to me.

The following morning, I drove into Saint Andrew's parking lot fifteen minutes before Mass was scheduled and waited. From Zorba's large bay window, I watched for an elderly woman, or anyone else, approaching the church from the pale-yellow house. But it did not bear fruit. With a few minutes to spare, I entered the church, blessed myself, and found a seat in a pew near the back. Even though I have not practiced Catholicism for almost fifty years, a Mass always feels like a familiar experience. As much as I resist it, and review the litany of reasons I left it behind, there is still something comforting in the ritual. It takes me back to a simple time when all big decisions belonged to my parents, and my job was to torment my sisters and wreak havoc in the neighborhood with my friends. I sat back and enjoyed the service.

Having no idea what Evelyn looked like, I needed help finding out if she was there. When the service ended, I waylaid the gentleman in the pew in front of me with whom I had exchanged the "sign of peace" just moments before. I figured that gave me the right to ask a favor. I inquired about Evelyn, and he replied that he was familiar with her, but had not seen her at St. Andrew's for quite a while. Thanking him, I headed for the line of parishioners winding out the door, exchanging greetings with the priest who had offered the Mass.

Having stood in these lines before, I knew it was bad form to attempt a real conversation with the priest while parishioners queued up behind you. People wanted to get home for the game on TV, head to the nearest donut shop, or grab a cold beer as a chaser to the bad altar wine. Thank him for the sermon and move on—that's the protocol. Knowing this, I requested a word with him once he was free and quickly moved on. Priests are not allowed to say no to requests like this, so he smiled and said he would look for me once he finished with his flock.

I stepped to the side to wait and thought back to my seminary days and the path I had chosen in life. No one was waiting in line to thank me for anything, but I was content with my decision to leave the seminary and with the journey that followed. I felt satisfaction with my career as a social worker, and I was fortunate to have experienced an abundance of love, both giving and receiving. Finally, the thought of not having my two daughters in my life dispelled any doubts I had in my mind about my choices.

Bishop Gilmore interrupted my reflection when he came over and introduced himself. I was surprised to learn he was a bishop given the size of the town and its flock. "The pastor is traveling, and I like to get out to all my parishes, so I took the opportunity to fill in for him," he explained.

Since it was not his parish, I guessed he would not know Evelyn, but I ventured into the conversation anyway. "I'm looking for a member of this parish, Evelyn Steimel."

"I'm sorry. I do not know Evelyn. I really can't be any help with that. I wish Father Schremmer were here to help you."

His flock having dispersed, Bishop Gilmore had the time to chat, and I shared with him the journey I was on. He surprised me when I mentioned my uncle, Father Charles, saying he remembered him. "Father Charles always made people laugh." Then he added with a smile while lowering his voice some, even though there was no one nearby, "He was a good person to have a drink with." Thus proving he knew my uncle.

"I'm going to bless your journey, and I hope you find what you are looking for. You might want to check out the book *Blue Highways*, by William Heat Least-Moon. He took a journey similar to yours. I think you would enjoy the read."

I thanked the good Bishop and headed out to the parking lot, which was heating up under the noonday sun. I pondered my next move—or if I even had one. I was running out of ideas.

"Love the bus!" I heard someone call out from across the parking lot. This had been shouted to me many times over the course of my trip, but this proved to be the most beneficial of all. Allen Burkhart walked over and introduced himself as we shook hands. We made some small talk about VW buses, and then I threw my Hail Mary pass—appropriately in the parking lot of a church.

"Allen, would you happen to know Evelyn Steimel?"

"I sure do. In fact, I'm the one who looks after her house," pointing over to the small yellow ranch home I had visited the day before.

"She's the reason I'm here in Wright today," I told him, and shared with Allen the history that brought me there.

"Sorry to tell you she is not in Wright anymore. She became ill, and since several of her children were living in Albuquerque, she now resides in a nursing home there. The kids haven't decided yet what to do with the house, so I look after it until they do."

I was happy to hear that Evelyn was near her children during her final years, and knew that would mean more to her than anything. Disappointed that I was not going to meet her, I thanked Allen who had given me some closure on this important part of my journey. I gave him the hug I had intended for Evelyn, which he accepted.

Until this time, I had delayed visiting Gregg's gravesite in the cemetery next to the church, hoping that Evelyn would be able to visit it with me. I knew that was not possible now, and it was time for me to go see Gregg. I opened the gate to the simple chain-link fence surrounding the graves and walked toward the two graves that stood off from the others, close to the bay window of Evelyn's house.

The stone on the left, closest to the house, had Alfred's name inscribed, along with the dates of his birth and death. Above his name, the image of the Alliance Ag & Grain silo, where Alfred had worked his entire life, was etched into the stone. On the right side of the stone was Evelyn's name, along with her birthdate. Above her name, a writing tablet and a pencil were etched in the stone, a symbol of her dedication to writing. Alfred was patiently waiting for her.

To the right of their gravesite, a similar stone, though smaller and with darker granite, marked where Gregg lay. Under Gregg's name, the marker stated that Gregg "Gave His Life for His Country." As Ron Hughes would say, he also gave his life for his fellow soldiers. Standing at the grave, I asked myself unanswerable questions: *Why did Gregg have only nineteen years to live his life, while I received so much more? Why did Alfred and Evelyn have to carry such a heavy burden?*

I had no answers, of course, and I wanted to believe that Gregg did not have any regrets. His selfless actions that day in Vietnam led to many full lives, such as Ron Hughes's and so many others in his platoon. His gift was multiplied like the loaves and the fishes, and the ripple he created in the universe continues to this day.

I don't know if Gregg and I would have ever met if he had been able to live a long full life. We were distant relatives, a fourth cousin by my best calculation, and I found him only because his name was on the Wall. But still, I felt a sense of loss. I think he would have enjoyed this trip in an old air-cooled VW, and probably would know a lot more about fixing it when it broke down than I did. I could have used his help, and I would have enjoyed his company as we compared notes on our childhoods, one on the plains of Kansas and one in Louisville, Kentucky.

As I stood at Gregg's gravesite, I remembered Evelyn describing the "peace funeral" that she insisted on for Gregg. She wrote that "the family wore the peace symbols around our necks that were loved and also hated as unpatriotic at the time." That gave me an idea. Before I departed Boston, a friend gave me a small model of a VW bus as a kind of traveling companion. It was dark brown with a white top, and plastered with peace symbols that made it the quintessential "hippie van." I kept it on Zorba's dash, a lookout scouting the road before me. In my belief that Gregg would have enjoyed a trip like this, I retrieved it from Zorba and placed the small VW bus atop his gravestone.

I thanked Gregg for helping me find my way to his hometown of Wright and asked him to keep an eye on me as I continued my journey. With that, I walked from the cemetery and returned to Zorba and the road ahead. I had completed the most anticipated stop on my 5,000-mile journey. It was time to put Bleeding Kansas behind me.

Gregg's grave marker with VW bus

*I was happy, I knew that. While experiencing
happiness, we have difficulty in being conscious
of it. Only when the happiness is past and we look
back on it do we suddenly realize - sometimes
with astonishment - how happy we have been.*

—Nikos Kazantzakis, *Zorba the Greek*

ROCKY MOUNTAIN HIGH

I picked up Route 50 outside of Wright and headed west toward the Colorado state line, 115 miles away. As the Alliance Ag & Grain silo receded from sight in my rearview mirror, I was disappointed in not meeting Evelyn, who had sent me so many kind notes and Christmas cards over the years. But even without meeting Evelyn, I felt I had completed an important part of my journey, a quest that started when I first saw Gregg's name on the Vietnam Memorial Wall.

The image of the small VW bus resting on Gregg's grave marker brought a smile to my face, the only smile I could recall regarding Gregg since I discovered my connection to him sixteen years ago. I guessed that Evelyn was also tired of all the sadness, so I allowed the smile to linger as I drove west. My goal was to cross the state line into Colorado before dark, find a good spot for the night, and collect myself for the challenge that lay ahead—crossing the Rocky Mountains.

Route 50 is a historic road that stretches from Ocean City, Maryland, to Sacramento, California—just over 3,000 miles in length. After Route 30, the Lincoln Highway, Route 50 is the country's second oldest cross-country highway. But while interstate highways have largely replaced Route 30, Route 50 remains a two-lane highway across most of the United States, particularly in the western states. Along its route, you still find the old motor courts, diners, and odd tourist attractions that entice motorists to stop for a spell.

The one I could not resist was the World's Largest Hairball in Garden City, Kansas. Found in the stomach of a cow that had been slaughtered, it weighed fifty-five pounds at the time of the butchering. It had dried out some since then and now weighs in at thirty-eight pounds. Still impressive. There are also giant hairballs in Webster, South Dakota, and East Lansing, Michigan, each laying claim to the "World's Largest" title. I don't have a dog in this fight, but since the one in Garden City was the one I was gazing at, it gets my vote.

Just west of Garden City, and a few miles off Route 50 in Holcomb, Kansas, is the house made famous by Truman Capote's *In Cold Blood*. In this house, Richard Hickock and Perry Edward Smith impulsively shotgunned the Clutter family— just because they could. For me, this did not qualify as a "tourist attraction," and I'm not sure what looking at a murder scene across an open field does for you. I had wisely spent my time looking at the cow's hairball and zipped past Holcomb.

I arrived at the Colorado state line just as light began to fade and made my way to the John Martin Reservoir State Park. There was nothing remarkable about the park, just a body of water in the middle of a long stretch of flat prairie, but it was a peaceful, perfect spot to end the day. Zorba and I had a significant challenge ahead of us—crossing the Rockies—and what I needed most was some solitude to reflect on my time in Wright. I settled in for the night.

Before departing on this journey, I had researched the best route for traversing the Rockies in an underpowered VW bus. There was no shortage of opinions, each making a case for why you were least likely to die if you took a particular route. I settled on taking Interstate 70, which heads west out of Denver. While my intent was to avoid the interstates on the trip, this seemed like a prudent time to take advantage of Eisenhower's vision for highway travel in the US. Road engineers reliably design interstates to be as dull as possible. As such, they avoid steep inclines and sharp curves, while providing a passing lane for faster vehicles—in my case, all other vehicles. I also deduced that if I got into trouble, help would not be far away.

Between the John Martin Reservoir and I-70 in Denver, however, I had planned a rendezvous with some cousins. Our family in Kentucky referred to them as our "Colorado Cousins." We had only a few occasions to interact with them when we were young and then very little contact once we became adults as the various branches of the family tree no longer gathered in Kansas. This particular meeting was significant for me because one of the cousins was Ernie, whom I had shot on the farm in Oklahoma nearly sixty years ago. I informed him in advance that cousin Pete had lifted the ban on my possession of guns in the past week, and I was looking forward to seeing him. Would Ernie dare show for lunch?

Zorba and I rolled into Colorado Springs and began looking for the rendezvous spot, a place called Johnny's Navajo Hogan. For someone from the East, it seemed a strange name for a restaurant, and I assumed there was some history behind it. My assumption proved correct; the restaurant is on the National Register of Historic Places. It was opened as a roadhouse by a labor organizer, Nicholas Fontecchio, who came to Colorado as a representative of the United Mine Workers in hopes of organizing miners working in the Rockies.

Many of the Navajo in the area were working the mines, and having spent considerable time with them, Fontecchio became familiar with the "hogan," a traditional dwelling for Navajos where they often practiced their religious traditions. He modeled his structure in Colorado Springs after a hogan on the nearby reservation, and it included two large domes constructed without a single nail. In addition to providing food and other sustenance, Fontecchio hoped to provide a place for miners to gather and bond as friends and neighbors. It seemed like an appropriate place for Ernie and me to meet and pass the peace pipe. I assumed they would check all guns at the door—for Ernie's sake.

Just as Fontecchio had envisioned in 1935, when he built the hogan, the restaurant was a perfect meeting spot. I gathered with cousins I had not seen since my teenage years, and we re-bonded over food and cold beers. There were laughs over the infamous shooting incident on Doherty Farm and some incredulity that cousin Pete had lifted the ban. Memories of my reckless behavior seemed remarkably fresh. Ernie showed me the scar he had over his left eyebrow—not in the center of his forehead as I remembered it—and I realized how close I had come to turning my cousin into a pirate with a dashing eyepatch. No smoking was allowed in the current hogan, so instead of a peace pipe, I bought Ernie a beer, which seemed to do the trick. After hugs in the parking lot, I headed north on Highway 85, feeling lucky I was from a family with so many kind and generous people—not to mention forgiving.

By the time I reached the outskirts of Denver, darkness was approaching, and I was looking for a place to park Zorba for the night. I didn't feel like putting a lot of energy into it, so I located a nearby Marriott and tucked Zorba into a parking space. I retired for the night, looking forward to some of their fresh lobby coffee in the morning. One concern hung over me as I settled in. On the way to Denver, the brakes on Zorba had begun to malfunction. In addition to a frightening grinding noise every time I applied pressure, the front of the bus would jerk to the right. I began to anticipate it and compensate by steering to the left as the brakes took hold.

I thought about seeking out a mechanic in Denver, but that would have involved navigating city traffic. The thought of that, combined with my desire to attack the Rockies first thing in the morning, convinced me I could live with the problem until I got to the other side. That is, the other side of the Rockies, not the ultimate "other side"— although the brake problem may have something to say about that.

After a friendly greeting from the Marriott front desk staff, I helped myself to some coffee from the breakfast buffet. The scrambled eggs looked good—but again, I didn't want to push my luck. I also needed to get an early start on the climb over the Rockies before the temperatures started to rise, so I passed on a leisurely breakfast. The chances of an air-cooled vehicle overheating increase significantly when you combine high temperatures with a long, steep climb. My road map told me that once I jumped onto Interstate 70 just west of Denver, I had a fifty-mile climb to Loveland Pass. At that point, I-70 enters the Eisenhower Tunnel and passes under the Continental Divide. The brakes would have to wait, and I trusted the condition would not worsen.

About the only part of this plan that went well was the coffee in the Marriott lobby. After filling my mug, I drove north on Route 470 before sunrise, and merged onto I-70 heading west, the lights of Denver behind me. Before beginning the climb, I stopped at a truck turnoff area to empty the seven-gallon container of water used for cooking and washing dishes. Lightening my load by sixty pounds could not hurt, and I wanted every edge I could muster to increase the odds of a successful climb. The brakes were still acting up but had not worsened, so neither did my anxiety.

After lightening my load, the climb up the Rockies steadily steepened. Soon I needed to downshift to third gear, chugging up the mountain at a steady forty mph. One of the suggestions I had read for driving an old VW bus over the Rockies was to wait until a large semi-trailer passed you, then draft off of it by pulling into its slipstream as it glided by. The only problem with this strategy was that the semis were passing me so quickly, that getting close behind them proved to be beyond Zorba's capabilities. We would have to do it on our own.

Wanting to keep my gas tank as full as possible, I pulled off at the Idaho Springs exit with the gas gauge still showing half a tank and found a Valero Station nearby. I pulled up to the pump, shut the engine off, and pulled back on the emergency brake. The handle flew back with no resistance, and I discovered that I no longer had an emergency brake. The emergency brake on an old VW bus engages the rear wheels, and with the difficulty I was already having regarding my front brakes, I now had genuine concern.

I filled Zorba's tank and pulled forward into a spot near the front door of "The Sasquatch Store," an adjunct to the Valero gas station. Zorba did not roll into the store, so I surmised I still had some braking action on the vehicle. The morning sun was still below the horizon, and I sat for a bit, weighing my situation. The map told me there was very little in Idaho Springs, and a quick search on my phone told me the nearest mechanic was thirteen miles further up I-70 in a hamlet called Georgetown. Retreating to Denver was not an option, as I deduced going uphill was preferable to going downhill when you have no brakes. Rocket scientist on board.

Before getting back on I-70 and confronting my fate, my curiosity induced me to see what "The Sasquatch Store" was all about. The sign had a giant foot emblazoned on it, so I surmised it had something to do with the infamous Big Foot—the mythical creature some have claimed to have encountered in the woods. I had always associated Sasquatch sightings with the Northwest region: Oregon, Washington

State, and perhaps up into British Columbia. Had Sasquatch wandered south and entered the Rockies? I needed to know.

Becky was behind the counter and gave a friendly greeting, particularly given how early it was in the morning. I wandered past the usual items you see near a gas station checkout: butane lighters, maps, beef jerky, and the always-present Slim Jims. Deeper into the store, I encountered stuffed Sasquatches, Sasquatch bandanas— the pink ones embroidered with "Real Women Believe"—and Sasquatch key chains. Even deeper into the store, the selection of items for sale oddly changed to chain saws. I guess if you truly "believe," you might want to have one of those handy.

I returned to the counter with a fresh cup of coffee and quizzed Becky on whether there had been any sightings of Big Foot in the area. She informed me there were frequent sightings in Colorado, the most recent nine months ago, fifty miles north of where we stood. Becky was a real woman who believed. I refrained from buying a chain saw, paid for my coffee, and returned to Zorba. I had my own problems to deal with.

I took a couple of spins around the Sasquatch Store in Zorba, testing my brakes. Reassured that I at least had some ability to slow Zorba down, I headed back onto I-70. Zorba comfortably returned to third gear and continued the slow climb. By the time I pulled off I-70 and glided into Georgetown, the sun was up, but the temperature was still in the 30s, not unusual for September and an altitude of over 8,500 feet. We arrived at the auto repair shop and waited in the cold until the announced opening time of 8:00 am. Someone approached the door and opened the shop at 8:10 am. Duly noted.

Unlike many people I encountered on this trip, the sight of an old air-cooled VW bus sitting outside the mechanic's bay door did not make him smile. I explained Zorba's symptoms. The mechanic's dour response was that he would try to look at it, but he had a busy day ahead. Handing him the keys, I informed him I was taking my bike with me and would wait for a call.

Pedaling in the cold, I headed back in the direction from which I had entered the town. I had seen some motels along the road, and I hoped to find a vacancy. I wanted to get into a room despite the early hour and warm up as I awaited the verdict on my brakes. The first hotel I stopped at was full, but a room could be available at noon after some folks had checked out. The rate was a bit high, which did not surprise me given it had a French name, Hotel Chateau Chamonix, but I did not rule out the option entirely. My next stop down the road was the non-French America's Best Value Inn. The price was right, and they could get me into a room and out of the cold immediately. I checked in, cranked up the heat in the room, and crawled under the covers to await the call from my newest mechanic. I wasn't feeling hopeful.

By the time noon rolled around, the outside temperatures had risen into the 60s, and with no word from the mechanic, I was ready to forage for lunch. I biked toward the garage where I had left Zorba, keeping an eye out for a place to eat. The Roundabout Burgers & Dogs was quickly deemed the winner, and I leaned my bike against the large bear carved from a tree trunk out front. He was holding the "Open" sign and didn't seem to mind watching my bike.

I realized as I entered that I had not had a hot dog—although lots of bratwursts—since I left Boston. For anyone who knows me, this is probably a record of sorts. I consider myself something of a connoisseur, and during my time at Boys & Girls Clubs, I kept a personal hot dog rotisserie in my office. I would occasionally fire it up and treat the entire staff to a Hot Dog Day. At the Roundabout, I went with the Chili Cheese Dog and the Kraut Dog. They did not disappoint.

The pedaling was a little slower after consuming two large dogs—they don't cheat you at the Roundabout. Luckily, it was just a short way up the road to where Zorba was sitting, unmoved from the spot I had left him in that morning. The mechanic said he had not looked at it and wasn't sure if he would before the end of the day. Not promising to say the least. Meanwhile, the dogs in my stomach had settled a bit, so I decided to spend the afternoon exploring Georgetown on my bike. I discovered that once you get away from the strip where I had found the mechanic and hot dogs, it is a charming little town. In the old town area, brick buildings dating back to the late 1800s line the streets with antique shops, small boutiques, and an occasional outdoor cafe populating the storefronts.

Established by two prospectors from Kentucky in 1859 during the Pike's Peak Gold Rush, Georgetown became the center of the Colorado mining industry in the nineteenth century. It earned the name "Silver Queen of Colorado." At one time, when the population exceeded 10,000, there was a brief push to move the state capital from Denver to Georgetown. But the silver was soon mined out, and with a population today of only 1,000, it primarily serves as a watering hole for skiers returning to Denver from Vail and other ski areas farther up I-70.

While I appreciated the charm of Georgetown, I needed to get over the Rockies, and could not afford a significant delay if I were going to make it to California for my appointed rendezvous with Dianne. Late in the afternoon, I biked by the garage and spied Zorba, still sitting where I had left him that morning. I accepted the idea that I would be in Georgetown for the night and returned to the motel.

I returned to the garage the following morning with little hope of receiving a diagnosis on Zorba's brakes. The mechanic surprised me, however, saying he had "gotten to it."

"The front brakes need new pads and rotors, and your emergency brake needs a new cable."

"Great. You got the parts?"

"Of course not. It's an old VW bus," he laughed. I didn't laugh.

"How long until you can get the parts?"

"Three days should do it."

I let out a sigh and excused myself from my now least favorite mechanic. A three-day delay was more than I could live with. I decided to call Damon, my local mechanic back in Boston who had worked on Zorba. After I described the brake situation, Damon guessed it was probably safe to drive. Perhaps because that was what I wanted to hear, I readily agreed. I reasoned I didn't need the brakes going up the mountain, and you aren't really supposed to use your brakes going down. And besides, that's why those runaway truck ramps are there. The clincher may have been when Damon said: "A lot of old hippies drive around with no emergency brakes."

Damon promised to get his hands on the brake pads that day. My task was to find a repair shop on the other side of the Rockies that was willing to accept delivery and install them onto Zorba. Damon would overnight them there. I paid the mechanic in Georgetown for his time and drove back to my motel and made some calls. A shop in Grand Junction, 200 miles down the road and beyond the Rockies' crest, agreed to the task, and I promised to be there the following afternoon. Zorba and I needed to get rolling. It was before 10 am, not too hot, and time to crest the Rockies.

Departing Georgetown, back in third gear, and chugging along at a constant thirty-five mph, Zorba became the little VW bus that could. It was then that I experienced a revelation as a vehicle quickly passed me. It was a light-blue VW bus, and it was traveling at nearly sixty mph up a steep incline. A smile came to my face as I realized it was sitting on a trailer pulled by a large Dodge Ram truck. The best way to get an old VW bus over the Rockies? Tow it, of course.

AIRCRAFT ARCHAEOLOGY

Zorba had been traveling in third gear for a while, gradually making his way up the eastern slope of the Rockies. It was time for him to take a break. Not wanting to challenge his limitations, I had planned a diversion off the Interstate near the crest of the Rockies. The diversion involved a rather odd hobby my brother John and I have become engaged in.

One day, early in September 2007, an article in the *Boston Globe* caught my eye. Bob Fossett, the famed balloonist, had taken flight in his small single-engine plane and disappeared. After a week of searching, the Civil Air Patrol had found eight previously undiscovered plane crashes, but not Fossett's. The article went on to describe the remote terrain being searched and added that over 300 flights had disappeared in the Western United States, never to be found. Fascinated by that fact I discovered a pursuit called "aircraft archaeology," which involved searching for airplane crash sites. I called my brother, and easily convinced him we needed to get involved in this endeavor.

Since then, my brother and I have dedicated one week every year to wandering in the western desert, and occasionally New England, looking for airplane crash sites. To be clear, committing one week per year to aircraft archaeology does not put us in the serious category when it comes to doing this work. Most of the sites my brother and I attempt to locate have already been discovered by someone else, but remain a challenge as they are in remote locations. Seldom are there existing trails that lead you to the plane wreckage, and the land navigation skills my brother learned during his Green Beret training are invaluable. A fair amount of research is required perusing old FAA and military crash reports. While we will probably never make any significant contribution to the field of aircraft archaeology, it gives me a good excuse to wander around the desert with my brother.

The diversion I planned to take off Interstate 70 was a hike to a crash site, a crash which had occurred near Interstate 70 and the Eisenhower Tunnel at the crest of the Rockies. A hike to the site would give me a chance to stretch my legs, give Zorba a rest, and allow me bragging rights over my brother if I could find it. I was also motivated because the site was a particularly tragic one, and I wanted to pay my respects.

The flight, scheduled on October 2, 1970, was carrying the Wichita State Shockers football team to Logan, Utah, for a game against Utah State. There were two flights that day, code-named Gold and Black after the school's colors. Gold carried the head coach, Athletic Director, and the starting players, while the reserves and assistant coaches were flying in the plane, code-named Black. Both aircraft were Martin 4-0-4s, twin-prop aircraft operated by Golden Eagle Aviation, and after leaving Wichita on their first leg of the trip, both stopped in Denver to refuel.

Given Denver's proximity to some of the Rockies' tallest peaks, the typical flight plan out of Denver would head north toward Wyoming, giving a plane sufficient time to gain altitude and then turn west to cross the Rockies. The pilot flying Gold was Ronald G. Skipper, President of Golden Eagle Aviation. He had visited with the coaches and players in the main cabin during the first leg of the flight from Wichita to Denver, telling them they would be taking a "scenic route" out of Denver. This route would allow them to see Mount Sniktau, the alpine skiing venue for the upcoming 1976 Winter Olympic Games. The pilots in Black planned to take the traditional and less scenic route heading north out of Denver. Before departing Denver, Skipper purchased aeronautical charts, which he planned to use in picking out various landmarks and points of interest for the football team. After takeoff in clear weather, the two planes separated, each taking their chosen route for crossing the Rockies.

Witnesses that day at Loveland Pass, at an altitude 11,990 feet, reported seeing an aircraft flying below them. Crash survivor Rick

Stephens, a senior guard, stated that as the plane flew along I-70, he saw abandoned mines and old vehicles in the hills above them. Seeing the mountain tops above him, he became concerned enough that he walked up to the cockpit, not an unusual activity on a flight such as this. Peering out the cockpit windows, he was shocked to see nothing but green in front of them.

The aircraft had become trapped in a box canyon as it flew up Clear Creek Valley and was unable to climb above the mountain ridges surrounding it on three sides. At 1:14 pm, Gold struck trees on the east slope of Mount Trelease, 1,600 feet below its summit, and crashed only 400 yards from I-70. Based on the testimony of survivors and rescuers, it is believed that many survived the initial impact. The nearly full fuel tanks did not immediately ignite, allowing some survivors to escape, but eventually, the tanks caught fire. The intense flames from the resulting explosion consumed the passenger cabin and doomed the survivors who had not yet escaped the wreckage.

Of the forty souls on board Gold flight, thirty-one perished, including the captain and two flight attendants. Fourteen of those who died were Wichita State football players. Ronald G. Skipper, the Golden Eagle Aviation CEO and first officer on the plane, was at the controls when it crashed, and he survived. When the second plane, Black, arrived in Logan, Utah, they received news of the tragedy that had befallen their teammates and returned to Wichita. The Utah State team held a memorial on the field where the game was to have been played, placing a wreath on the fifty-yard line.

The NTSB attributed the crash to "pilot error," referencing the "intentional operation of the aircraft over a mountain valley route at an altitude from which the aircraft could neither climb over the obstructing terrain ahead nor execute a successful course reversal." While the FAA shut down Golden Eagle Aviation after the crash, CEO Ronald Skipper denied any responsibility and claimed the right engine caught fire, causing the crash. The NTSB found no evidence of this. While

Skipper's pilot's license was revoked, he eventually recovered it, and near the end of his career, he was flying 747s for Transamerica Airlines.

Wichita State University placed a memorial along I-70 for those who died in the crash. Every year on October 2, representatives from the school place a wreath at the memorial. I located the memorial along I-70 near mile marker 217, and pulled onto the shoulder of the road to pay my respects. The large bronze plaque is affixed to a granite slab, the names of the crash victims engraved upon it. A mile further up the Interstate, Exit 216 provides access to a trail leading to the crash site. I took the exit, then made a sharp right-hand turn onto a dirt road that doubled back, heading east alongside the highway. A half-mile after exiting the Interstate, a locked gate blocked the dirt roadway, and I parked Zorba there.

I filled my CamelBak with water, packed a small lunch, and began the 1.2-mile hike to the crash site. I knew the trail was not well marked; however, a previous hiker had posted some photos online that proved helpful. I hiked first the dirt road past the gate and then began looking for a turnoff that would take me in a westerly direction to the site. A small rock cairn at the juncture alerted me to the turn, and the final mile was a gradual ascent up the southern slope of Mount Trelease.

As I began to question whether I had taken the correct trail, I saw sunlight reflecting off a piece of aluminum in the distance. I have been to several aircraft crash sites where people have perished, but I have never visited a location where the tragedy was so immense. My brother and I treat crash sites where people have died as hallowed memorials and never move objects or take souvenirs of any kind. Always, we observe a moment of silence for the people whose journey in life ended at the crash location. This site was particularly sobering given the youth of the passengers, the bond they felt for each other as a team, and the senseless cause of the crash.

There is considerable debris from the Martin 4-0-4 scattered along the side of Mount Trelease. Among the twisted pieces of aluminum and aircraft parts, there are Wichita State Shocker hats and other mementos left by previous visitors. In a secure plastic sleeve, held in place by a rock, are pictures of the players along with the coaches and administrators who died. Included in that sleeve is a touching memorial written by some of the surviving players. As I read the testament to their teammates, I thought back to when I was standing at Gregg's gravesite, and the same question came to mind. *Why do some of us get to live long lives while others' are cut short?* I had no better an answer at this place where Gold flight met its end. After my moment of silence, I reflected on how fortunate I was to have been gifted the opportunities I had in life.

Along the trail back to Zorba, I recalled a passage from Kazantzakis's writings. Zorba—the Greek, not the bus—once encountered an old man planting an almond tree. He laughed at the idea, knowing the old man would never reap the fruit from the tree. Mocking him, Zorba called out "What, Grandfather! Planting an almond tree?" The old man, bent as he was, turned and said: "My son, I carry on as if I should never die." Zorba replied: "And I carry on as if I was going to die any minute." I meditated on who had it right as I followed the trail back to Zorba—the bus.

Debris at Wichita State crash site

HAPPY HIPPY LANE

The sun was directly above me when I finished the hike, and the temperature was rising. It was time to finally crest the Rockies. Chugging back onto I-70, I was soon approaching the Eisenhower Tunnel, bored through a mountain and under the continental divide, sixty miles west of Denver. I-70 enters the Eisenhower Tunnel at an elevation of just over 11,000 feet. It is the longest tunnel on the Interstate Highway System and is the highest point on the 46,876 miles of interstate in the United States. It is a dual-bore tunnel and was the last section of the original Interstate design completed in 1973. Seven workers died constructing it, and now more than 32,000 vehicles pass through it every day. This section of I-70 replaced old Route 6 as the primary car route west out of Denver. Route 6 winds through Overland Pass nearby and still carries trucks with hazardous materials considered unsafe to enter the tunnel.

In 1970, during its construction, the tunnel surprisingly became a focus point of the women's rights struggle. Janet Bonnema, a civil engineer, applied for a job as an engineering technician on the project and was hired when her résumé was mistakenly read as that of "James" Bonnema. When Janet showed up for work, and the supervisor realized his mistake, he promptly transferred her to a position doing office work. There was a common superstition among miners that women were bad luck in a mine, and the supervisor feared the men would walk off the job if Janet entered the tunnel.

Janet had no patience for male superstitions and promptly sued the Colorado Department of Highways for sexual discrimination. The case was settled in her favor two years later, and Janet, accompanied by an entourage of reporters, entered the tunnel in November 1972. There was a minor rebellion among the miners, and some did walk off the job. Janet was not deterred and re-entered the shaft several days later dressed in overalls and without reporters. No one seemed to pay her much mind, and she worked on the tunnel until its completion in 1973.

I hold Janet in high esteem for another reason as well. Prior to this commotion over her working in the tunnel, she had quit her job with Boeing in Seattle in 1963, after men with less experience were promoted over her. She proceeded to hitchhike around the world for six years until she ran out of money in 1969. It was only after her years of wandering the globe that she stepped into history at the Eisenhower Tunnel. I embrace Janet as a fellow wanderer. She was posthumously inducted into the Colorado Women's Hall of Fame in 2012 in recognition of her fight for equal rights—not for her wandering.

Zorba and I exited the 1.7-mile-long tunnel and began our descent, knowing it would be temporary. Interstate 70 begins to climb again ten miles west of the tunnel as it reaches up toward Vail Pass. It was only after crossing Vail Pass that I could declare the Rockies behind me. The long descent from Vail, with its multitude of runaway truck ramps, had amazing views in every direction. Without a doubt, it is the most scenic stretch of interstate I have ever traveled. It provided some distraction from the gnawing fear inside me that I could lose my brakes entirely at any point during the descent.

After coasting down to Rifle, Colorado, using the brakes as little as possible, I wound through the congested streets of the town to Rifle Gap State Park. The Park campground appeared to be even more crowded than Rifle, so Zorba and I pulled into a small roadside stop with picnic tables. It looked like I had found a good spot for the night until the park ranger stopped by just before dark and asked, "You're not planning to spend the night here, are you?"

"Of course not," I replied. "Got any suggestions for a campsite nearby? The state park looks a little crowded."

"There's some BLM land about five miles east of the park. Shouldn't be too hard for you to find and you can park anywhere within the boundaries and spend the night."

The Bureau of Land Management (BLM) was created in 1946 by President Truman and manages one-twelfth of the country's entire landmass, predominantly in the western states. Originally the BLM lands were known as "land nobody wanted," since all the homesteaders heading west had judged them unfit for habitation. Ranchers have grazing rights on nearly 25 percent of the land, and large tracts of land are leased for mining and oil exploration. But the parts I value are the wilderness areas, national monuments, and conservation lands, which total thirty-six million acres. BLM camping sites tend to be primitive, sparsely inhabited, and often free. Just don't look for electrical hookups and comfortable bathrooms.

The ranger's directions were about as exact as the ones Donna gave me back in Harlan, Kentucky, but I had no choice except to give it a shot. Darkness was arriving quickly, so Zorba and I set off in search of the BLM lands. Unfortunately, the headlights on an old VW bus do little more than emit a warm, inviting glow, and it was hard to see more than thirty feet in front of me as I looked for the dirt turnoff he had described. This was the only nighttime driving I did on the trip, and I'm glad of it. We found a turnoff, but it led to a locked gate. Not wanting to back out onto the road in the dark, I decided it would be my place for the night. If anyone needed to get through the gate, they would just have to wake me up. I settled in.

No one pounded on Zorba during the night, and at first light, I headed back to the roadside picnic table the ranger had chased me from the night before. I waited for him to return and accuse me of having spent the night there, but he had apparently slept in. After eggs and the last of my bratwurst from Missouri, Zorba and I headed out. Our destination was Grand Junction, an easy sixty miles farther down I-70, where we anticipated a rendezvous with the brake pads Damon had overnighted to me.

I found the shop without too much trouble, and sure enough, Damon had done his part. The man at the counter brought out the box of vintage VW brake pads. I remembered his voice from the day before, and although it was late on a Friday afternoon, I was confident they would get the job done as promised, and I could be on my way. My confidence was misplaced.

"We got a little problem here," he said somewhat sheepishly as he leaned in toward me.

"We do?"

"Well, my boss… he's bein' a stickler. I didn't mention this to him yesterday. He's sayn' he ain't gonna just slap pads on a vehicle without also doing the rotors."

I wasn't happy to hear this, but my options were limited. "Okay. Let's do it."

"Well, we don't have the rotors. I could get them by next Tuesday, though."

Tuesday was four days away. I didn't need to say anything. I'm sure the expression on my face said it for me.

I leaned into the counter as well, and lowering my voice, I wondered out loud, "Do you think there's anyone in town who might be willing to just slap these pads on the bus for me?"

He leaned in even farther, and after glancing over his shoulder to be certain his boss was out of earshot, he said, "Call Steve at Foreign Aid. He might be the guy you want."

I took my box of brake pads and retreated out the door to Zorba. It was now after 3 pm on a Friday, and my prospects looked bleak. I found the contact information for Foreign Aid on my phone and gave Steve a call. After a brief laugh over my request that he work on my car at 3 pm on a Friday, he suggested I come over so "We can have a little talk." Talking I'm pretty good at, so I headed over to Steve's place, and I took it as a good sign that he was at least willing to let me in his front door.

The first thing I saw when I entered Steve's shop was a street sign on the wall that said "Happy Hippy Lane" with a flower-bespeckled VW bus on it. I took that as a good omen. Steve appeared from the shop's work area, and I placed the box of brake pads on his counter.

"I'm the guy with the VW bus." I smiled but did not get a smile in return. I wondered if the "Happy Hippy Lane" sign belonged to someone else.

Pulling the brake pads from the box, Steve stated, "Well, you got the right ones." Then he added, "It would be irresponsible for me to just slap pads on your bus without also dealing with your rotors. No good mechanic is going to do that."

Great. Here we go again.

But Steve wasn't done. "Look, here's the deal. I will do this, but it's off the books. You pay me cash, and you're not getting any damn receipt for the work. This never happened. I've got several other customers waiting for their cars, but hell, I ain't gonna finish them today anyway."

Loving a good coverup, I quickly responded, "My friend, you have a deal."

"Well, we're not friends yet. Pull your bus into the bay."

I hustled out to Zorba before Steve could change his mind and drove through the bay door and into Steve's shop. I got a pleasant surprise when I did. Sitting in the next bay over was a fully restored 1965 VW bus. I concluded I had found "Happy Hippy Lane" after all, and it turned out that Steve's hard-ass exterior was a very thin facade. He put his mechanic to work on my brake pads and began showing off his bus, nothing but smiles now.

"Ain't she something? I bought her twenty-three years ago, and I've been working on her ever since." Any VW bus owner could identify with that statement.

Steve opened the side door revealing an immaculate interior that appeared as if no one had ever stepped into it, while Zorba's interior was beginning to look like a toxic waste dump. He showed me the spotless engine, with no road dust or oil residue clinging to it, as pretty and immaculate as the day it rolled out of the plant at Wolfsburg. Steve had painted the exterior a creamsicle orange with French vanilla coloring on the roof. It looked so good it was making me hungry.

I looked over at Zorba and suddenly noticed he had every possible insect you could encounter between Massachusetts and Colorado plastered onto his front. He was leaking oil, the side door was beginning to get finicky again, and his interior looked and smelled like someone was living in it—for good reason. But I wasn't jealous. Zorba was a workhorse, while Steve's bus was a show pony. One would never try to drive a show pony across the country and certainly not on some of the roads that Zorba and I had ventured on. Zorba looked worn and tired in comparison, which made him a perfect partner for me.

"Take a look at this." Steve began pulling some photos out of his wallet. "I got married three months ago."

"Congratulations!" I said.

Expecting to see photos of his bride, I saw pictures of his wedding cake instead. In place of the traditional bride and groom perched on top, holding hands, there was a replica of his VW bus. I wondered how Steve got away with this, but I assume whoever married Steve knew what the pecking order was when she signed on.

I waited until Steve's mechanic started working on Zorba before I shared a small fact with him.

"You know, Steve… I'm a little low on cash right now. Is there an ATM within walking distance? I don't wanna come up short when we conclude our deal."

Steve tossed me the keys to his Audi A6 and gave me directions. "This job is gonna take about an hour, so if you need to run any errands, now is the time."

I eased myself into the brown leather seats of the Audi and pulled away from Steve's shop. After four weeks of driving Zorba, the comfort of the Audi was very enticing. The driver's seat gave me an inviting embrace, the ride was as quiet and smooth as butter, and then there was the air-conditioning. It was all too seductive. I found the ATM, stopped at a pharmacy, and got back to Steve's shop as soon as I was able. I knew the longer I sat in the Audi, the more difficult my return to the open road in Zorba would be.

When I returned to Steve's shop, the work was nearly complete. Steve retrieved his Audi keys then loudly complained about the oil that Zorba was leaking onto his shop floor. The problem I had first recognized on the Mass Pike had followed me to Colorado and was getting progressively worse. I would have no trouble following the trail back home if I chose to do so.

"You better keep an eye on that," he said with some genuine concern in his voice.

Soon the work was finished, and what Steve asked for in payment was the equivalent of about twenty minutes of a mechanic's time in Boston. I paid in cash and, as promised, got no receipt in return. What I did get was an invite.

"I just got back from a fishing trip to Alaska with some buddies of mine. We've got some fresh salmon we plan on throwing on the grill tonight. Why don't you stick around and have some? We're taking some disabled vets on a hunting trip tomorrow, and we need to get this salmon eaten while it's still fresh. I promise the beer will be cold."

And that probably tells you more about Steve than his "Happy Hippy Lane" sign and his willingness to help a traveler late on a Friday afternoon. But I regret to say, I declined his offer. I was anxious to get some miles under my belt and nervous about the delay I had already incurred. I passed on the cookout, which turned out to be my biggest regret from the entire trip. I'm sure it would have been epic, and when epic chances come your way in life, you need to slow down and experience them. I think of Steve and the kindness he showed me every time I have salmon, knowing it's not as good as what would have come off his grill.

Steve Stewart at The Foreign Aid   Steve's wedding cake topper

MAKHA OF THE LAKOTA SIOUX

The sun was getting low on the western horizon when I finally departed Steve's shop with hundred miles to travel to my destination for the night, Moab, Utah. I crossed the state line into Utah on I-70 but shortly after ducked onto Highway 128, which took me southwest toward Moab. Highway 128 in Utah is nothing like Boston's Route 128, which I have traveled hundreds of times. Boston's 128 creates a semicircle around the city and has the worst rush-hour traffic in the area. Gridlock every morning and evening is guaranteed. I smiled as I looked at the Utah highway marker indicating the route number, and I knew that it being late on a Friday, gridlock was at its absolute worst back in Boston.

What I encountered on Utah 128 was an endless stretch of picture-postcard views out Zorba's big bay window. For nearly forty miles, the two-lane roadway followed the Colorado River as it wound through chiseled canyons on its way to Moab. My only delays were when I stopped to take photos of the red rock formations stretching up to the deep blue sky. It was the kind of "stop and go" driving that I embraced.

As the road neared Moab, small BLM campgrounds began to appear alongside the road. I picked the one that looked least inhabited and pulled in for the night. After grilling some chicken and making a salad, I sat and watched the stars in the night sky appear. I had nine days and 953 miles until my rendezvous with Dianne in Glen Ellen, California, but the canyon walls around me convinced me to linger in Moab for as long as my schedule would allow.

For the next two days, I hiked Arches National Park and rode my bike on the endless number of trails that emanate from Moab out into the desert. I also abandoned my cooking, opting instead for breakfasts and lunches at the Eklecticafe on Main Street in Moab. Their various Mexican breakfast dishes made me eager to rise each morning, and for lunch, their Greek Gyros took me back to my days in Chicago, where gyros cafes are as common as Dunkin Donut shops are in Boston.

When I wasn't hiking or biking in Moab, I was sitting on the outdoor patio at Eklecticafe and checking out the passing foot traffic on Main Street, Highway 191. My observations led me to conclude that in Moab, there are more white-guy dreadlocks than in any other square mile in the country—an unfortunate occurrence in my mind. But having experienced some hair shaming myself back in Bethel, New York, the site of Woodstock, I kept my opinion to myself.

My final morning in Moab, as I finished my huevos rancheros smothered in green chili at Eklecticafe, I decided to do one more bike ride before I departed this scenic enclave. Departing the cafe for the last time, I thanked the staff who now knew me by name, and I drove to a bike trailhead north of Moab near the entrance to Arches. The temperature was in the low 80s, with a forecast rising into the mid-90s. I pulled my bike off its rack on the back of Zorba, and feeling the heat on my neck, I filled an extra canister with water before heading onto the trail. I planned to cycle ten miles out, execute a U-turn, then return to the trailhead and the bus before continuing my journey west.

When I saw her walking ahead on the trail, she immediately struck me as out of place. As I passed her, I saw she was a small Native American woman carrying an oversized gym bag nearly as big as she was. I gave her a nod as I passed and headed on toward my turnaround point, but something didn't feel right. The bike trail was paved and headed north, parallel to Utah's Highway 313. I had studied Highway 313 on the map since I planned on traveling it once I finished my time in Moab, and the map showed that the highway didn't take you anywhere except deeper into the unforgiving desert.

Returning to Moab on the trail, I stopped when I re-encountered her. Asking if she'd like some water, she replied with a soft "Yes, please," and I handed her one of the canisters from my bike. Tilting the bottle up and her head back, she took a long drink. Her thirst convinced me that she was not carrying any water in her large black bag, and I was both puzzled and alarmed. Asking her where she was headed, she responded, "Fort Duchesne."

I did not know the location of Fort Duchesne, but I knew it could not be nearby as open desert and rough terrain stretch out from Moab for great distances in every direction. I shared with her that I planned on driving Highway 313 once I returned to my vehicle, and if she could navigate herself over the fence separating the trail from the highway, I would stop and pick her up. She murmured, "Okay," but not with a lot of conviction. I didn't have the heart to tell her I would be driving an old VW bus with no air-conditioning and an interior temperature perhaps a few degrees higher than what she was experiencing now.

I returned to Zorba, and after an hour of getting my gear squared away, I headed onto Highway 313, silently hoping not to see her along the road. For her sake, my wish was someone with an air-conditioned vehicle, and one with a little more zip, had stopped to give her a ride.

But there she was, her fragile frame standing by the road, her large bag sitting on the ground next to her. She had found a way around or over the fence that bordered the highway and was patiently standing in the hot sun. I pulled onto the sandy red dirt that tapered into a ditch alongside the highway, and she climbed into the bus with her bag.

Before heading back out onto the road, I pulled out my Rand McNally to see where Fort Duquesne was located. I could only shake my head as the map showed it was over 200 miles to the north.

"I can get you as far as Green River," I said, pointing at the map. "That's fifty miles north of here. But then I need to head west, and you need to keep going north."

She murmured, "Thank you," and with that, Zorba sputtered back onto Highway 313 and we headed north away from Moab.

"Can I ask your name?"

"I am Makha, of the Lakota Sioux tribe. Our tribal land is in South Dakota. My spirit animal is the white wolf." She pointed to the white wolf emblazoned on her T-shirt.

"What are you doing in Moab, Makha?"

"Camping." By every appearance "camping" translated into "homeless," and I was confident that everything Makha owned was packed into her gym bag.

"Why do you need to get to Fort Duquesne?" I inquired.

"My uncle died, and I want to get to his funeral."

"And your plan is to walk there?"

"Yes."

I didn't know what to say to that. Over the next fifty miles, Makha shared her story in bits and pieces, always speaking softly, and parts of her life were lost to the wind and the road noise that are constant traveling companions in Zorba. I did learn she had a six-year-old daughter, currently in the custody of the State of Arizona, and Makha had not seen her in over a year. She did not know her exact whereabouts but hoped to be reunited with her soon. I was not as hopeful. The sadness of the situation grew heavier than the desert heat, and I made a point of not asking her many more questions. The answers were overwhelming me.

The Lakota Sioux are a proud tribe; one of the three tribes of the Great Sioux Nation. It was the Lakota Sioux, with a little help from the Cheyenne, who wiped out Custer on his ill-fated trip west. Learn the history and you will know that Custer had it coming. The Lakota Sioux had a more recent victory against the Federal Government when they sued to reclaim their land in the Black Hills of South Dakota after it had been taken from them in violation of the Fort Laramie Treaty of 1868. In *United States* vs. *Sioux Nation of Indians,* decided in 1980, the Supreme Court ruled that the land had been illegally taken from the Lakota and they were owed compensation. The amount was based on the quantity of gold that prospectors had removed from the land, valued at $102 million in 1980. But the Lakota do not want compensation—they want their land. They have refused to accept the money, which sits in a trust and is currently valued at $1.3 billion. This legal battle began in 1923, and the Lakota Sioux still await justice.

Zorba got Makha and me to Green River, which is just off Interstate 70 in Utah, and we stopped to get some gas. I bought Makha several water containers in the small store at the station, and then we headed a short distance down the road to a taco truck, which appeared to be the only lunch option in town. But are there ever better options than a taco truck? I remember during the recent presidential campaign, one particularly xenophobic politician warned that if Hillary Clinton won the election, there would be a taco truck on every corner. That pretty much sealed my vote for Hillary. This particular taco truck in Green River did not disappoint, and I happily consumed three chicken tacos, while Makha outdid me, easily downing six.

From Green River, I took Makha to the juncture of I-70 and Utah Highway 191, which headed north and toward the general direction of Fort Duchesne. We pulled onto the shoulder of 191, and I lamely asked, "Are you going to be okay?" I think it'd been a long time since Makha was "okay," but she said, "Yes," and we both climbed out of Zorba. She slung her bag onto her back, shook my hand, and with a smile and a thank-you, she turned and headed north on 191.

It was noon, the temperature was in the mid-90s, no shade for miles, and dressed all in black, Makha began taking steps towards an uncle's funeral 150 miles away. I stood and watched her for a while and became increasingly concerned when she did not stop and assume the normal hitchhiker pose with her thumb extended and a hopeful look cast toward the passing drivers. She just put her head down and walked as the sporadic traffic on 191 zoomed past her.

Climbing back into Zorba, I followed her with my eyes a little longer and then turned the key. Zorba came to life, and we made a U-turn on 191 heading back onto I-70 and our westerly course. One last glimpse in the rearview mirror showed Makha taking her small but steady steps to the north—another lost soul traveling on America's highways. I wrestled with the questions swirling in my head. *Did I help her? Or did I put her in a more perilous situation, deep in the desert, and along a sparsely traveled road? Would another traveler see her and stop to offer help?* Of course they would, I reassured myself. Surely, someone seeing a woman walking alone along the highway under the hot desert sun would slow down to assist. Absolutely. Just as I met many people willing to help me on my journey, there would be many to help Makha on hers. That is what I told myself every night for the remainder of my trip to help me find my sleep and take the image of Makha from my mind.

Makha of the Lakota Sioux   Makha heading north on Utah Highway 191

THE TORCH IS PASSED

Perhaps it was knowing Makha was hiking in 90-degree heat, but the temperature in Zorba seemed to spike even higher than usual. Opening the side vent, I directed the breeze onto me as I leaned forward with my forearms resting on the large steering wheel of the bus. I felt road-weary and resented that I was traveling on Interstate 70, which had replaced old Highway 50 in that part of Utah. But the options for westward travel in Utah are limited, and I slogged on knowing I could exit the Interstate 100 miles ahead and rejoin Highway 50 just past the midpoint in the state.

I hardly noticed the scenery as I drove—the heat, the road noise, the sudden gusts of wind that rocked Zorba put me into survival mode. Highway 50 took me into the town of Delta, past the midpoint in the state, and darkness had enveloped the road. I did not have the energy to look for a parking spot for the night, and when I saw the sign at the Delta Inn advertising rooms for $29, I pulled in.

There was no one in the Delta Inn's lobby but the phone sitting on the counter had a note instructing you to call a specific number if you wanted a room. I made the call, and the woman with the raspy voice at the other end said she would be there shortly to take care of me. I sat in the vinyl-covered chair in the lobby and looked at the tourist brochures in the rack near the door. There weren't many. After a while, Evelyn came in the door and welcomed me to the Delta. She assumed without asking that I needed a room for just one night. Delta did not appear to be a destination site, but an "I'm just passing through" place on the map.

Evelyn fetched a room key for me. The room she directed me to was at the far end of the one-story motel, and I pulled Zorba up to the front door. The adjacent room had a pickup truck parked in front with two flat tires. They looked like they had been flat for a while, and the truck had settled in for the duration. The duration of what I don't know.

After getting into my room, I considered the limited food options I had in Zorba. I was down to the freeze-dried meals I kept for emergencies. I pulled the curtain back on the window in my room, and it was just clean enough for me to see the lights emanating from the McDonald's across the street. As treacherous as a Big Mac can be, it still seemed more inviting than freeze-dried chicken, so I put my shoes back on and crossed the street.

Eating a Big Mac always has the same effect on me, and it's not terribly different from Arby's. I love it going down, but within thirty minutes my stomach is rebelling and my self-image suffers as much as my gastrointestinal tract. Between Makha, the heat, Interstate 70, the pickup truck with two flats, and the Big Mac, I felt more spent and empty than at any point in my journey. Fortunately, I knew the cure, and it was 300 miles down the road. With some luck and determined driving, I could get to Spencer Hot Springs in northern Nevada within two days.

The route to Spencer Hot Springs is a long stretch of Highway 50, which *Life* magazine in 1986 declared to be "The Loneliest Road in America." It was meant to be pejorative, but the state of Nevada adopted it as a marketing slogan. In the 280-plus miles from Ely,

Nevada, on the eastern border of the state, to Fallon, Nevada, on the western border, you pass through only two towns, Austin and Eureka, with a combined population of just over 800 people. Route 50 crosses seventeen named mountain passes, and the grades will challenge any vehicle, not to mention a VW bus. Word to the wise: stop for gas whenever you have the opportunity.

A romanticized piece of history associated with Highway 50 is that it traces in the West the route of the Pony Express, and you can still see remnants of some of the way stations for the riders. Despite the Pony Express's relatively short history, a total of nineteen months from 1860 to 1861, something about it captures the spirit of the American West. The Express ran from St. Joseph, Missouri, to San Francisco, and a letter could be delivered in just under ten days. It has taken Zorba and me thirteen days to cover the same distance, but I am calling this the Peace Out Road Trip—not the Peace Out Express. The existing telegraph line at the time extended only as far as Kearney, Nebraska. One of the most important pieces of news ever delivered by Pony Express to the West Coast was the election of Abraham Lincoln.

Shortly after crossing the line into Nevada on Route 50, I noticed a red convertible closely following me and making no effort to pass despite my slow progress and a wide-open road ahead. After several miles, it finally sped around me but then slowed considerably. A young woman's arm appeared out the driver-side window and motioned for me to pull over to the side of the road. Not many men can ignore a woman in a red convertible (Dianne drives one), so of course, I pulled over. I climbed out of Zorba to see what was up and met Nurse Laurie and her Welsh Corgi, Queenie.

"I love VW buses!" she exclaimed as she blew right past me and up to Zorba. "I'm going to own one someday and just wander around the country," she said as she eyed Zorba up close.

"I hear that a lot. But I left Boston five weeks ago, and I seem to be the only one doing it."

Sensing my skepticism, Laurie turned from Zorba and pointed to her tank top. Sure enough, it had a VW bus on it.

"Let me show you something," she added as she blew past me again to her car. She popped her trunk and pulled out a piece of luggage. Her luggage had a VW bus on it along with "Peace and Love" scrawled in bright red.

I was starting to take Laurie more seriously, and after she offered to buy Zorba, I realized the bus she wanted to own was mine. I laughed, telling her, "My bus is not for sale—at least not yet," hoping Zorba didn't overhear that last part.

"You can ask me again when I get to California. Where are you heading?"

"California, too. I've got a nursing gig waiting for me in San Francisco."

Laurie is a traveling nurse; her wanderlust prevents her from staying in one place for long. I knew Zorba would be in good hands with her, and I suggested she follow my blog, so she would know when I was ready to sell Zorba. I handed her a card with my blog address and contact information and encouraged her to read about my journey before taking off in her own VW bus.

Looking at the card, Laurie paused, and then a light seemed to go off.

"I saw something on Facebook. You're the guy in the bus traveling the United States and blogging about your experiences!"

Even though I hadn't seen any other VW nomads on the road, I knew I was probably not the only person doing this—but who doesn't want to be "the guy," so I claimed it.

"Yeah, I'm the guy."

I wished her well in San Francisco, and Nurse Laurie and I promised to keep in touch. Before she parted, she exclaimed she had a gift for me and ran to her car to retrieve it. Laurie returned with an air freshener tagged with the phrase "Always on Vacation." I thanked her and made a mental note to take a shower at my next stop.

Re-entering our vehicles, we both headed west on Route 50. Laurie and her red convertible were soon out of sight. Zorba and I trudged along in the hot desert sun, in no particular hurry. Twelve miles short of Austin, Nevada, I turned south onto Highway 376 and then took a quick left turn onto unpaved National Forest Road 001. I followed the dirt road for six miles leaving a cloud of dust behind me until I saw a turnoff to the left that took me to Spencer Hot Springs.

The springs are undeveloped and available to anyone who wants to take the time to find them— and willing to cover their vehicle in road dust. Two sources for spring water exist at the site. One is an open pool on a small rise in the desert, and as you slide into the hot water, clothing optional, you ooze into the muddy bottom as well. The other site is a little more civilized. There the spring feeds into a pipe that diverts the water into a large metal basin, about the size of your standard hot tub. You can adjust the temperature of the water in the tub by directing the spring water flowing from the pipe either into or away from the tub.

My first stop was at the spring which provided the mud treatment, no additional charge. Exiting the pool were two young women.

"How's the water?" I asked.

"Muddy. You own the VW bus that we saw pull in?"

"I do. But I think at this point, it owns me."

Ari and Jessie introduced themselves. Ari was from Chicago, and Jessie was a New Yorker.

"How long you been on the road?" Jessie asked.

"Started this trip five weeks ago. The old bus is starting to feel a little small at this point. Heading to California, but couldn't resist stopping at the hot springs. I was here about twenty years ago with a friend. It hasn't changed much."

"We're heading to San Francisco. I expect we'll get there tomorrow."

"Probably going to take me a couple more days. That's the way it is in an old VW bus. You can't be in a hurry to get anywhere."

Jessie and Ari were lifelong friends. College had temporarily separated them, but now they were taking their new degrees, in social work and graphic design, and road-tripping to San Francisco.

"Don't know what we'll do once we get there," Ari said.

"We don't have jobs. But we'll figure something out," Jessie added.

It all had a familiar ring to it. These two young women fresh out of college had no more of a plan than Art and I did in 1972. Concerned, I asked them what they were driving and was relieved when they pointed out a green Subaru stuffed with all of their belongings. It had some years on it, but it looked roadworthy. Mimicking Billy back in Pennsylvania, I said: "A Subaru will get you anywhere." I trusted I hadn't jinxed them.

The look of hope and optimism on their faces rejuvenated me more than any hot spring could, and as they headed off toward their car, I yelled out, "Don't rule out working on a fishing boat once you get there." I'm sure they thought that was an odd comment, but they did not have time to listen to an old man's story. They returned to their Subaru and their journey into their future.

I watched the dust cloud they left in their wake as they drove off toward Highway 50, and then I climbed into the hot springs thinking about my own journey and how it was nearing its end. For the next two days, I stayed at the hot springs, reluctant to depart, knowing a lifelong goal was now within my reach. I relished my encounter with two young people, just out of college, and as open to life and whatever surprises it brought as I was back in 1972. They didn't know it, but I felt the torch had been passed. I would soon put my dream behind me, knowing the spirit thrived in Nurse Laurie, Ari, and Jessie.

Nurse Laurie

Nurse Laurie's luggage

Ari and Jessie at Spencer Hot Springs

DONNER PARTY

A fter spending two days in the hot springs, I eagerly fired up Zorba
with only one more night on the road before my rendezvous with
Dianne in Glen Ellen, California. The Loneliest Road in America took
me across northern Nevada to Reno. There was one more mountain
range to cross, the Sierra Nevadas, and Zorba and I hopped onto I-80
just west of Reno. Mirroring my strategy for the Rockies, I reasoned
my best option was to utilize the Interstate Highway System again with
its passing lanes and available breakdown lane.

I followed I-80 knowing it was the same route the infamous
Donner Party had taken more than 170 years earlier on their own road
trip of sorts. It was mid-September and warm, but as I-80 climbed
toward what is now named Donner Pass, I could feel the temperature dropping. I knew the view of the surrounding mountains was
unchanged from what the Donners saw from their wagons as they
struggled up the eastern slope of the Sierras. The pass crests at just over
7,000 feet, and there I pulled into Donner Memorial State Park. For
my last night on the road, I planned to stay where the Donner Party
had become stranded in 1846. I may have been tempting fate just a bit.

In the 1840s, there was a significant migration of people heading to California, and they were motivated for various reasons. Some
believed they could live a fully Catholic lifestyle, not complicated
by prejudice, in a place initially settled by the Spanish, where most
communities had a Catholic mission as its central point. Others were
motivated by Manifest Destiny, the belief that the land between the
oceans was destined to be occupied by European Americans. Many just
wanted a new start in life. I doubt there were any who felt compelled to
go west because they had failed a similar endeavor in their youth and
had put it on a bucket list of sorts. In those times, a "bucket list" was

something that you did with an actual bucket, and failing on a "road trip" generally meant you were dead.

The journey for these travelers lasted four to six months and followed the well-established, but extremely difficult, Oregon Trail. The trail begins in Independence, Missouri, and covers 2,170 miles spanning the current states of Kansas, Nebraska, Wyoming, Idaho, then into California and Oregon. In Idaho, the Oregon Trail continued west to Oregon City, Oregon, but a spur called the California Trail headed southwest to Fort Sutter in Northern California. The most challenging part of the trail was the last hundred miles over the Sierra Nevada Mountains. Timing was critical since snow generally came to the mountains in October.

The Donner Family left Independence, Missouri, in May of 1846 as part of a wagon train of almost 500 wagons. They were traveling with the Reed Family, and the families' nine wagons were positioned near the end of the train. When the group reached Fort Bridger in Southwest Wyoming, the Oregon Trail headed north, but some members of the party unfortunately encountered a man named Lansford Hastings.

Hastings was promoting a shortcut he claimed to have discovered that would cut 350 miles off their journey. Just as we have all gotten poor directions, and other misleading advice from a convincing stranger, the Donners, Reeds, and some others opted for the shortcut and left the main party of the train. Their party consisted of sixty wagons and nearly a hundred people, and Hastings went ahead, saying he would leave directions nailed to trees along the way. What could possibly go wrong with this plan?

While the Oregon Trail was frequently traveled and well marked, the Hastings Cutoff was not, and the directions that he left for them were unclear. They encountered difficult canyons, were forced up steep inclines, and required to move boulders in their path. The days were exceedingly hot, and the nights were frigid. In addition to summiting mountain ranges, they were forced to cross long stretches of salt flats which had no water source. Oxen, crazed by thirst, would bolt off into the desert; wagons were abandoned when damaged beyond repair. All told, the "shortcut" added nearly a month to their travel time.

In early November, they found themselves finally crossing the Sierra Nevada Mountains. The snows arrived with the Donner Party, and what few wagons they had left came to a halt. Their party now consisted of eighty-seven souls, and they had no choice but to hunker down in an attempt to survive the winter while a small number of them went ahead to Fort Sutter to organize a rescue party. When the rescuers arrived three months later in early February, the party of eighty-seven had dwindled to forty-eight. With supplies exhausted, they had resorted to cannibalism to survive. Patrick Breen, a member of the party, recorded the following in his diary:

> *Mrs. Murphy said here yesterday that she would commence on Milton and eat him. I don't think she has done so yet; it is distressing.*

Indeed.

Milton was a teamster for the Reed Family, and nearing death, he was sent from the Reeds' cabin into a snowstorm because some felt his death would disturb the children. He made it as far as the Murphys' cabin, and there he apparently ended up in Mrs. Murphy's chowder.

Boldly, I had chosen to spend my last night on the road in a place where thirty-nine souls had perished, and poor Milton was put into a stew. Entering the campground, I found a secluded spot among the tall pines as the temperature continued to drop, and darkness settled in. For the first time on the trip, I pulled out my sleeping bag—rated for 10 degrees. After a quick meal, I crawled into the bag, covered it with two blankets, and pondered the Donners' difficult situation as I tried to keep myself warm. I mostly thought of Milton, who, after surviving all the hardships crossing the desert and mountain ranges, was sent outside to die alone so as not to disturb anyone. Thankfully, there was no one else to disturb in Zorba, so I did not have to worry about banishment as the temperature fell below freezing, and I tucked my head down inside my sleeping bag.

Waking the next morning, it required a supreme effort to crawl out from under my blankets and extradite myself from the bag. It was 20 degrees outside, the first time I had experienced below freezing conditions on my trip. The drop in temperature was over 70 degrees from the previous day spent crossing the Great Basin Desert in northern Nevada. I had not packed a jacket of any kind, so I put on several layers of clothing and boiled some water inside Zorba for coffee.

I did not want to push my luck any longer in Donner Pass, wishing to exit the area and the altitude as soon as possible. With my hot coffee in hand, I climbed into the driver's seat and turned the key. Nothing. The battery was as dead as poor Milton. Donner Pass had claimed another victim. The irony of being trapped in Donner Pass on the last night of my five-week journey was not lost on me. I finished my coffee and kept my eye out for Mrs. Murphy.

I waited for the sun to rise a little higher above the horizon before I stepped out into the cold to address the situation. Because of my preference for solitude on my last night, I had parked Zorba in the far corner of the campground, and there were no other vehicles in sight. I thought about walking back to the ranger station at the entrance of the park for assistance, but whether it was laziness or just the desire not to ask for help on my last day of the journey, I decided I would try to MacGyver my way out of the situation. My challenge seemed small compared to what the Donners had faced.

My first thought was to run my jumper cables from my auxiliary battery to my primary battery and jump-start the car off the auxiliary. I was not hopeful about this strategy, since the auxiliary battery tended to hold a charge for an even shorter period than my primary battery. After running the cables from one battery to the other, I was proven right; turning the key produced the same dead response.

As the sun rose higher it began to warm the air around me, it also turned on a light inside my head. I pulled out my solar panel, which, when placed atop Zorba›s roof, was wired to send a charge to the auxiliary battery. By changing some connections, and using my jumper cables, I was able to redirect the solar charge to the primary battery. Once this was completed, I made some more coffee, pulled out my camp chair, and waited for the sun to do its job. After an hour, the sun was shining brightly, the temps were in the high 30s, and I turned the key to see if my battery was back from the dead. Zorba chugged to life, and I allowed myself some satisfaction at having outwitted Donner Pass…and Mrs. Murphy.

Exiting the park, I jumped onto I-80, and from there, Zorba and I could almost coast down the western side of the Sierra Nevadas into the wine country of Northern California. The dream of driving an old air-cooled vehicle across the United States to California was complete. I smiled and gave Zorba a pat on the dash.

"We did it," I said.

"Job well done," Zorba replied.

I hope for nothing. I fear nothing. I am free.

—Epitaph on Tombstone of Nikos Kazantzakis

REPORT TO NIKOS

Near the end of his life, Nikos Kazantzakis authored *Report to Greco*, which can be best described as an intellectual autobiography. It is the story of his moral journey through life as he searches for what gives man meaning. The "Greco" referred to is El Greco (The Greek), a painter, sculptor, and architect of the Spanish Renaissance. Like Kazantzakis, he was born in Crete, but El Greco spent most of his life working in Toledo, Spain, and was buried there after his death. Kazantzakis viewed El Greco as a model for himself and a hero of sorts. He was attracted to El Greco's willingness to be different, his genius in the arts, and his denial of hope and fear—two traps which Kazantzakis believed equally inhibit a person's ability to embrace the present.

I did not intend to write a book when I began this journey, but upon its completion, I felt compelled to provide an accounting of myself to Kazantzakis just as he did to El Greco. I have shared as accurately as possible the events and incidents that occurred during the trip. My passage across the United States began on August 13, 2017, in Newburyport, Massachusetts, and ended on September 16 in Glen Ellen, California, thirty-five days later. Zorba and I passed through seventeen states and covered 4,682 miles. When I began the trip, the manifest goal was to accomplish what my friend Art and I failed to do in 1972. In many ways, reaching California was not the most demanding part of the journey. The real challenge was to stay true to myself and to Kazantzakis and my other mentors along the way.

The quotes from *Zorba the Greek* I share at the beginning of each chapter embody the lessons I learned from reading the literary works of Kazantzakis. He became a mentor for me in life just as El Greco was a mentor for him. Throughout my life, and throughout this journey in an old VW bus, I had chased this role model of mine and felt his presence during every moment of the journey.

CHAPTER I—*Once more there sounded within me the terrible warning that there is only one life for all men, that there is no other and that all that can be enjoyed must be enjoyed here. In eternity no other chance will be given to us.* -NK, *Zorba the Greek*

Live in the present. And live in your present life. If we spend our lives hoping for another existence, or even an afterlife—a life we are not promised—we will never fully experience the life we have within our grasp. If my thoughts while traveling in Zorba were only focused on the goal of California, then opportunities I saw from Zorba's big bay window would pass as quickly as a missed exit sign along the highway. My biggest failure in this regard was declining the invitation to join the mechanic Steve in Grand Junction, Colorado, to share some beers and some Alaskan salmon. I was tired, anxious about the delay, and too focused on the goal of California. I missed an exit sign that would have deepened the experience for me.

And did I do enough for Makha of the Lakota Sioux? I kept my bearing heading west and left her at a barren intersection in the desert. *Should I have forsaken my destination and adopted hers? Did I take her only as far as it was convenient for me?* The memory of Makha still haunts me.

On the other side of the ledger, my willingness to take a detour up Bonny Blue Hollow with Tim, the Zorba-like coal miner in Virginia, was a detour that was true to Kazantzakis. Tim took me in a direction away from California but toward my vision of what the journey was really about. My detour south into Oklahoma, to risk reconnecting with cousins unseen in fifty years, proved to be both rewarding and redemptive. I hope those detours, and other times when I wandered from my course, balance the scale in Kazantzakis's eyes.

CHAPTER II—*Man is able, and has the duty, to reach the furthest point on the road he has chosen. -NK, Zorba the Greek*

In the simplest terms, I reached the furthest point on the road when I arrived in California. The dream I deferred for so many years had been realized. Along with the exhaustion I felt, there was a great sense of satisfaction finishing what I had started forty-five years earlier. My dad would be proud.

Traveling alone provided an abundance of time to reflect on my life and the road I had chosen. I weighed my successes and my failures. I had stood in the rye fields as Holden longed to do, and I hope I spared some children from the precipice. But many questions remained. *Did I do enough with the opportunities I had? When it was time to make a change in my life and "Jump!" did I make the leap, and in so doing, did I leave anyone behind? Were the leaps selfish and attempts to avoid the difficult? Did I embrace my life as a journey as Siddhartha taught me or become blinded by whatever goal I was working toward? And most important to me—did I see god in every person I met along the way?*

More questions remain than answers, and while I did not arrive at the end of my journey with a final accounting of my life, I got closer to my personal truth. And, as Kazantzakis demands, I will struggle with my mentors to the very end.

CHAPTER III—*Every man has his folly, but the greatest folly of all… is not to have one.* -NK, *Zorba the Greek*

If I accomplished nothing else on this trip, I demonstrated my commitment to my folly. For this, I believe Kazantzakis will embrace me as a brother.

CHAPTER IV—*You have everything but one thing: madness. A man needs a little madness or else he never dares cut the rope and be free.* -NK, *Zorba the Greek*

We spend a good portion of our lives seeking comfort and contentment. And is it not mad to cast off what we enjoy and makes us feel safe? This is why a full life requires a little madness. There is nothing comfortable or easy about raising children, and their vulnerability makes every parent feel unsafe and unsteady themselves. Yet, most parents would describe it as the most meaningful thing they have done in their lives. I know it was for me.

I found the most significant experiences in my life occurred when I pulled away from my comfort zone: choosing graduate school in Chicago, packing up my Datsun truck and heading east with no job or place to live, taking jobs for little pay but which offered an opportunity to learn. Growth does not happen without shedding our protective shells, and a little madness can be very helpful in this regard. The whole idea of driving an old VW bus across the country called for a small amount of madness. Or, as Jeff, the mechanic in Louisville, put it a little differently, "You are ballsier than I am."

CHAPTER V—*Life is trouble. Only death is not. To be alive is to undo your belt and look for trouble.* -NK, *Zorba the Greek*

When I shared with friends that I intended to pick up every hitchhiker I met along the way, they expressed concern and some even implored me to reconsider. I'm sure they felt I would be opening myself up to trouble. They were, of course, correct. The act of hitchhiking is often an act of last resort, perhaps by a person with few resources and with nothing to lose—the very definition of desperation. The danger is there. And like a good father, I always admonished my daughters never to do it.

But as Kazantzakis states, life itself is taking a risk, and only death is not. Either we choose to live and accept the trouble that accompanies it, or we are just waiting to die. While I encountered few actual hitchhikers on my journey (Tim is the only one who truly had his thumb out), I gave several rides, and my decision to undo my belt and look for them reflected an essential part of the trip for me. I saw everyone standing by the road as another Zorba... someone I could learn from.

CHAPTER VI—*Happy the youth who believes that his duty is to remake the world and bring it more in accord with virtue and justice, more in accord with his own heart. Woe to whoever commences his life without lunacy.* -NK, *Zorba the Greek*

More madness from Kazantzakis. President Obama phrased it differently when he spoke of "the audacity of hope." Audacious or mad, the idea we have in our youth that we can shape the world and align it with our view of what is virtuous and just, is no doubt, just a little crazy. Yet Martin Luther King Jr. said, "The arc of the moral universe is long, but it bends towards justice." As I traveled, I encountered many people living on the fringes of society, forgotten and seemingly cast aside. They deserve more justice in their lives. Should we not do our part to bend that arc just a bit more during our time here? According to Kazantzakis, it is the only way to save ourselves: *The sole way to save oneself is to save others. Or to struggle to save others... that is enough.* -NK, *Report to Greco*

When I was exiting my youth, I tried to get to California in an old VW Beetle. And now, as the clock is ticking down on my life, I attempted the same irrational act. During the intermittent years, I hope I retained the same lunacy that I could bend that arc of history just a little further toward justice. I believe every act of kindness does that. When I met the students at Berea College, I felt I was talking to younger versions of myself. I hope, in me, they saw perhaps an older version of themselves.

CHAPTER VII—*To think things out properly and fairly, a fellow's got to be calm and old and toothless. When you're an old gaffer with no teeth, it's easy to say: 'Damn it boys, you mustn't bite!' But, when you've got all thirty-two teeth....* -NK, *Zorba the Greek*

Rational versus irrational. Thoughtful versus impulsive. My father, the chemist, certainly embodied the rational, and my brother John seems to have inherited all of it—leaving little for me. When I informed my brother of my plans to buy an old VW bus and, once retired, drive it across the country, he summed it up as "the craziest thing he had ever heard of." But then my brother is an engineer. I am a social worker. We view the world through different prisms. He is also the person I have relied on the most in my life. His compass is true and steady, and the litany of scrapes he has gotten me out of is endless. Would Kazantzakis say he grew old and toothless while I retained all thirty-two? I think not. My brother never shies from the difficult, but he does shy from the foolish.

I know my brother's steady thoughtfulness allowed me to be less thoughtful at times, a little more mad, a little more audacious. It was a gift I have always appreciated. Many of the people I met as I traveled in Zorba agreed with my brother and implied that I was a bit mad for attempting this journey—starting with Maggie in Pennsylvania, who then asked if she and her dog could join me in the madness. I was not bothered by her comments or the expressions of others regarding my questionable sanity. Their reasoned position is a sound one. However, the people I met who didn't question my sanity—Jimmy in Bonny Blue Hollow, all the students at Berea College, and Ari and Jessie at Spencer

Hot Springs—gave me strength and lifted me up. They embodied the "audacity of hope."

But I always knew the only one who would come get me if I got into trouble along the way…would be my brother John.

CHAPTER VIII—*God changes his appearance every second. Blessed is the man who can recognize him in all his disguises.* -NK, *Zorba the Greek*

I met many gods as I traveled west: Naomi in Bethel, New York, as she reached out for a helping hand; Ira as he rode his mower and gave me guidance; and Makha as she turned and headed north alone on Highway 191 in Utah. From my view, out the bay window of an old VW bus, the disguises they wore were thin at best. Their godliness shone through, and for brief moments, we shared the grace of living.

So many other gods gave me the support I needed to complete the journey, and I tried to give back as much as I could along the way—to pay it forward. The gifts I have received from others in my life have been abundant, and I know I will never balance the ledger. But as Kazantzakis says, the struggle to do so is what matters.

CHAPTER IX—*I was happy, I knew that. While experiencing happiness, we have difficulty in being conscious of it. Only when happiness is past and we look back on it do we suddenly realize—sometimes with astonishment—how happy we have been.* -NK, *Zorba the Greek*

My road trip was something I had dreamed of my entire adult life. It was the one goal I set for myself once I retired. I knew it would be a challenge when I set out, and even then, I underestimated how weary I would become at times. As I stated earlier, the real challenge in the journey was not to get to California in Zorba. As Ira wisely said as he sat on his riding mower in Berea, "Of course you will get there—if you have enough money." I had enough money. The challenge was to be alive and present in each day, to experience the "joy of being" in each moment, even when things were difficult—especially when things were difficult.

We too often wait until something is completed and only then allow ourselves to feel satisfaction that we finished the task. Find the joy in the doing. Whether it is raising our children, managing challenges at work, or driving an old VW—appreciate what you are feeling in the moment, even if it is making you wish you were somewhere else. There were mornings on this journey when a wave of fatigue would wash over me just as I was climbing into Zorba and turning the key for the first time. I dreaded that feeling. But I miss it now. It was real, and I may never have been so alive as at those moments.

Nikos, you have been my mentor—a guide for me throughout my life. I can only imagine your thoughts regarding this little adventure of mine. Was I true to you? Was I faithful to myself? I believe everything we do creates a ripple that gradually expands beyond our existence. The ripple you created with your writings in some way made this road trip possible. I hope, in some way, the ripple from this trip will touch another person.

This concludes my report to you.

Peace Out

EPILOGUE

As promised, Dianne met me at a nice hotel and spa in California. We spent five days enjoying the vineyards of the Sonoma and Napa countryside and celebrating my completion of a lifelong dream. The wine, the excellent food, and the time with Dianne revived me. After a week, Dianne returned to Massachusetts, while I stayed behind and completed the ALS Ride I had prepared for while driving across the country. Luckily, the course was as flat as the American prairie that I trained on. I survived and managed to raise some money for a good cause.

Embarking on this journey, I had planned to continue after a brief respite in California and drive Zorba home, taking a more southern route. However, I found the trip west had left me physically drained, so I put the return trek off to a future date. Zorba was still waking up each morning and getting me where I needed to be in California, but he needed some work done. The trip had taken a toll on him as well.

Before the start of my journey in Newburyport, I met a woman from San Francisco who owns a 1976 VW Beetle. She told me of a wise mechanic she relies on for her air-cooled VW. She suggested I look him up once I got to California in the event my VW bus needed work. That is how I was able to meet Elliott Zalta, owner of Elliott's Garage in San Rafael. When I dropped Zorba off at his shop, he insisted I come to his home for some ribeyes on his grill to celebrate my accomplishment. It's difficult to say no to a ribeye, and I don't think many people under any circumstances can say no to Elliott. His positive energy pulls you in, and once you are in Elliott's amiable orbit, it is hard to escape.

Elliott lives on an ark that is grounded in Corte Madera Bay, along with a fleet of other arks. These vessels had once floated on the bay until forced onto land when they were determined to be navigational hazards. This community of ark dwellers is known for being home to an eclectic cast of characters, and Elliott fits right in. Knowing I needed a place to stay while he worked on Zorba, he took me in. For the next five days, I relaxed on the deck of his ark watching the water traffic in the bay pass by, while Elliott addressed the list of Zorba's mechanical issues I had given him. The oil leak that Steve in Grand Junction warned me about was at the top of that list; Zorba and I had left a visible trail from Newburyport to Elliott's shop.

While Elliott worked on Zorba, I looked for a place to store my traveling companion until I could return to California and continue my journey. I secured a spot for Zorba forty miles farther north at Ace Vehicle Storage in Santa Rosa. Ace Storage is comprised of a large field, secured by chain link fencing, and many of the vehicles in the lot appeared to have been long ago abandoned by their owners. After Elliott's work was complete, and feeling a little guilty, I drove Zorba north and tucked him into a spot between a VW Westfalia and a drab green Plymouth station wagon with three flat tires. I had purchased a cover for him, and as I secured it around him, I promised to return; he would not be abandoned. From Santa Rosa, I took the bus to the San Francisco Airport and took a plane back across the country—something Debbie at the rest stop in West Virginia had suggested I should have done in the first place.

Dianne worked her magic with the hodgepodge of video I gave her from the trip and produced a documentary entitled *Peace Out*. Art came up from Kentucky for the premiere, and Elliott flew in from California. The film has won several awards and was an official selection for the Annual Newburyport Documentary Film Festival. *Peace Out* is available on YouTube. Dianne's gentle mocking of my idea of retirement continues, but none of this would have been possible without her support.

Finally, I did not abandon Zorba in the field at Ace Storage, nor did I sell him as Dave the mechanic in Bethlehem, Pennsylvania, suggested. I flew to California in April 2018 and brought Zorba home, taking an even longer route through the Deep South and up the Eastern Seaboard. The return journey lasting forty-five days covering nearly 6,000 miles. John met me in Arizona for some aircraft archaeology, and again he needed to pull me—literally—out of one more predicament when I tore my hamstring.

Art met me in Louisiana, and we had one more road trip together. We explored the back roads of Mississippi, seeking out the blues and BBQ wherever we could find them. And I continued to meet more engaging and generous mechanics along the way: Jim in Modesto, California, and David in Montgomery, Alabama. I've written about my experiences on that road trip on my blog: PeaceOutRoadTrip. wordpress.com.

When I finally returned to Newburyport, I was as exhausted as when I had arrived in California. But I had kept my promise to Zorba—he was home and is now retired from cross-country road trips. While Zorba enjoys his retirement, Art and I have begun building a shantyboat (a houseboat built out of repurposed materials) and plan to launch it onto the Ohio River. We will see if we can float to New Orleans in it—but that is a story yet to be written.

FINAL NOTES TO READER

On March 15, 2018, the plaque on the Jefferson Davis statue in the rotunda of the Kentucky State Capitol declaring him to be a "Patriot—Hero—Statesman" was removed. On June 13, 2020, the entire statue was removed from the Capitol rotunda.

On June 29, 2020, the Mississippi State legislature voted to remove the Confederate battle flag from their state flag.

In May 2018, the State of Kansas dedicated the section of Route 50 that stretches from Wright, Kansas to Dodge City, as the SGT Gregg Steimel and PFC Richard Conrardy Memorial Highway after the two young men from Wright who lost their lives in Vietnam. Rest in peace, Gregg and Richard.

The Lakota Sioux still await justice and the return of their tribal land in the Black Hills. The trust fund is now valued at $1.3 billion and still untouched by the tribe.

The arc of history continues to bend toward justice.

PEACE OUT ROAD TRIP SOUNDTRACK

Every good road trip has a soundtrack, and below are the sounds that carried me across the country in Zorba—with some bonus tracks for Chapters I, II, and III.

CHAPTER I

The Big Muddy — Pete Seeger

VW Bug Song — Denny Brening (NemesisSquirrel on YouTube)

You've Got a Friend — James Taylor

Brother — Kodaline

CHAPTER II

Hey Jack Kerouac — 10,000 Maniacs

CHAPTER III

VW Bus Song — The Newbies

CHAPTER IV

Watching the Wheels Go Round — John Lennon

America — Simon & Garfunkel

With a Little Help from My Friends — Joe Cocker

Allentown — Billy Joel

Battle Hymn of the Republic — Odetta

If This Is Goodbye — Mark Knopfler & Emily Lou Harris

CHAPTER V

Take Me Home, Country Roads — John Denver

The Coal Miner Song — Jimmy Joe Lee

Rocketman — Elton John

CHAPTER VI

You'll Never Leave Harlan Alive — Darrell Scott

Imagine — John Lennon

Me and Bobby McGee — Janis Joplin

Kentucky Rain — Elvis Presley

Hometown — Bruce Springsteen

CHAPTER VII

San Francisco —Scott McKenzie

Small Town — John Mellencamp

Dead Man's Curve — Jan & Dean

Thuringer Bratwurst Blues — Dittmar Loewe

Kansas City — The New Basement Tapes

California Dreamin' — The Mamas & The Papas

CHAPTER VIII

Gimme Shelter — The Rolling Stones

This Land Is Your Land — Woody Guthrie

Bony Fingers — Hoyt Axton

Here's To the Farmer — Luke Bryan

I Love This Bar — Toby Keith

Brothers in Arms — Dire Straits

Fortunate Son — Creedence Clearwater Revival

CHAPTER IX

Ain't No Mountain High Enough — Marvin Gaye & Tammi Terrell

Stuck in Lodi — Creedence Clearwater Revival

Wichita — John Corbett

Rocky Mountain High — John Denver

The Talkin' Song Repair Blues — Alan Jackson

Bridge over Troubled Waters — Simon & Garfunkel

Life Is a Highway — Rascal Flats

Hotel California — The Eagles

CHAPTER X

Zorba's Dance — Mikis Theodorakis

THE ROUTE

Points of Interest

A) Newburyport, MA
B) Bethel, NY
C) Shanksville, PA
D) Coalwood, WV
E) Louisville, KY
F) Tipton, MO
G) Wright, KA
H) Moab, UT
I) Spencer Hot Springs, NV
J) Glen Ellen, CA

AUTHOR BIO

Jerry Steimel was born in Louisville, Kentucky, where he spent his youth and undergraduate college years at the University of Louisville. He departed Louisville in 1974 to attend graduate school at the University of Chicago, receiving a Masters in Social Work. During a forty-five year career in youth work, he worked in various settings assisting disadvantaged youth. These included the court system of Chicago, a residential program in Maine, an outdoor adventure program in Massachusetts, and as the director of a shelter for runaway teens in the Boston area. The final years of his career were with Boys & Girls Clubs of Boston as Director of the Charlestown Club and Executive Vice-President of Operations. He is married and has two daughters. Now retired, he lives in Newburyport, Massachusetts—when not wandering the country in his 1973 VW bus named Zorba.

ACKNOWLEDGEMENTS

My heartfelt thanks first to my wife Dianne, who had the dreadful task of reading all of my first drafts. My sister Mary Lee Younger and her husband, Allen —a dear friend for fifty years— became my primary editors, cleaning up my work considerably. Gratitude also to my friend and dock sitting buddy, Ed Hoell, for all of his feedback and contributions. Many more friends took the time to read the manuscript and steer me in the right direction. I am forever grateful.